ENVIRONMENTALLY SUSTAINABLE DEVELOPMENT
STUDIES AND MONOGRAPHS SERIES NO. 11

Biodiversity and Agricultural Intensification

Partners for Development and Conservation

Jitendra P. Srivastava
Nigel J. H. Smith
Douglas A. Forno

The World Bank
Washington, D.C.

This report has been prepared by the staff of the World Bank. The judgments expressed do not necessarily reflect the views of the Board of Executive Directors or of the governments they represent.

Cover illustration by Stefano Padulosi, courtesy of the International Plant Genetic Resources Institute, Rome.

Library of Congress Cataloging-in-Publication Data

Biodiversity and agricultural intensification : partners for
  development and conservation / Jitendra P. Srivastava and Nigel J.H. Smith, and
  Douglas A. Forno, editors.
     p.   cm. — (Environmentally sustainable development studies
  and monographs ; no. 11)
   Includes bibliographical references.
   ISBN 0-8213-3759-9
   1. Agriculture ecology. 2. Agriculture productivity.
 3. Biological diversity. 4. Agriculture conservation.
 5. Biological diversity conservation. 6. Sustainable agriculture.
 7. Sustainable agriculture. I. Srivastava, Jitendra P. 1940– .
II. Smith, Nigel J.H., 1949– .   III. Forno, Douglas A. , 1946– .
IV. Series.
S589.7.B56
1996
333.95—dc20   96-36166
                                               CIP

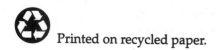 Printed on recycled paper.

Contents

Foreword

Agriculture is both a threat to biodiversity and a key to its survival. Unless agriculture is sustainably intensified, many remaining wild areas will succumb to the plow, ax, or herds of grazing livestock. With global demand for food and other agricultural products expected to at least double—and perhaps even triple—over the next fifty years, the productivity of existing farms and rangelands will have to increase dramatically. How this intensification process plays out in the decades ahead will largely determine how many species—and their habitats—will survive into the coming century.

This volume on biodiversity and agricultural intensification argues that biodiversity must be better managed and conserved if the twin challenges of improving living standards and enhancing the environment for all of humanity are to be met. The publication of this volume reflects an evolution in the World Bank's thinking about agriculture and the environment. These disciplines no longer can be seen as discrete, much less antagonistic.

For some time now the World Bank's Agriculture and Natural Resources Department has been engaged in discussions with environmental groups and Bank staff on how to better harmonize agricultural development with the need to safeguard natural habitats and the integrity of ecosystems. At times progress has been slowed by different perspectives and varying interpretations of terminology. Both sides

have learned. We have found a strong consensus emerging that agricultural development and conservation of natural resources and the environment must go hand in hand.

The authors of this volume explore the many links between biodiversity and agricultural development and suggest that there is much common ground between environmentalists and the agricultural development community. Both conservation and development interests have a stake in the survival of natural habitats. They harbor wild populations and near-relatives of numerous crops and livestock that contain genes for agricultural improvement. Forests and other natural habitats also contain a wealth of plants and animals that could be domesticated to enrich our diets. These could benefit both consumers in industrial countries and residents of difficult environments in which standard crops and livestock have trouble surviving.

Several authors argue that one of the surest ways to further the survival of traditional crops and breeds, many of which are on the verge of extinction, is to find new markets for them. Much of the world's biodiversity is affected by altered or cultured landscapes, especially in farming areas. Land-use practices thus have major implications for species survival. How agriculture can be changed to enhance biodiversity is a major focus of this volume.

Numerous examples are given of how *agrobiodiversity*—that portion of biodiversity used directly or indirectly for agricultural production—

is being tapped to intensify agriculture in a sustainable manner. The authors also highlight an emerging research and development paradigm that departs from conventional approaches to crop and livestock breeding. Policies that can accelerate better use and conservation of agrobiodiversity are relevant to all partners in conservation and development, from multilateral development banks to governments, foundations, and nongovernmental organizations.

We hope that this volume contributes to the articulation—and ultimately to the adoption—of policies that will enhance agrobiodiversity, promote sustainable agricultural intensification, and protect global biodiversity.

Ismail Serageldin
Vice President
Environmentally Sustainable Development
The World Bank

About the Contributors

Harvey Blackburn has a Ph.D. in animal breeding from Texas A & M University and has been involved in developing animal breeding models. From 1992 to 1996 he worked as a livestock specialist at the United States Agency for International Development (USAID), the past two years under a cooperative program with the World Bank. During that period he worked extensively on livestock-environment interactions, including the impact of livestock on biodiversity.

Gordon L. Bultena is professor of sociology at Iowa State University.

Sanjiva Cooke has a master's degree in economics from the University of Toronto and is a long-term consultant to the World Bank's Agriculture and Forestry Division.

Michael D. Duffy is professor of economics and associate director of the Leopold Center for Sustainable Agriculture at Iowa State University.

Douglas A. Forno, chief of the World Bank's Agricultural and Forestry Systems Division, has two decades of experience in World Bank operations in agriculture as well as in sectoral and policy analysis. A Ph.D. plant nutritionist from the University of Queensland, Australia, and a Woodrow Wilson Fellow at Princeton University, Forno worked at the International Rice Research Institute in the Philippines before joining the World Bank.

Cornelis de Haan has a Ph.D. in animal production from the University of Wageningen, the Netherlands, and has worked on livestock development in Africa and Latin America for twenty years. Since 1990 he has served as livestock adviser to the World Bank and is responsible for policy development and livestock quality concerns. De Haan is currently leading a review of livestock-environment interactions to help prepare guidelines for enhancing the contribution of livestock to sustainable agriculture.

Sakti Jana holds a Ph.D. in genetics from the University of California at Davis. He is currently professor in the Department of Crop Science and Plant Ecology at the University of Saskatchewan in Canada, and he has participated in plant exploration and collection missions in the Mediterranean, southwest Asia, and the Tibetan Plateau. His current research focuses on both *in situ* and *ex situ* conservation of crop genetic diversity.

Steven E. Jungst is professor of forestry at Iowa State University.

Ramesh S. Kanwar is professor of agricultural and biosystems engineering at Iowa State University. Kanwar's research interests encompass water quality, water and chemical management practices for sustainable cropping, and environmental management.

Steven Kyle is associate professor of economic development in the Department of Agricultural, Resource, and Managerial Economics at Cornell University. His specialization is macroeconomic policy, and as a Portugese speaker he has been particularly involved in advising the governments of Brazil and Mozambique. Before joining Cornell, he was at the World Bank.

William Lesser is professor of marketing in the Department of Agricultural, Resource, and

Managerial Economics at Cornell University. Lesser's research has focused extensively on the transfer of new agricultural technologies, particularly the role and impact of intellectual property rights on the exchange of living organisms. More recently, his work has expanded into questions dealing with the sustainable use of genetic resources under the Biodiversity Convention.

Bruce W. Menzel is professor and chair of the Animal Ecology Department at Iowa State University.

Manjit K. Misra is director of the Seed Science Center and professor of agricultural and biosystems engineering at Iowa State University.

Piyush Singh is a postdoctoral research associate in the Department of Agricultural and Biosystems Engineering at Iowa State University.

Nigel J. H. Smith is professor of geography at the University of Florida and has worked on several natural resource management issues of the humid tropics, especially Amazonia. Smith has been a consultant to the World Bank on environmental issues in the Latin American region, has collaborated extensively with the secretariat of the Consultative Group on International Agricultural Research (CGIAR), and is now also consulting on the Pilot Program to Conserve the Brazilian Rain Forest on agroforestry issues.

Jitendra P. Srivastava, a Ph.D. agronomist and plant breeder, is principal agriculturist in the Agricultural and Forestry Systems Division of the World Bank. He was involved in launching the Green Revolution in India under the auspices of the Rockefeller Foundation. Before joining the World Bank, Srivastava was agricul-

tural specialist for the Ford Foundation's agricultural development program for arid lands in the Near East and North Africa; director of the cereals program at the International Center for Agricultural Research in Dry Areas (ICARDA) in Aleppo, Syria; and deputy director general for international cooperation of ICARDA.

Henning Steinfeld is a Ph.D. agricultural economist from the Technical University of Berlin. Mainly oriented toward production and resource economics, he has worked in a number of associated fields, including agricultural policy and farming systems analysis, and with technical assistance projects in Africa. Since 1990 he has been with the Food and Agriculture Organization (FAO), currently as senior officer (livestock development planning) in the Animal Production and Health Division.

Janette R. Thompson is associate scientist in the Department of Forestry at Iowa State University.

Arnold van der Valk is professor of botany at Iowa State University.

Noel Vietmeyer has served as a staff officer at the National Academy of Sciences since 1970. He holds a doctorate in chemistry from University of California, Berkeley. Vietmeyer is best known for his innovative work on bringing underused plants and animals to the attention of the global community. He has published more than a hundred articles and has directed study teams that have delivered more than forty published reports on topics ranging from the lost crops of the Incas to the lost crops of Africa.

Richard L. Willham is distinguished professor of animal science at Iowa State University.

Acknowledgments

This volume has drawn extensively on comments of individuals both within the World Bank and from outside organizations. Some exchanges occurred during two workshops held at the World Bank in 1995 to explore the issues raised in this volume.

Within the World Bank special mention is due Alexander McCalla, Andrew Steer, and Lars Vidaeus. Alexander McCalla is director of the Agriculture and Natural Resources Department. In addition to encouraging the pursuit of ways to enhance biodiversity in agricultural development, he provided substantive, insightful comments on the concept paper that helped to launch this volume. Andrew Steer, director of the Environment Department, also early recognized the importance of trying to reconcile the need for agricultural development with environmental concerns and has supported collaboration between the two departments in this regard. Lars Vidaeus, chief of the Global Environment Division, has played a major role in ushering this effort forward on behalf of the Environment Department, and he has made many useful comments on individual chapters.

Among individuals who generously gave time to comment on presentations at the two workshops are Roger Blobaum, Lea Borkenhagen, Brian Brandenburg, Marjory-Anne Bromhead, Wanda Collins, Peter Dewees, Masa Iwanaga, Narpat Jodha, Jacob Kampen, John Lambert, Walter Lusigi, Kathleen Mackinnon, William Magrath, Miranda Munro, Stefano Pagiola, Louise Scura, Frances Seymour, Shiv Singh, Ann Thrupp, Joachim Voss, Anthony Whitten, and Montague Yudelman.

The editors and authors are particularly grateful to Cal Qualset for his thoughtful comments on the individual presentations as well as for serving as moderator of the second workshop.

The editors and authors extend their thanks to the following individuals for their helpful comments on all or parts of the manuscript at various stages of development: Stephen Brush, Derek Byerlee, Wanda Collins, Norman Jones, John Parrotta, Frances Seymour, and Ann Thrupp.

In addition many other people kindly shared their thoughts on biodiversity and its relationship to agriculture, and these insights have enriched this volume. Among those who discussed these issues with the editors or authors of this volume are Janet Abromovitz, Lester Brown, and Kate Newman.

The editors and authors also thank Sharon Bluico for her insights and for editing this publication. We wish to acknowledge the patience and hard work of Vandana Pradhan in preparing and finalizing the manuscript. Amy Smith Bell copyread the final version, and Virginia Hitchcock also contributed to the editorial process. Glenn McGrath desktopped the volume, and Tomoko Hirata designed the cover.

Overview

This volume is a product of ongoing collaboration between the agriculture and environment divisions of the World Bank on ways to better integrate biodiversity concerns in agricultural development. To help clarify thinking on this issue, *Biodiversity and Agriculture: Implications for Conservation and Development* (Jitendra, Smith, and Forno 1996) was produced in early 1996. In the meantime several scientists had been commissioned to explore some dimensions of this complex issue in more detail. A small group of specialists from inside and outside the World Bank brainstormed about the building blocks that would provide a solid foundation for the Bank's eventual strategy for tackling agriculture and biodiversity concerns. Preliminary ideas were vetted among World Bank staff and others, mainly in nongovernmental organizations, then presented at a workshop in December 1995. Based on exchanges at the workshop and reviews of individual papers, the authors revised their contributions for this volume.

While no claim to consensus is being made, the issues raised here were widely discussed and will continue to be debated. The path to sustainable agricultural development and biodiversity conservation is a long and arduous one, and this volume is only a modest step in that direction.

The contributors to this volume come from a wide assortment of disciplines and institutions. A broad array of perspectives was deliberately sought to enrich the debate (see "About the Contributors").

The dynamic borders among biodiversity, agricultural intensification, and rural development are explored in eight chapters. In chapter 1, "Agriculture as Friend and Foe of Biodiversity," the volume editors present a conceptual framework and identify major cross-cutting themes. In chapter 2, "Harmonizing Biodiversity Conservation and Agricultural Development," Noel Vietmeyer illuminates the very narrow base of plants and animals on which humans rely for the bulk of their sustenance and other products. While staple cereal and root crops will continue to feed humanity for some time to come, the jettisoning of many useful plants and livestock is an unwise course. Many neglected crops and traditional breeds have special characteristics that render them superior to the few dominant types used commercially today. Often better adapted to difficult environments, traditional crops and breeds could be used to tackle two related problems: enhancing the biodiversity of transformed—and in some cases degraded—landscapes while improving local living conditions.

In the third chapter, "Policy Considerations along the Interface between Biodiversity and Agriculture," William Lesser and Steven Kyle focus on the impact of policies, regulatory mechanisms, trade agreements, and intellectual property rights on biodiversity in the agricultural context.

The clear need for better scientific and economic understanding of the costs and benefits of *in situ* and *ex situ* conservation is underscored. Without such understanding it will be difficult to formulate adequate policies to safeguard genetic resources for agricultural development. The authors also explore how intellectual property rights might impart economic value to biodiversity, thereby creating incentives for conservation.

No evidence has emerged to support the idea that intellectual property rights have been a major factor in the dwindling use of traditional varieties. Much of the genetic erosion of traditional varieties was well under way before legislation supporting patents and breeders' rights was passed.

The authors also pinpoint some issues related to how local communities could benefit from the conservation of genetic resources that they have identified and protected over time. Competitive claims and the lack of national policies to clarify the rights of traditional peoples to their ancestral lands are highly political issues in some countries. But countries need at least to specify what genetic resource rights can be claimed by governments and what are available for landowners and other claimants. How local communities can claim rights over traditional knowledge separate from the resources themselves should also be defined.

Chapter 4, "Effects of Land-Use Systems on the Use and Conservation of Biodiversity" by Nigel J. H. Smith, explores ways to better integrate biodiversity in the process of intensifying agriculture. Although the differential effects of major agricultural production systems are discussed, more emphasis is placed on remedial measures such as crop diversification. Smith argues for balancing the mosaic of land uses rather than trying to pick the right land use for a given area. He examines land-use dynamics and the driving forces behind changes in land use. Land-use systems investigated include intensive cropping with short-cycle crops, shifting agriculture, agropastoral systems, agroforestry, plantation systems, and forest extraction.

The policy recommendations in chapter 4 span research priorities for agricultural research and development organizations, socioeconomic infrastructure and property rights, agricultural development schemes, and conservation projects. Smith highlights current trends toward a new agricultural research paradigm and proposes that agrobiodiversity survey teams assess an area targeted for development before the project is carried out. The potential for agrobiodiversity as a new dimension to ecotourism is also discussed.

The case study in the fifth chapter, "Effects of Agricultural Development on Biodiversity: Lessons from Iowa," reflects many of the themes that thread through this volume. Iowa is one of the most transformed pieces of real estate on earth. Virtually all of Iowa's prairies and wetlands are gone, and two-thirds of the state's forest has been cleared. Agricultural development, with its concomitant blessings and woes, is at its peak in one of the world's most important bread baskets.

Iowa is often flagged as a textbook case of how not to develop a region because of the widespread destruction of natural habitats, drastic loss of biodiversity, serious loss of topsoil, and water pollution by agricultural chemicals. Yet the authors of the Iowa case study point to recent and promising efforts to rectify at least some of the environmental damage while still maintaining high crop yields. Practices adopted by increasing numbers of environmentally aware farmers include crop rotation, conservation tillage, strip cropping, reduced applications of agrochemicals, and buffer strips of natural vegetation along watercourses.

To better show the severity of environmental change in Iowa, the chapter traces the state's settlement history. The authors highlight the relevance of settlers' agricultural practices to the state's main habitats: forests, prairies, and prairie-wetlands. They describe various practices that enhance biodiversity on farmland and help conserve the natural resource base for agriculture and then analyze state- and federal-level policies and programs that enhance biodiversity.

In chapter 6, "Livestock Production Systems and the Management of Domestic Animal Biodiversity," Harvey Blackburn, Cornelis de Haan, and Henning Steinfeld underscore the alarming loss of animal genetic resources and explore the implications for livestock improvement. They analyze various livestock production systems for their impact on animal genetic diversity, which is diminishing because of shifts in consumer preferences, adoption of large industrial-scale operations, and widespread breeding techniques that concentrate on fewer and fewer breeds. The authors discuss important synergies between livestock raising and wildlife.

Analysis of pressures on animal genetic resources includes a review of important indicators that can alert livestock owners, government agencies, and development organizations when the genetic health of livestock may be endangered. Such indicators include a reduced number of herds and diminishing herd size, and the authors suggest minimal thresholds. They explore patterns of genetic movement into livestock populations. In industrial countries this information is usually readily available, but few data on this important aspect of breed conservation are available for most of the tropics and subtropics.

The authors also look at how livestock owners (the actual breeders in many cases) breed associations, national governments, and international agencies respond to the need to better safeguard animal genetic resources and how they work cooperatively toward the goal of conserving breeds within economically viable farming systems. The cost-effectiveness of various approaches to conserving breeds is also explored. The authors conclude that a bias toward importing exotic breeds at the expense of indigenous stock has been based on faulty analysis. The assumption that imported breeds would outperform local breeds has largely ignored genotype-environment interactions.

In chapter 7, "Biodiversity and the World Bank's Agricultural Portfolio," Sakti Jana and Sanjiva Cooke review how the World Bank handles biodiversity in its agricultural projects. They analyze several types of policy documents—from country assistance strategies to national environmental action plans—to identify biodiversity concerns, particularly as they relate to agricultural biodiversity. They examine the World Bank's sector analysis, such as agriculture and forestry sector reviews, that relates to biodi-

versity for several countries, paying particular attention to megadiversity countries (areas especially rich in species and unique life forms).

Reviewing the World Bank's agriculture sector portfolio between 1988 and 1995 based on a checklist of positive attributes, the authors find that agricultural projects are increasingly biodiversity-friendly. They conclude that a long-term perspective is needed when dealing with biodiversity and agricultural development and that social and economic considerations are just as important as biodiversity concerns. A focus on biodiversity alone will not work.

In the final chapter, "Toward a Strategy for Mainstreaming Biodiversity in Agricultural Development," the volume editors bring together major policy recommendations within a framework that both highlights the multiple dimensions of agriculture-biodiversity interactions and suggests some ways to proceed. Chapter 8 explores fresh approaches to *in situ* conservation of plant and animal genetic resources, underscores the value of work on the systematics of plants and animals to help us better understand variation within species and relationships among species, and makes a case for assembling interdisciplinary teams to assess agrobiodiversity before agricultural development projects are carried out. Major policy recommendations include promoting quality pricing, extending credit to traditional varieties as well as modern cultivars, and further reducing agricultural subsidies that often exacerbate environmental problems. The editors also examine various dimensions of the emerging agricultural research paradigm that stress sustainability.

Reference

Srivastava, Jitendra P., Nigel J. H. Smith, and Douglas A. Forno. 1996. *Biodiversity and Agriculture: Implications for Conservation and Development.* World Bank Technical Paper 321. Washington, D.C.

1. Agriculture as Friend and Foe of Biodiversity

Jitendra P. Srivastava, Nigel J. H. Smith, and Douglas A. Forno

The conservation of biodiversity has now emerged as a priority across many levels of society in virtually all countries. It is no longer just the concern of bird watchers and a handful of field botanists. Citizens and politicians alike have rallied to the cause of saving biodiversity. But few people are sensitive to the fact that the destiny of biodiversity and people are connected. Biodiversity is not separate from the human experience, a category to be compartmentalized and hermetically sealed off from people (Abromovitz 1994). Biodiversity is harnessed by cultures in various ways to produce food and other products, and much of the planet's remaining biodiversity will be lost unless future needs can be met from areas already cultivated or grazed.

The 5.8 billion people on earth are already stressing the natural resource base that ultimately supports the global economy. The world's population is expected to at least double before it stabilizes. But demand for food and other agricultural products is likely to triple within the next fifty years (Avery 1996). As societies on every continent become more urban and income levels rise, especially in Asia and Latin America, consumption patterns shift, often up the food chain. As more livestock products are consumed, greater demands are placed on landscapes to produce feed for cattle, pigs, and other animals. This process is unfolding especially rapidly in East Asia (Brown 1995), and is likely to exert further pressure on biodiversity unless a concerted effort is made to adopt more environmentally sound agricultural practices.

Some dramatic changes will be needed in the ways that people raise crops and livestock if much biodiversity is to survive the next fifty years. How agriculture is transformed and intensified in a sustainable manner will be the key to how many species and how much genetic variation is still around in the next century. A focus on conserving biodiversity in "protected areas" alone will not work (box 1.1). This book aims to make the case that agriculture and biodiversity are intimately connected; one cannot survive without the other. Continued progress in raising and sustaining agricultural yields hinges on better protecting and harnessing the planet's biological riches.

Agriculture is often seen as the "enemy" of biodiversity rather than as part of it. This perception arises because raising livestock and crops inevitably alters vast expanses of the earth's surface. Population growth and other factors propel farmers into forests; pastoralists are squeezed into ever-diminishing spaces and sometimes overgraze the land; and high-input, modern farming practices frequently pollute the water and soil with chemicals. All of these activities trigger a widespread and potentially dangerous loss of biodiversity. But some land-use systems and agricultural practices enhance biodiversity within managed landscapes. For example, the judicious use of livestock waste as organic manure enhances the species diversity of macrofauna (Bohac and Pokarzhevsky 1987). Also, inappropriate agricultural practices can be modified to mitigate their adverse effects on the environment.

Box 1.1 Holistic approach to biodiversity conservation

Protection of a sample of natural habitats is neither sufficient nor desirable for conserving biodiversity for two simple reasons: most of the world's biodiversity exists in human-managed or -modified systems, and land-use patterns and sociopolitical factors in areas adjacent to parks and reserves have major implications for the integrity of biological diversity in "protected" areas.

This relationship has clearly been demonstrated by the fate of sixty-two bird species in an 86-hectare woodland in West Java. After several square kilometers of surrounding woodland were destroyed, twenty bird species disappeared, four declined almost to extinction, and five more declined noticeably (Diamond, Bishop, and Van Balen 1987). The remaining species appeared to be unaffected. This example highlights the need for regional conservation (Ricklefs 1987) and the need for integration of biodiversity conservation for both protected areas and agricultural ecosystems.

Source: Pimentel and others 1992.

The fates of agriculture and biodiversity are intertwined. Wildlife habitats provide environmental services to agriculture, such as protecting water sources for irrigation. Relatively undisturbed habitats also contain wild populations of domesticated plants and animals, and these populations contain useful genes that are often absent in the domesticated gene pool. It will be possible to secure at least some of the remaining habitats that are home to endangered plants and animals only if agriculture is intensified in a sustainable manner. Doing so should reduce pressure on forests, grasslands, and other habitats important for wildlife.

Agricultural Intensification: Bane or Blessing for Biodiversity?

To many *agricultural intensification* means more purchased inputs such as fertilizers, pesticides, herbicides, and machinery. Understood in those terms, intensification is akin to jumping out of the frying pan into the fire. Eutrophication of lakes and estuaries, loss of soil microorganisms, accelerated soil erosion, contamination of groundwater, and draining of wetlands—to mention a few of the adverse effects of some agri-

cultural practices—attest to the dangers inherent in intensifying agriculture without regard to the long-term consequences for the natural resource base. But agricultural intensification is not synonymous with such externalities; these are environmental signals that intensification is being approached the wrong way.

Agricultural intensification is not the same as maximizing yield at all costs. Farmers are not interested in this approach anyway. They want to increase output per area, but only as long as it is profitable. If it is profitable to intensify agriculture, is that always acceptable? If long-term damage to the environment and biodiversity results, the answer is no. But how does society provide the incentives to turn agricultural intensification into more rational directions? Is agroecological intensification—as opposed to modern, high-input agriculture—feasible?

This volume does not purport to provide all the answers. It is only a step in that direction. But sustainable agricultural intensification would include such approaches as:

- More rational use of nutrients, space, and energy in all land-use systems
- Greater recycling of nutrients
- Better use of biological resources to raise and maintain yields of crops and livestock
- Greater appreciation for and use of indigenous knowledge, especially of neglected crops that could help improve livelihoods and the environment
- More effective measures for soil and water conservation
- The deployment of "environmental corridors" in landscapes that have been transformed by agriculture and livestock raising.

We are not talking about simply going back to "traditional" practices, whatever that means in the context of ever-evolving agricultural systems. A blend of modern science and indigenous knowledge will be required to face the challenges of increasing agricultural production in the decades ahead. Purchased inputs and their judicious use are essential to raise and maintain crop yields in many areas. Application of purchased inputs can be effectively managed to minimize environmental damage. The process of crop and livestock intensification needs to be explored across a range of land-use systems to highlight specific strategies for raising yields while alleviating biodiversity loss. For some land-use systems, purchased inputs are hardly a part of the intensification process. Several chapters in this volume explore the theme of intensification in some detail, especially the discussion of promising undervalued crops (chapter 2), land-use systems (chapter 4), and the Iowa case study (chapter 5).

Core Issue

How agriculture can be intensified while enhancing biodiversity is the critical question this book tackles. Our goal is to identify some of the critical dimensions of this issue, illuminate their many facets, and suggest policies that mitigate adverse effects of agriculture on the environment. When agriculture provokes excessive soil erosion, loss of forage cover, or pollution of streams, it assaults the home of species, and thus often diminishes biodiversity. But unsound agricultural practices can be transformed so that productivity increases while the adverse effects on biodiversity decrease.

Our concern is not simply to highlight ways that agricultural practices can be tailored so that they are more "environment-friendly." We are especially concerned with incorporating greater biodiversity within agricultural production systems. New approaches to agricultural research and development are being tried in various places around the world, and virtually all of them emphasize a much better harnessing and management of biological resources than has prevailed in the past. Instead of excessive reliance on an arsenal of potent chemicals to improve soil fertility and thwart the attacks of insects and disease-causing organisms, agricultural research is geared increasingly to manipulating genes and releasing predators of crop pests, among other biological assets. When crops and livestock are bred so that they can thrive under the incessant onslaught of challenges to productivity, agricultural production systems become more resilient.

Agricultural intensification does not automatically trigger greater harm to the environment. On the contrary it can save and enhance biodiversity. Benign policies and practices that enhance agricultural productivity as well as biodiversity conservation are possible. This book pinpoints ways this has already been accomplished in certain areas and suggests measures that might accelerate wider adoption of sound practices. It is hoped that such information will be useful to those engaged not only in designing and carrying out agricultural development projects but also in helping to establish priorities for agricultural research. Individuals involved primarily in conserving biodiversity as it is most widely understood—safeguarding wildlife and natural habitats—might also find the discussion on the complementarities between agriculture and environmental conservation useful.

Biodiversity and Agrobiodiversity Defined

Before exploring in more detail the complex issues surrounding agricultural development and biodiversity, it would be useful to define what we mean by biodiversity and the subset of biological resources that support agricultural production: agrobiodiversity.

Biodiversity has three main dimensions: the genetic variation within species and populations, the number of species, and habitat preservation (Srivastava, Smith, and Forno 1996). The significance of variation within a species is less widely appreciated but is critical, particularly for agriculture. Continued productivity of existing crops and livestock hinges in large part on harnessing the genetic variation found within each species.

In biodiversity the number of species is fairly straightforward: it is an index of species richness, or the numbers of distinct plants and animals in a given environment. Thus tropical rainforests are especially rich in species, and their fate has major implications for many crops important for subsistence and cash income in the tropics and subtropics (box 1.2). To protect species and genetically distinct populations of each species, it is necessary to safeguard their environments. Without a home, species and populations cannot survive.

The issue of habitat conservation has two parts: safeguarding natural habitats for wild species and populations and wisely managing habitats that have been modified for human use, such as farmland. The second item is less well

Box 1.2 Biodiversity and the tropics

Conservation and management of biodiversity is particularly critical in lower latitudes because they contain infinitely more species than typically found in temperate areas. Agrobiodiversity is also exceptionally high in the humid tropics. Tropical rainforests cover only 7 percent of the earth's surface but are home to more than half of the world's biota (Wilson 1988). A couple of specific examples illustrate the extraordinary levels of biodiversity found in tropical rainforests and underscore their importance for conservation and the need for careful management of their biological riches. A 13.7-km² portion of the La Selva reserve in Costa Rica contains almost 1,500 plant species, more than are found in all of the United Kingdom (Myers 1988). The Malayan Peninsula is only about a third as large as the United Kingdom, but it contains five-and-a-half times as many plant species (Whitmore 1985). Throughout geological history the tropics have been a major source of evolutionary novelty, not simply a refuge that has accumulated diversity because of low extinction rates (Jablonski 1993). Tropical forests contain wild populations of hundreds of crops, such as mango, coffee, and rubber, as well as candidates for new crops and livestock. The loss of tropical forests also forecloses on options for future agricultural development. Humankind has a collective responsibility to ensure that such novelty is available for future generations.

understood among the general public and many policymakers. Economic growth and poverty alleviation hinge in large measure on managing biodiversity in habitats transformed by humans, such as farmland, rangeland, and forests exploited for lumber and nontimber forest products. How farmers and livestock owners manipulate natural resources is therefore critical to the question of conserving biodiversity.

It is in habitats that have been modified for crop and livestock production that one finds agrobiodiversity. All plants and animals that contribute directly or indirectly to raising crops and livestock can be considered. Agrobiodiversity includes crops and their varieties, as well as livestock and the different breeds that have been developed over the ages to suit different cultural needs and to fit a wide array of environments. Some managed habitats, such as agroforestry systems, can be surprisingly rich in both species and varieties.

Plants and animals that indirectly constitute agrobiodiversity include weedy populations that exchange genes spontaneously with crops, thereby helping them become more hardy; crop pollinators; biocontrol agents that suppress crop pests; and soil microfauna and microflora. Some land-use practices, such as the indiscriminate use of pesticides, destroy some crop pollinators and therefore have a tangible negative effect on agrobiodiversity. Overuse of pesticides can also create a boomerang effect by eliminating predators of crop pests, which then develop resistance to pesticides. Microorganisms in the soil are critical in nutrient cycling and may be destroyed or enhanced by certain agricultural practices (Lal 1991). Policies can be formulated to help mitigate the adverse effects of agricultural practices on agrobiodiversity and as off-site effects on other species that are not currently incorporated in agricultural production.

Although it is conceptually useful to differentiate agrobiodiversity from the larger array of species and habitats, it is worth emphasizing that the boundaries between biodiversity and agrobiodiversity are not clear-cut. All of biodiversity is potentially of use to agriculture, particularly with the power of emerging biotechnologies. Agriculture is highly dynamic, and the interface between domesticated plants and animals and wild species is constantly shifting. A wild plant or animal of little or no current market value could provide significant employment and income in the future. The fact that it is not easy to draw a firm line between biodiversity and agrobiodiversity only underscores the importance of conserving as much biodiversity as feasible for its future value for agricultural development, among other reasons.

Agriculture has a direct stake in safeguarding wider biodiversity. Wild species are essential for agricultural improvement because they are sources of new economic plants and animals and provide important services such as pollination and pest control (figure 1.1). Advances in biotechnology are also pushing back the limits to exchanging genes between unrelated organisms.

Given the ultimate importance of biodiversity to agriculture, a strategy for mainstreaming biodiversity in agricultural development should

Figure 1.1 Habitat biodiversity enhances natural pest control mechanisms

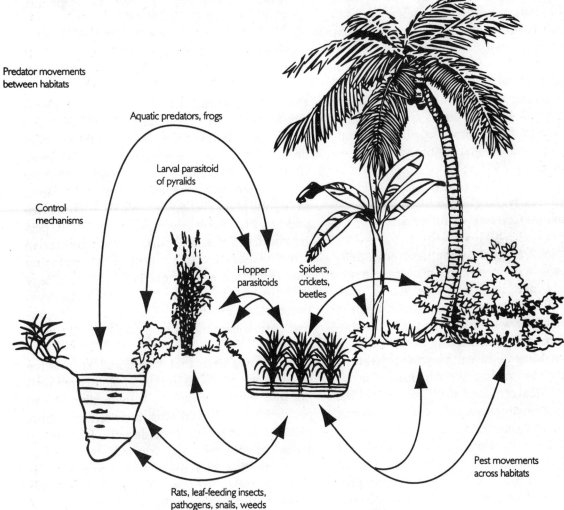

Predator movements
between habitats

Aquatic predators, frogs

Larval parasitoid
of pyralids

Control
mechanisms

Hopper
parasitoids

Spiders,
crickets,
beetles

Pest movements
across habitats

Rats, leaf-feeding insects,
pathogens, snails, weeds

Source: International Rice Research Institute 1996.

address the off-site effects of land-use systems. Steps in this direction are outlined in the call for a new agricultural research and development paradigm. Work is already under way to address a range of issues related to off-site effects, including reduction or elimination of agricultural pollutants in groundwater and in run-off and greater emphasis on integrated pest management strategies.

To conserve and better use biodiversity, it is essential to preserve and manage a diverse array of habitats, ranging from areas with little human disturbance to environments that are managed for a variety of products. A species cannot thrive if its environment is destroyed or seriously impaired. Agricultural scientists—including

breeders, farmers, and ultimately consumers— thus share a common concern for the conservation of "natural" areas with their wild plant and animal life as well as "cultural" habitats—environments that have been significantly altered by human activities.

Biodiversity is both a product of evolution and the essential raw material for future diversification of life on earth (Wood 1993). If species and genetic variation are diminished by human activities, options are closed for improving agriculture and many other activities that are essential for human survival and economic growth. For all its glamour the marvels of genetic engineering can never be a substitute for the myriad trajectories of evolution.

Humankind cannot afford to dispense with species and their genetic variation just because we now have the power to synthesize genes in the laboratory or to create deoxyribonucleic acid (DNA) libraries. Such feats are no match for the laboratories of evolution that continuously create novel biodiversity in the broad range of cultural and natural habitats. Rather, recombinant DNA techniques are gradually being added to the toolboxes of plant and animal breeders and underscore the value of conserving biodiversity.

Agrobiodiversity: Neglected Stepchild in the Rush to Conserve Biodiversity

To many biodiversity conservation is essentially synonymous with protecting showcase mammals, birds, and wild and spectacular landscapes. While efforts to safeguard the habitats of wildlife certainly warrant support, this conventional approach to conserving biodiversity is insufficient. Most of the earth's surface has now been modified in various ways by human activities. On a global scale less than 5 percent of the land is in nominally protected parks or reserves, and some 70 percent of the total land surface is in agriculture or managed forests (Pimentel and others 1992). Considerable biodiversity is often found in areas managed for agricultural production or extractive products in both industrial and developing countries. In Germany, for example, only about a third of the species found in that country are in protected areas. And in northeastern Italy the number of arthropod species in the soil and litter of natural forest and a maize field were about the same, although species composition differed (Paoletti 1988). In the past, efforts to promote biodiversity conservation have largely ignored the value of agrobiodiversity.

The neglect of agrobiodiversity in the portfolios of lending and development organizations, as well as in treaties and conventions that deal with environmental conservation, is striking. Chapter 7 of this volume explores the agricultural and rural development portfolio of the World Bank. A recent examination of U.S. funding for biodiversity conservation revealed that of 873 projects, only four dealt with genetic resources for agricul-

ture. In contrast numerous projects focused on the conservation and management of elephants, birds, and pandas (Wood 1993).

Agrobiodiversity, Cultural Habitats, and Indigenous Knowledge

Human cultures are interwoven in the biodiversity fabric. Most of the habitats on earth have been modified to some extent by people, usually deliberately but sometimes inadvertently. Cultural habitats range from grasslands that are frequently burned to improve forage for cattle, to highly managed environments such as rice paddies. National parks encompass only 3.2 percent of the earth's land surface, whereas human activities have modified most of the remaining area (Pimentel and others 1992). Any strategy that purports to address biodiversity conservation must take into consideration the wide spectrum of habitats modified by a diverse array of cultures.

It follows then that traditional knowledge systems are critical to the sustainability of farming and natural resource management. Local peoples have evolved with their environments and have acquired considerable knowledge about the locations and appropriate strategies for harvesting and managing their resources (Thrupp 1989; Thrupp, Cabarle, and Zazveta 1994). The integrity of cultural systems that have adapted to the numerous habitats on earth is therefore an essential part of biodiversity conservation.

How and why rural people conserve, enhance, and use biodiversity has rarely been taken into account when designing management interventions and devising policy for agricultural development and natural resource management. The active participation of farmers, ranchers, and pastoralists—and especially resource-poor operators—is essential in designing and carrying out biodiversity and agricultural development projects (Thrupp, Cabarle, and Zazveta 1994; Wilcox and Duin 1995). Incorporating indigenous knowledge is thus an integral part of the new paradigm for agricultural research and development that is emerging at various speeds in different parts of the world.

The Critical Role of the Business Community

All stakeholders must be involved in the wise management and conservation of agrobiodiversity. Often the importance of the private sector is ignored in such discussions. The roots of this oversight probably arise from the idea that the profit motive is a major force propelling environmental destruction and overexploitation of plants and animals. Degradation of habitats has occurred across a broad spectrum of political systems reaching far back in time. Today few would take issue with the notion that the business community has an important role to play in better using and helping to manage biodiversity.

A recurring theme in this volume is that market forces can be harnessed to ferret out crops or old varieties that are in danger of slipping into extinction and promoting them. The same idea applies to ancient but dwindling livestock breeds and some unconventional livestock species such as iguanas. If markets can be found for forgotten crops and livestock breeds, they are more likely to survive. Gene banks and embryo stores cannot be relied on to save all the varieties and breeds that are no longer commercially viable. Markets are constantly changing, and new opportunities are emerging for tapping some of these dwindling pockets of agrobiodiversity to generate income for locals and to enrich the diets of people around the world.

Many of the innovative approaches to marketing the untapped wealth of biodiversity in Latin America are likely to come from relatively small-scale enterprises. One example is Kapok International, based in Chagrin Falls, Ohio. Kapok has a Brazilian subsidiary in Manaus, Brazil, and markets Amazonian fish. Kapok soon expects to begin marketing some unusual Amazonian fruits for the juice and candy industries in North America (box 1.3).

With assistance from the International Finance Corporation (IFC) an innovative trust fund has been established to spur greater private sector investments and better use and management of the wealth of biological resources in Latin America (box 1.4). As experience accumulates about what works and what to avoid with such specialized investment funds, expansion of these efforts should be considered in Latin America and in other regions.

The private sector has critical roles to play at various steps in the process of better using agrobiodiversity. In planting material multinational seed companies dominate the production and sale of major cereals, but opportunities also exist for small-scale private seed companies to exploit the

---

Box 1.3 Opportunities in Amazonian agrobiodiversity

Turning the tide on the rapid destruction of species-rich rainforests will happen only if the economic needs of the local people are addressed. To that end Kapok International is seeking to develop new markets for some intriguing Amazonian fruits little known outside the region. Based in Chagrin Falls, Ohio, the company is exploring the potential of nontimber forest products and promising crops that can be grown or collected on a sustainable basis. In this manner economic value will be added to forests, and locals can improve their standards of living.

Market opportunities in the United States abound for "cause-oriented" foods. U.S. and other consumers are increasingly interested in novel foods, especially if they come from exotic locations such as the Amazon. And some consumers are willing to pay a premium for extractive and agricultural products that have been obtained without damaging the environment or the cultures of local people, especially indigenous groups.

One product Kapok International expects to market in the near future is *cupuaçu*. Pronounced *coo-poo-a-su*, this relative of cacao renders a fine chocolate-like drink with a hint of citrus. Cupuaçu makes a creamy-tasting cocoa without milk, a big plus for the millions of people who suffer from lactose intolerance. Fine cupuaçu chocolate bars also may soon grace supermarket shelves. Drinks containing cupuaçu pulp have appeared recently in several U.S. markets.

Lack of infrastructure in most parts of the Amazon is a major impediment to exploring the full potential of the region's numerous tropical fruits. Poorly maintained roads impede the timely delivery of fruits to processing plants. Unsanitary conditions and inadequate refrigeration at the few agroindustrial plants in the region also hinder the export of frozen pulps and purees to demanding markets in North America and Europe. With supportive agricultural policies and an improved investment climate, such barriers can be overcome to the benefit of consumers, local people, and biodiversity.

Box 1.4 Biodiversity Enterprise Fund for Latin America

The private sector can help prevent the loss of biodiversity by generating income from intact systems such as ecotourism receipts and by promoting more sustainable farming operations. More biodiversity-friendly agriculture includes organic farming and creation of markets for underused crops or traditional varieties of megacrops. The Biodiversity Enterprise Fund for Latin America hopes to help achieve these aims by providing $20–$30 million of venture capital for small-scale enterprises starting in late 1996.

The market for certified organic or sustainably harvested products is growing not only in Europe and North America but also in some developing country markets. In Europe alone sales of certified organic produce was in the vicinity of $7 billion in 1994. Demand in the United States for similar produce has grown 25 percent a year for the last three years.

---

growing demand for unconventional crops, particularly in areas where the crops have recently been introduced. Although the private sector is still a relatively minor player as a source of new varieties in most developing countries, this picture is gradually changing (Dalrymple and Srivastava 1994). National and international policies are needed to facilitate this encouraging trend.

Undergirding Themes

Three main ideas underpin this book. First, biodiversity conservation is essential to efforts to make agricultural development more sustainable (box 1.5). Biodiversity furnishes a constant source of new genetic material to improve crops and livestock and of new crops and domestic animals. Second, agriculture must be intensified in an environment-friendly manner to reduce pressure on remaining habitats for wild plants and animals. Third, it will be easier to conserve and better use biodiversity if its value is more widely appreciated. This does not necessarily mean placing monetary value on all biodiversity in a given area, an extremely difficult task. Rather, it means assessing the cultural as well as market value of plants and animals. For example, if local people no longer have any use for a variety, it will be difficult to convince them to continue producing it.

Rationale for the Fund

- *Business case.* Many opportunities exist in Latin America to invest profitably in biodiversity projects.
- *Need for equity.* The availability of long-term resources for small and medium-size projects in Latin America is scarce, particularly in the nascent industry of biodiversity-related enterprises.
- *Timing.* The growing threat to biological resources has underscored the importance of involving all stakeholders—including the private sector—in managing and safeguarding biodiversity.
- *Catalytic role.* The fund will demonstrate the economic viability of private sector approaches to the sustainable uses of biodiversity.

Investment Focus

- Sustainable or alternative agriculture (organic farming, aquaculture, recycling of agricultural wastes, and underused species)
- Sustainable forestry (selective harvesting, mixed-species plantations)
- Sustainable harvesting of nontimber forest products
- Ecotourism.

Sponsors and Investors

Sponsors and investors include private sector investors from South America and abroad, foundations, bilateral and multilateral organizations, and other strategic investors. The IFC will invest $5 million or 20 percent of the initial capitalization, whichever is lower.

Management

A new fund management company led by experienced personnel in Rio de Janeiro, Brazil, will direct the fund. The fund management company has a board of directors and an investment committee to decide on investment proposals. In addition an advisory board of scientists, nongovernmental organizations (NGOs), and business organizations counsels the fund on biodiversity issues.

Box 1.5 Biodiversity and sustainability of agricultural systems

As with any ecosystem the functioning and sustainability of agricultural systems depend greatly on biological diversity. Through an experimental study, Tilman, Wedin, and Knops (1996) demonstrated that more diverse plant communities use and retain nutrients more efficiently, thereby attaining greater productivity and reducing nutrient-leaching losses from the ecosystem. Various soil microbes also effectively recycle nutrients. Earthworms, insects, and fungi all play a vital role.

Biological diversity also enhances natural pest control mechanisms in agroecosystems. In fact every species that exists in agroecosystems has intrinsic value. Insects provide a virtually untapped source of food (Defoliart 1989), dyes (C. L. Metcalf, Flint, and R. C. Metcalf 1962), and pharmaceutical products (Eisner 1990). Elimination or addition of even one species can have profound effects. Pimentel and others (1992) cite a remarkable example to illustrate this. Until a few years ago pollination of oil-palm trees in Malaysia was done manually—an inefficient and expensive way of performing the task. Ten years ago the government introduced a tiny weevil from West Africa's forests associated with palm pollination. The pollination of palm trees in Malaysia is now entirely accomplished by the weevil, lending to annual savings of $140 million (Greathead 1983).

Contact Information
International Finance Corporation
1850 I Street, N.W.
Washington, D.C. 20034
Michael Rubino
Tel.: 202-473-2891
Fax.: 202-334-8705
Evan McCordick
Tel.: 202-473-0674
Fax.: 202-676-0746

The connection between agricultural intensification and biodiversity preservation is frequently debated. Some would argue that agricultural intensification only exacerbates environmental problems, such as eutrophication of lakes through excessive use of fertilizers or pesticide contamination of soils and waters. A strategy for sustainable agricultural intensification will have to incorporate a blend of modern, scientific approaches to increased agricultural production and some traditional methods.

Agricultural intensification is not necessarily synonymous with mechanization and the heavy use of purchased inputs. In the agenda for action section of chapter 8 elements of a new research and development agenda are highlighted that promise to help intensify agricultural production without assaulting biodiversity. The premise is that without sustainable agricultural intensification, little biodiversity of developing countries will survive the next century.

Although intensification alone will not guarantee the survival of wild biodiversity, it at least creates the possibility. For those unconvinced that intensification is the way to go, a question arises: How can the world's population, which will double before it stabilizes, find sufficient food and other products from landscapes currently managed or abused? Most of the population growth will take place in developing countries, precisely where most of the world's biodiversity is concentrated. If agricultural intensification is not pursued, then the only way production can increase is by clearing—and destroying—much of the remaining wild heritage of plants and animals.

References

Abromovitz, J. N. 1994. "Biodiversity and Gender Issues: Recognizing Common Ground." In W. Harcourt, ed., *Feminist Perspectives on Sustainable Development.* London: Zed Books.

Avery, D. T. 1996. "Low on Farm Science, High on Pledges," *Des Moines Register.* 9 June.

Bohac, J., and K. Pokarzhevsky. 1987. "Effect of Manure and NPK on Soil Macrofauna in Chernozem Soil." In J. Szegi, ed., *Soil Biology and Conservation of Biosphere.* Vols. 1–2. Proceedings of the Ninth International Symposium. Budapest: Akademiai Kiado.

Brown, L. R. 1995. *Who Will Feed China? Wake-Up Call for a Small Planet.* New York: W. W. Norton.

Dalrymple, D. G., and J. P. Srivastava. 1994. "Transfer of Plant Cultivars: Seeds, Sectors and Society." In J. R. Anderson, ed., *Agricultural Technology: Policy Issues for the International Community.* Wallingford, U.K.: C.A.B. International.

Defoliart, G. R. 1989. "The Human Use of Insects as Food and as Animal Feed," *Bulletin of the Entomological Society of America* 35: 22–35.

Diamond, J. M., K. D. Bishop, and S. Van Balen. 1987. "Bird Survival in an Isolated Javan Woodland: Island or Mirror?" *Conservation Biology* 1: 132–42.

Eisner, T. 1990. "Prospective for Nature's Chemical

Riches," *Issues in Science and Technology* 6 (2): 31–34.

Greathead, D. J. 1983. "The Multi-Million-Dollar Weevil That Pollinates Oil-Palm," *Antenna* 7: 105–7.

Jablonski, D. 1993. "The Tropics as a Source of Evolutionary Novelty through Geological Time," *Nature* 364: 142–44.

Lal, R. 1991. "Soil Conservation and Biodiversity." In D. L. Hawksworth, ed., *The Biodiversity of Microorganisms and Invertebrates: Its Role in Sustainable Agriculture.* Wallingford, U.K.: C.A.B. International.

Metcalf, C. L., W. P. Flint, and R. L. Metcalf. 1962. *Destructive and Useful Insects.* New York: McGraw-Hill.

Myers, N. 1988. "Threatened Biotas: 'Hotspots' in Tropical Forests," *The Environmentalist* 8: 1–20.

Paoletti, M. G. 1988. "Soil Invertebrates in Cultivated and Uncultivated Soils in Northeastern Italy," *Firenze* 71: 501–63.

Pimentel, D., U. Stachow, D. A. Takacs, H. W. Brubaker, A. R. Dumas, J. J. Meaney, J. A. S. O'Neil, D. E. Onsi, and D. B. Corzilius. 1992. "Conserving Biological Diversity in Agricultural-Forestry Systems," *Bioscience* 42 (5): 354–62.

Ricklefs, R. E. 1987. "Community Diversity: Relative Role of Local and Regional Processes," *Science* 235: 167–71.

Srivastava, J. P., N. J. H. Smith, and D. A. Forno. 1996. *Biodiversity and Agriculture: Implications for Conservation and Development.* World Bank Technical Paper 321. Washington, D.C.

Thrupp, L. A. 1989. "Legitimizing Local Knowledge: from Displacement to Empowerment for Third World People," *Agriculture and Human Values* 6 (3): 13–24.

Thrupp, L. A., B. Cabarle, and A. Zazueta. 1994. "Participatory Methods in Planning and Political Processes: Linking the Grassroots and Policies for Sustainable Development," *Agriculture and Human Values* 11 (2–3): 77–84.

Tilman, D., D. Wedin, and J. Knops. 1996. "Productivity and Sustainability Influenced by Biodiversity in Grassland Ecosystems," *Nature* 379: 718–20.

Whitmore, T. C. 1985. *Tropical Rain Forests of the Far East.* Oxford: Clarendon Press.

Wilcox, B. A., and K. N. Duin. 1995. "Indigenous Cultural and Biological Diversity: Overlapping Values of Latin American Ecoregions," *Cultural Survival Quarterly* (Winter): 51–53.

Wilson, E. O. 1988. "The Current State of Biological Diversity." In E. O. Wilson and F. M. Peter, eds., *Biodiversity.* Washington, D.C.: National Academy Press.

Wood, D. 1993. *Agrobiodiversity in Global Conservation Policy.* African Centre for Technology Studies (ACTS), Biopolicy International Series No. 11. Nairobi: ACTS.

2. Harmonizing Biodiversity Conservation and Agricultural Development

Noel Vietmeyer

For most of human history people have depended on hunting, fishing, and gathering for their sustenance. Finding food was fraught with danger because many of the world's 250,000 plant species are poisonous. Over tens of thousands of years of trial and error, however, our ancestors identified about 20,000 species of plants with leaves, seeds, stems, fruits, pods, shoots, flowers, stems, tubers, or other parts that were safe to eat. They also found 2,000 edible mushrooms. And they probably regularly ate most of the world's 3,500 mammals and 9,000 birds, not to mention some reptiles (such as iguanas), amphibians (especially frogs), and about 1,000 insects. In sum prehistoric people collectively employed an enormous reservoir of food biodiversity—all of it wild.

During this trial-and-error period a few useful plants were probably protected or encouraged near campsites. Then about 10,000 years ago agriculture began in earnest as people started to cultivate some promising plants. Plant domestication began independently in Africa, China, the Middle East, South and Central America, and Southeast Asia. But during the transition to agriculture no one understood pollination, genetics, fertilizers, microbial pest organisms, or the other knowledge that we now consider indispensable for domesticating any species.

Narrowing Used Species

With the passing millennia farmers understandably focused on the plants most amenable to their conditions. From the 20,000 edible species about 3,000 were sampled. Eventually only a few hundred became seriously cultivated in fields and gardens. In the last fifty years or so less than 100 crops and 24 domesticated animals have been significant enough to be included in global lists of agricultural crops.

Today the food base is smaller than ever: a dozen crops now feed most of humanity. These pillar crops include cereals such as barley, maize, millet, rice, sorghum, and wheat; several root crops such as cassava, potato, and sweet potato; and a handful of legumes such as beans, peanuts, and soybean; and bananas, coconut, and sugarcane (figure 2.1).

In the same way the number of species used in forestry has also narrowed. At least 50,000 species of trees exist, yet conifers comprise 70–80 percent of the roughly 100 million hectares of forestry plantations. Even among cultivated conifers only a small range of the available species is grown. Most commercial plantings include only a few species from the genus Pinus. Among non-conifers one or two species of poplars and eucalypts dominate.

Animal husbandry followed a narrowing course as well. Most of the world's 3,500 mammals and 9,000 birds—not to mention numerous reptiles and insects—have been trapped, snared, speared, netted, or grabbed for food at one time or another. But over the millenia only a couple dozen were domesticated, such as the turkey, duck, goose, water buffalo, horse, donkey, camel, and alpaca. Today almost all meat, milk,

Figure 2.1 Annual production of crops that feed humanity

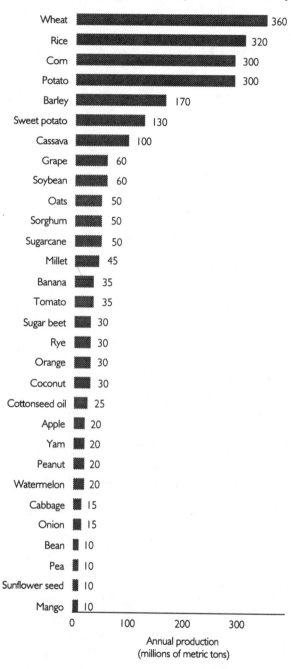

Annual production
(millions of metric tons)

Source: Vietmeyer 1986.

harvest then provided slightly better food: roots became plumper, fruits sweeter, seeds quicker cooking, or vegetable leaves more tender. For livestock farmers bred types that gained weight faster, gave more milk or more wool, or were better at pulling carts or laying eggs. In some cases this age-old selection process has produced the good-tasting, high-yielding, attractive crop varieties and productive livestock that we rely on for the bulk of our food. Horticulture depends on the same approach, cloning elite varieties such as Red Delicious apples, for example. Forestry is moving in the same direction and is now starting to clone top-performing tree specimens.

Reliance on a select array of crop varieties and livestock breeds produces record harvests and is the basic reason the earth's 5 billion people are as relatively well fed as they are. The narrowing process has reached dangerous thresholds, however. Large numbers of farmers now employ the same varieties and breeds over wide areas, even on different continents. The seeds that farmers sow may come from different companies, but they often contain much the same genetic material. In the United States, for example, all commercially grown maize comes from just six strains, two-thirds of rice from four, half the cotton from three, and half the wheat from nine. Wheat on the Great Plains can actually be the same variety from horizon to horizon.

In animal husbandry genetic uniformity is such that a handful of breeds now dominate worldwide. In North America, for instance, virtually all beef comes from two breeds (Angus and Hereford), while Holsteins produce most of the continent's milk. In industrial nations virtually all broiler chickens are a cross between White Cornish and White Plymouth Rock, and chickens destined for commercial egg production are also derived from the interbreeding of just two strains. The world's turkey farmers buy more than half of their chicks from a single corporation.

Increasing Vulnerability

Genetic uniformity raises the danger that crop and livestock resources could succumb to diseases or pests. Domesticated organisms are par-

eggs, and other animal products come from just five animals: cattle, pigs, goats, sheep, and chickens.

Genetic narrowing in crop production, forestry, and animal husbandry is even greater than we realize because farmers have selected individual specimens whose qualities stood out from the rest. For crops farmers have tended to save only seeds of elite plants. The subsequent

ticularly at risk because from nature's perspective they are unnatural. Because people have chosen plants for traits such as tender leaves, large seeds, good flavor, and synchronized germination, the transformed plants are often ill-adapted to cope with nature, where hard leaves, small seeds, bad flavor, and variable germination are necessary protections. The danger is not so much that disease will break out but that—with all the specimens so genetically similar—a small outbreak will explode into a catastrophic epidemic and devastate the primary production that keeps humanity fed.

In addition to the specter of an uncontrollable disease farmers must cope with shifting demands for agricultural products. Contrary to public perceptions agriculture is never static; it must constantly adjust to a changing environment triggered by new technologies, emerging consumer preferences, rising fuel prices, alterations in pricing policies, and even climate change. A narrowed genetic base reduces the options for adapting to change.

The ability of agricultural and pastoral systems to adjust to change and meet ever-increasing demands for food and other agricultural products thus hinges on the availability of a broad range of plant and animal resources. Only when the integrity of this genetic safety net is assured can agriculture remain productive and resilient in the face of unexpected shocks. And those unexpected shocks can be very real. Consider these examples from the history of agriculture and forestry.

Agriculture

All the major crops have their own natural enemies that can bring on catastrophic collapse. The history of agriculture is replete with examples of such collapses:

- *Wheat*. Ancient writings of the Middle East and Mediterranean describe devastating grain losses that brought famines and even the downfall of whole societies. Thousands of years later a disturbing succession of stem, leaf, and stripe rusts and major outbreaks of viruses, smuts, and other microbes are still concerns. In the United States, for example, a stem-rust epidemic destroyed almost all of the wheat crop in 1904. In 1917 another rust mutant rose up so destructively that the government had to institute wheatless days. In the 1950s yet another rust caused similar destruction. Most Americans could find alternative foods, but other nations are not always so lucky. In 1943, for instance, the wheat crop's failure in eastern India brought on a disastrous famine and the death of millions of people.

- *Rice*. In Indonesia a serious rice pest, the brown planthopper, became resistant to virtually every insecticide by the 1980s. This hardy insect threatened to wipe out all of Asia's hard-won self-sufficiency in rice.

- *Potato*. In 1846 Ireland's potato fields fell victim to a Mexican fungus that the potato plant (which hails from South America) had not previously encountered in Europe. Today at least a dozen fungi capable of similar devastation are known; if any of them reached epidemic proportions in potato fields, they could threaten the lives and fortunes of millions of Africans Asians, Latin Americans, and Europeans. One such fungal threat, a variant of the same species that once devastated Ireland, is already on the rampage, and current potato varieties appear to be susceptible to it.

- *Cassava*. A mealybug that destroys cassava—the food of last resort for millions of the world's poor—was detected in Zaire in 1973. Within ten years this insect had penetrated some thirty-four countries where 200 million Africans depend on this resilient crop for their lives. By 1982 yields had plummeted as much as 60 percent, forcing millions to abandon the root that for generations has been their staple.

- *Citrus*. In 1985 citrus canker suddenly appeared in Florida where the few strains of oranges and grapefruit are all susceptible to this disease-causing agent. Nothing could be done to combat the newly arrived bacterium other than sacrifice 12 million valuable trees before the whole crop became infected.

- *Banana*. Black Sigatoka, a fungal plague that kills banana plants, appeared in Fiji in the 1920s and is now moving inexorably around the globe, bringing disaster to the world's biggest fruit crop. Even worse in human terms would be the loss of the plantains and cooking bananas upon which millions of lives depend. Most varieties of bananas and plantains are susceptible to black Sigatoka.

Forestry

The risk inherent in relying on a handful of species or clones is also evident in forestry species:

- *Poplar.* In France a single poplar clone grown throughout the country succumbed to disease in recent years. New Zealand had a similar experience in the 1980s.
- *Pine.* New Zealand has instituted military-style operations to keep out bark beetles and gypsy moths that have devastated pine plantations in other regions. Radiata pine is planted over vast areas in New Zealand and is so important that the national economy could collapse without it.
- *Rubber.* Most of the world's rubber comes from just eight clones, each at risk should a pest or pathogen arrive. South America harbors a leaf-blight fungus that will wipe them all out if its spores ever manage to gain a foothold in Southeast Asia. The potential for devastation is therefore very real, with likely calamitous results for anyone who depends on wheeled vehicles.

Biodiversity Defense

Painful collapses of agricultural and forestry yields have taught agricultural researchers that to neglect diverse gene sources is to endanger humanity. Biodiversity is a sort of immune system husbanded by previous generations. To pass it on undiminished is each generation's charge.

Agricultural biodiversity encompasses the genetic foundations that support every type of land use: field farming, horticulture, pasturing, even aquaculture. And biodiversity underpins much more than food resources. Cultivated plants provide humankind with wood, paper, rubber, resins, dyes, medicinals, and insecticides, to name a few. In fact their biodiversity sustains most things in our lives: food, clothing, shelter, and many other items that we enjoy or need.

The problem now is that many landacres of old varieties and local breeds are being lost as farmers are attracted to the narrower base of higher-yielding and other premium varieties bred by modern science. If an African, Chinese, or Mexican farmer abandons a variety that has traditionally fed his or her family, that genetic line may become extinct in a year—even less if the family eats the seed that would have been used for replanting.

Just like last year's farm machinery, many plant varieties and animal breeds formerly held in high regard are considered obsolete and are nearly extinct. For example, the Rhode Island Red, once North America's premier chicken, is almost gone. Ten years ago the United States annually registered 10,000 Tamworth pigs; today there are some 1,000 Tamworths alive. A few decades ago Ayrshire, Guernsey, Jersey, and Milking Shorthorn were worldwide dairy breeds; today they are unknown in the dozens of countries that once relied on them.

The situation is hardly better in the wild. Until this century seemingly endless natural preserves such as tropical forests maintained crops' ancestors and botanical relatives. Even though wild crops may look unkempt next to their highly bred brethren they are vitally important: left to battle for survival, they have retained age-old immunities. Long buffeted by weed competition, drought and disease, insects, fungi, heat and cold, they are treasure chests of genes. After all, only the strong and adaptable have endured.

When specific genes are needed in the future, we now run the risk that they may not be available. Consider a recent close call with the coffee crop. Coffee production has been flirting with failure ever since an incurable leaf rust appeared in Ceylon in 1869, sapping the life out of coffee trees. It turned the British into tea drinkers and Latin Americans into the world's coffee producers. But in 1970 the fungus was spotted in Brazil, and in 1976 it showed up in Central America. Fearing that coffee production would collapse as it had in Ceylon, researchers began scouring the forests of Ethiopia, the original source of the main form of coffee. They were just in time.

Almost 90 percent of the forest had been removed, and new roads were slicing up the remainder. Most wild coffee trees had already been cut and burned, but a few samples were collected and planted in Costa Rica. Some have proven resistant to the leaf rust.

Vital Cradle Regions

Sites where crops emerged from the wild are particularly important sources of disease and pest resistance. Scientists can identify those cradle regions because there they find an array of ancestral varieties and wild relatives. For instance, Southwestern Asia (Afghanistan to Turkey) is the source of wheat, rye, peas, carrots, apples, and pears. China produced soybeans, peaches, and several vegetables; Southeast Asia, rice, sugarcane, and bananas; Mexico and the Caribbean, maize, sweet potato, beans, squash, and avocado; and South America, pineapple, potato, tomato, chili peppers, peanut, papaya, and chocolate. Most cradle regions are in the developing world.

Scientists have often dipped their nets into biodiversity riches and saved food supplies in probably every nation on earth. Examples of such genetic trawling include:

- The blight that devastated Ireland's potato crop in the last century was overcome with resistance genes found in a wild potato in Mexico, the home of the fungus that causes the disease.
- A nondescript Mexican maize saved the American maize crop in the early 1970s when another blight struck 50 percent of the crop.
- Rice grown in Southeast Asia is protected from four main rice diseases by genes located providentially in a single species of wild rice from India.
- A barley plant from Ethiopia has provided a gene that protects California's $160 million barley crop, as well as Canada's barley crop.
- Tomatoes could not be grown commercially without genes from at least nine wild relatives from Peru.
- On the eve of World War II Central America's banana industry was rescued by genes from a banana plant collected in a botanic garden in Saigon that provided resistance to the devastating Panama disease.
- The U.S. spinach crop is protected from blight and wilt by genes from a Chinese large-leafed spinach, whose seeds an American plant explorer picked up early in the century.

These few examples show that when it comes to biodiversity, no nation is an island; each depends on others for genes to sustain its crops.

Today's Precarious Situation

Pests and diseases have destroyed plants ever since both evolved millions of years ago, but the presence of uniform crops laid out in massive blocks can induce outbreaks on a global scale. Indeed, only stringent quarantine, intense plant breeding, a few biological controls, and synthetic pesticides have thwarted the hungry hordes in recent times. But the future is more uncertain than ever. For one thing concern over the hazards of chemical sprays is removing one of the four weapons.

The quarantine system is also breaking down because jet aircraft are giving insects, bacteria, and fungi that cannot survive long sea journeys a chance to globe hop. They may inadvertently stow away in the hold of an airplane, in soil on a person's shoe, or in the luggage of travelers convinced that one little fruit could not possibly hurt the next country. In the new home, however, the pests and diseases can find a paradise of gourmet dining and few natural enemies to block them.

Biological controls have proved no panacea. They take time to develop and are specific to certain predators and parasites that attack a given pest and nothing else. Indeed, the introduced controls can themselves become pests, as happened in Australia with a toad imported to eat sugarcane borers.

Because humanity must henceforth get along with a reduced chemical arsenal, a leaky quarantine system, and limited biological controls, boosting crops' own self-defenses through biodiversity has become the main hope for sustaining the supply of resources on which humanity depends.

Mobilizing more genes is also the main means of responding to changing needs. For instance, pressure to boost farm productivity is rising because another billion people will soon need food. Moreover, the food supply is faced with an increasing array of environmental challenges, including creeping deserts, dropping water tables, water and air pollution, floods, soil erosion, acid rain. In the face of these conditions biodiversity will be needed more than ever.

Changing Paradigm

Luckily, appreciation for biodiversity is mounting. People are increasingly aware of the importance of returning to nature in search of better ways to do things. Following fifty years of chemical breakthroughs (sulfa drugs, superphosphate, herbicides, nylon, and plastic foams)—some of which are being reevaluated or withdrawn (DDT, for example)—a more harmonious blend of approaches is now being attempted. Reinstating nature is creating a new and better balanced era of sustainability.

This shift in direction will have a particularly noticeable impact in developing countries in Africa, Asia, and Latin America. Vast new windows of opportunity are opening because those countries are crammed with species largely overlooked by science and technology.

For example, developing world food plants include 3,000 fruits, 1,000 vegetables, several hundred grains, and perhaps 100 roots and tubers. Even today their varieties are unsorted, their requirements unquantified, their potentials undetermined. Ignorant outsiders may see these unlisted food plants as obsolete, uncompetitive, and unwanted, but some of the foods—such as Africa's bambara groundnut, Asia's jackfruit, and Latin America's oca—are actually feeding millions and have exceptional qualities for global use (see chapter 4).

These lesser-known food crops have been generally neglected because the world's research centers are concentrated in the temperate zones. Some food crops are also ignored because they are considered poor people's plants (box 2.1).

Market Diversification

For many kinds of produce export opportunities are brighter than ever. New fruits and vegetables are being shipped around the world in ever-increasing quantities. Starfruit and kiwi are examples. The appetite for new taste sensations in affluent nations is driving the demand for novelty products, and modern technologies, such as packaging, chilled air-freight, and controlled-atmosphere containers help make it possible.

Even the pharmaceutical industry, a former bastion of synthetic resources, is returning to natural products in search of new possibilities for commerce. Moreover, as agricultural land or irrigation water becomes scarce in countries like Chile and Israel, producers are turning to new, high-value food crops.

A vivid broadening of agricultural diversity can be seen in Homestead, Florida, which is becoming one of the world's most diverse and dynamic farming areas. Many of its fruits and vegetables hail from developing nations and are being grown by immigrant farmers. These foods are being marketed nationwide and even worldwide, giving poor people's crops a chance to compete (box 2.2).

Changing Needs

Burgeoning recognition of sustainability (as opposed to just productivity) opens whole new fields for biodiversifying global resources. This is creating new opportunities for previously unconsidered plants. Here are a few examples:

- *Wastewater treatment.* Duckweeds and other aquatic plants are starting to be used instead of conventional methods for treating wastewater. Grown in man-made wetlands, they offer an inexpensive way to help relieve one of the world's worst public health problems, sewage-born disease. There is a wealth of aquatic plant biodiversity with formerly undreamed of potential.
- *Land stabilization.* Hedges placed on the contour are now seen as a new tool for erosion control, replacing terracing and land shaping, creating demands for formerly obscure plants such as vetiver, switchgrass, and various tropical shrubs.
- *Soil restoration.* A rising interest in green manures and cover crops is creating niches for many formerly unknown legumes that can restore fertility to soil in place of fertilizer.

Box 2.1 Poor people's plants

It is a universal phenomenon that certain plants are stigmatized by their humble associations. Scores of highly promising crop plants around the world receive no research funding, no recognition from the agricultural community; they are ostracized as poor person's crops.

For information on a poor person's crop one has to turn more often than not to botanists, anthropologists, and geographers. Only they will have taken an interest in the plant. Often there has been no agricultural research on it at all—no varieties collected or compared, no germination or spacing trials, no yield determinations or even nutritional analyses. And yet the crop actually may be crucial to the quality of life—even the survival—of millions.

Peanuts, potatoes, and other common crops once suffered this same discrimination. In the United States the peanut was considered to be slave food until little more than a century ago, and in the 1600s the English refused to eat potatoes because they considered them Irish food. Just fifty years ago the now-cherished soybean was itself a poor person's crop in the United States, where researchers had spurned it since Benjamin Franklin first introduced seeds from the Jardin des Plantes in Paris. To advocate soybean then was to risk being branded a crackpot. Early in this century Americans still considered the soybean a second-rate crop, fit only for export to poor people in the Far East. The crop acquired new status as a legitimate research target only in the 1920s, and its development gained so much momentum that it now is the nation's most valuable crop in dollar terms.

Nowhere is the neglect of poor person's crops greater than in the tropics—the very area where food is most desperately needed. The wealth and variety of poor people's species is staggering, but most agricultural scientists are unaware of their scope or potential. Some of the world's best crops are waiting in the poor person's gardens. Merely to have survived as useful crops suggests that the plants are inherently superior. They are already suited to the poor person's small plots, mixed farming, and poor soils. The plants poor people grow are usually robust, productive, self-reliant, and useful—the very type needed to feed the hungriest regions.

The marama bean is just one example. Known only in the Kalahari and neighboring sandy, semi-desert regions of southern Africa, this legume feeds some of the poorest of the earth's people: those in Botswana, Namibia, and South Africa who still subsist solely on wild fruits and plants, game, and birds. To the !Kung bushmen it is the second most important food. When roasted, its seeds have a rich, nutty flavor that has been likened to that of cashews or almonds. The seeds are exceptionally nutritious, with a protein content (37 percent) essentially the same as soybean and an oil content (33 percent) similar to the peanut. Marama bean is a poor person's plant whose nutritional content ranks with two of the world's best protein and food energy sources.

In addition to its seeds the marama bean produces tubers that can weigh as much as 40 kilograms and grow to 1 meter in diameter. People of the Kalahari region dig up the young tubers when they weigh about 1 kilogram. Baked, boiled, or roasted, they have a pleasant, sweet flavor and make a good vegetable dish. The succulent flesh, sometimes containing as much as 90 percent moisture, is an important emergency source of water.

With such attributes this poor person's plant should have been developed for large-scale cultivation long ago. Given its due share of research, this legume might become a valuable new crop for semi-arid lands everywhere.

- *Pest control.* Disillusionment with synthetic pesticides is opening possibilities for replacement materials derived from plants such as the neem tree (NRC 1992).
- *Water clarification.* Seeds of the moringa tree can clarify turbid water as effectively as alum, the chemical that most developing countries now import.
- *Global cooling.* Concerns over the buildup of greenhouse gases opens new opportunities for certain tropical trees and other plants—many of them previously considered of little value—that absorb carbon dioxide with high efficiency.
- *Healthcare.* Rising interest in medicinal plants used by people in developing nations is highlighting a wealth of biodiversity that agronomists have hitherto ignored. This includes many potentially high-value new crops (Srivastava, Lambert, and Vietmeyer 1996).

Biodiversity for Integrated Pest Management

One of agriculture's great hopes is integrated pest management, which uses wholly different biodiversity from that normally considered in farming. These organisms include:

Box 2.2 Tropical biodiversity comes to America

Susan Baterna and her husband Robert pick winged beans from vines growing along a high wire fence fronting a highway near Homestead, Florida. The couple is trying to grow every variety of Philippine vegetable. Their farm is a riot of mingled fruit trees and vegetable plants: calamondins (a sour, limelike fruit used to season fish and meats), snake gourds, bottle gourds, bitter melons, yard-long beans, horseradish trees (the leaves and pods are used as cooked vegetables), chayote (a pear-shaped squash with a taste halfway between cucumber and apple), and a sweet potato variety whose leaves are eaten like spinach.

The Baternas are part of impressive changes underway in the southern Florida agricultural scene. Orchardists who used to plant lemons and grapefruit now raise carambolas and mamey. Some farmers are cutting down limes and avocados and planting longan, lychee, atemoya, and sugar apple. One farmer is pulling out citrus and putting in jackfruit. The whole area looks like a transplanted bit of the developing world.

Scores of such African, Asian, and Latin American fruits—not to mention vegetables, herbs, spices, and even a dozen or so mushrooms—are now entering American kitchens. Supermarket shelves already carry foods of Central and South America, China, Cuba, Indochina, Mexico, the Philippines, and the West Indies. Many are selling briskly; some will end up as American as apple pie (probably originating in England), pizza (Italy), French fries (Peru via France), peanuts (Brazil), sweet potato (tropical America), black-eyed peas (Africa), soybean (China), and popcorn (Peru).

- *Spiders*. In China jumping spiders and wolf spiders (which stalk insects rather than build webs) can be so effective at controlling insects that insecticides are unneeded. Farmers now build straw houses in their fields to help the spiders survive the winter. Emerging from hibernation, the hungry spiders go to work consuming pests on the newly planted rice seedlings. This suppresses the insect population right from the start, and the eight-legged patrol force keeps it down throughout the critical part of the growing season.
- *Wasps*. When the cassava mealybug broke out in Africa, researchers scoured Latin America for its origin. In country after country they were unsuccessful, but in a remote area of Argentina they discovered both the pest and a predator that would attack it. A diminutive wasp proved a safe control, and dispersing it over Africa's cassava fields controlled the outbreak that threatened the lives of 200 million people.
- *Geese*. Because these vegetarian birds relish grasses and shun most broad-leafed plants, they can be used to rid grassy weeds among many crops (strawberries, for instance). They thus help the crop and provide high-value poultry.
- *Muscovy duck*. Following a lead from local farming practice, Canadian researchers have found that these domesticated ducks from tropical America are exceptionally effective at catching flies in the farmyard. In cattle stalls and on pig farms they save on insecticide and sell for a profit at season's end.
- *Wild ducks*. In Arkansas farmers formerly drained their rice fields for the winter, but now they keep them flooded. The watery expanses attract migratory ducks that eat the weeds and save the farmer a lot of later expense in herbicide purchases. Before the new crop is planted, the well-fed birds have flown back to Canada to breed.

Turning Pests into Resources

Pests can be turned into assets in some cases. Pest is a cultural term; it depends on one's perspective. Thinking of pests as potential resources opens up new and doubly useful biodiversity applications for creatures previously associated only with destruction. Examples of the organized exploitation of pests include:

- *Deer*. In New Zealand introduced deer wreaked havoc with the native forests until safe and economical methods for capturing and butchering them were developed. New Zealand venison has been selling well in Germany for several decades, and the local forests—now almost clear of the pests—are recovering their age-old splendor. New Zealanders consider this change the greatest improvement to their country's lush forests.
- *Rabbits*. Introduced rabbits are an equally serious problem in New Zealand. Now in an

extension of the success with deer, a local entrepreneur has started exporting field-shot wild rabbits to the game-meat markets of Europe.

- *Quelea.* This sparrow-like finch sweeps across much of Africa in flocks often containing millions of birds. These flying grain eaters descend on field after field, stripping each bare before moving on. In Zimbabwe, however, wildlife researchers have found that properly placed blocks of tall grass attract whole flocks to roost overnight. On dark nights people can approach these roosts and capture the birds by the thousands. Although small these grain-fed marauders make good eating and are even being exported to Hong Kong's poultry markets.
- *Armadillo and nutria.* The state of Louisiana has had at least modest success in reducing the populations of these creatures by developing recipes and holding cooking contests to encourage Americans to consume them.
- *Brush-tailed possum.* In Australia an entrepreneurial businessman and conservationist has found a market in Hong Kong for the meat of this arboreal marsupial, whose exploding populations are stripping trees bare and endangering the native forests of Tasmania.

Using Exotic Biodiversity

Although hunting and gathering began giving way to organized agriculture thousands of years ago, more wild biodiversity is used than people think. In Sweden, for instance, the 150,000 elk shot in sport each year represent more than a quarter of the national consumption of meat. In Africa the total contribution of wild animals, mainly mammals, to the diet is as much as 80 percent in Ghana, 70 percent in Zaire, 60–70 percent in Liberia, and 60 percent in Botswana. In the Leonardo da Vinci region of Amazonian Brazil wild animals supply about a fifth of the total protein intake. In Botswana hunters kill some 2.2 million springhares (a rabbit-sized rodent) a year and so provide as much meat as 20,000 cattle produce.

This type of biodiversity use is grossly overlooked by science. Yet there is much to be learned and gained by exploring the potential of new plant and animal domesticates.

New domestications. More organized production of creatures that to us seem impossibly exotic but to local people are valued and even vital food resources is now under way (NRC 1991). The domestication of new crops and livestock opens up exciting territory for harmonizing biodiversity use and wildlife conservation. These poor people's livestock include:

- *Iguana.* Costa Rica has an extremely successful program to raise these large, tree-living lizards. Green iguanas can now be produced routinely in large numbers and in simple facilities. To reduce operating costs, iguanas are left to live in the wild for a year or so, which means the farmers must have trees around. Iguana production is therefore a catalyst for reforestation (box 2.3).
- *Paca.* A researcher in Panama has learned how to rear this big forest rodent, which is a

---

Box 2.3 Mama iguana

Throughout much of Latin America large leaf-eating lizards called iguanas are a popular food. To fill demand, they are hunted by rifle, slingshot, trap, and noose; they are even run down by trained dogs. Because of human appetite for both the animal and its forest habitat, iguana populations are dwindling.

In Costa Rica biologist Dagmar Werner is showing how to produce large numbers of these alert, curious social reptiles. Her research farm looks more like a poultry run than a cattle ranch. The facility contains pens made of bamboo and corrugated roofing iron (constructed in ways that can easily be duplicated by farmers). Inside the pens short lengths of bamboo are piled up to form apartments into which the lizards squeeze to sleep. The hole is shaded by trees with thick branches where the animals indulge in their favorite pastime—sunning.

Despite their endangered status iguanas reproduce well. Each female produces thirty or more eggs a year, and most of the eggs hatch. If the young are protected from predators during their first year, iguana populations can build up rapidly. Once they reach adulthood, they have few natural enemies other than humans, so their populations can remain high.

This project demonstrates how locals can generate income while keeping the tropical forests intact. By farming an animal that lives in trees, people can benefit without cutting the forest. Iguana raising then is an alternative to the current destruction of the jungle to create fields for crops or pastures for cattle.
Source: NRC 1991.

delicacy throughout Central and northern South America. Because pacas in the wild are extremely territorial and fight each other to the death, domestication had been deemed impossible. But the aggressiveness turns out to be a learned behavior; raising the newborns with docile mothers eliminates this pugnacious trait from the population.

- *Grasscutter.* Across much of Africa this field rodent is considered a delicacy. It contributes to the nutrition of millions and can be seen in myriad meat markets. In Ghana researchers have pioneered the organized rearing of grasscutters. Other African nations are following this lead and raising this new addition to animal husbandry.
- *Duikers.* These rabbit-sized antelopes are prized for food throughout most of Sub-Saharan Africa. Demand is so great that scientists fear for the survival of the various species. Efforts are now under way in Zimbabwe and other nations to organize duiker husbandry. The timid little ruminants offer promise for household rearing as well as for ranching at forest edges, where they would provide locals with a powerful incentive to retain the trees.
- *Eland.* In Texas and Kenya this large antelope is reared on game park-like ranches.
- *Emu.* Ranching of this ostrich-like bird is taking off in the United Kingdom, United States, and New Zealand, much to the surprise of Australians who look on the native emu as something of a nuisance to farmers.

Exotic introductions. Even industrial nations are beginning to experiment with exotic animals. For example, emu steaks are selling briskly in London supermarkets, and not just because of a current scare over the safety of British beef. Among the exotic creatures being raised commercially in industrial nations are the following.

- *Ostrich.* These African birds are being farmed in Australia, New Zealand, and the United States.
- *Yak.* Canadians have reared this shaggy Asian bovine for more than fifty years. Before World War II several government research stations were devoted to adapting this extremely cold-tolerant creature to the rigors of Canadian winters.
- *Bison.* In the United States the return of the native buffalo from near extinction is something of a legend. Buffalo steaks are now common fare in the western parts of the nation.
- *Alpaca.* This relative of the camel produces the finest of fleeces. Light in weight and high in insulation, alpaca wool is woven into sweaters and comforters that fetch high prices. In Australia and the United States pioneering farmers have begun rearing alpacas, but in the Andes, where the donkey-sized animal is native, alpaca numbers have slipped below 3 million.
- *Llama.* Cousin to the alpaca, the mule-sized llama has risen from a few specimens in a California game park to a small industry. Although llamas produce good wool, they are mainly used to carry supplies for backpackers and others living in high-altitude wilderness areas served only by trails.

To some ranching exotic game may seem just an interest of the rich, the impractical, or the avaricious. That should not detract from the serious side of this effort, however. These challenging creatures contribute to biodiversification of resources. Some offer potential use for the global future. As an example both alpaca and llama can live at extreme altitudes, and both have soft-soled feet like a dog's that, unlike the hoofs of mainstream livestock, leave the hillsides unscarred.

Biodiversity Savers

People in various places are saving heirloom varieties of beans, apples, pears, potatoes, tomatoes, and other crops. Groups dedicated to saving the old breeds of livestock have sprung up in Britain, Germany, other parts of Europe, the United States, and elsewhere. Most of these barnyard conservationists are not scientists, but professionals are increasingly involved in rescuing bloodlines of family-farm livestock and old varieties of garden vegetables. This is people's participation in biodiversity conservation. Indeed in saving the genes of tomorrow, concerned conservationists can do much in their backyards and farms that the researchers cannot do in their sophisticated laboratories.

This new thrust in conservation holds out opportunities for direct involvement by millions of interested people. Those who can do little to save rhinos or whales can often keep alive some ancient strain of beans or chickens in their gardens and backyards. Already one enthusiast in the United States plants about ninety different strains of potatoes each year; a legendary Scot plants several hundred. These amateurs provide an internationally recognized service, and they guard a greater wealth of genes than most scientists. The Rhode Island Red and dozens of other chickens are being kept from complete extinction by backyard conservationists, as are certain pigeons, pheasants, sheep, pigs, rabbits, goats, and other livestock. Some may consider themselves hobbyists having fun, but scientists are beginning to see them as vital guardians of our genetic heritage. This homespun conservation is strengthening the foundations of agriculture.

Seed-saver movements are now taking hold in India. They started as programs to save varieties from extinction, but Indians now are equating biodiversity with freedom and self-reliance, and the movement has taken on a nationalistic importance and strength.

In the long run the people who save the genes of our crops and animals may be among the most important of all conservationists (box 2.4). A displaced crop or breed does not mean that it has no future. The modern homogenized breeds often cannot cope with uncommon environments or needs, and filling specialized niches is one of the most promising uses for rare breeds. Indeed many old types are already showing that they have the strengths to compete. Consider the following examples:

- *Texas Longhorn.* America's most famous breed of cattle in the past century, the Texas Longhorn, was down to ten animals in the 1950s. Herds of this distinctive breed are once again increasing because ranchers appreciate its hardiness and easy calving.
- *European oxen.* Limousin, Charolais, and Chiannina breeds, which were displaced by the tractor half a century ago, are coming back because their giant muscles make them ideal beef animals.
- *Soay sheep.* This antique sheep, a hold-over from the Bronze Age, has been put to use grazing spoil dumps near the China-clay pits in Cornwall, England. The great mounds of muck were formerly classified unsuitable for agriculture, but this little sheep is proving ideal for living off their thin grass. Hardy and inured to disease and harshness, the Soays need no shepherd, no shearing (the wool sheds naturally), no insecticide (their coarse hair deters biting flies), and they are so light that they do not scar the unstable spoil slopes, thereby reducing the risk of erosion.

Box 2.4 Importance of saving "useless" biodiversity

In the 1930s a farmer in Connecticut spotted a mutant maize plant whose kernels were soft and very different from all the rest in his field. Instead of throwing it away, he took it to the state agricultural experiment station, where it lay unappreciated on a shelf for thirty years.

Then in the 1960s chemists invented an instrument for analyzing the amino acids that make up protein. A Purdue University professor, analyzing all the maize samples he could obtain, discovered that this Connecticut mutant maize plant had a nutritional power far greater than any other. With about twice the lysine and tryptophan it provided two essential amino acids rare in plant proteins. For Africa and Latin America, where maize is the main sustenance for millions of poor, it seemed a magnificent breakthrough.

But the softness of the kernels was a deterrent because normal maize-based foods could not be made from them. The exciting development was subsequently dropped. But at the International Maize and Wheat Improvement Center in Mexico an analytical chemist and a maize breeder continued the effort by trying to produce a normal-seeded form that retained the superior protein content and matched the productivity of the world's best maize varieties. After fifteen years of dedication they succeeded.

Today this new crop called quality-protein maize is among the highest-yielding maizes in South Africa, Brazil, and Ghana. Its protein has a nutritional quality almost the equal of milk. A program in Ghana directed by Nobel laureate Norman Borlaug and former president Jimmy Carter is showing success with quality-protein maize on a considerable scale. Other African countries are testing it, and the crop has caught on in Brazil, where 100,000 hectares are now grown annually.

Source: NRC 1988.

Biodiversity-Friendly Farming

Seen in global perspective, today's agriculture disregards the true wealth of biodiversity; but pockets of diverse production can still be found, particularly in the fields of traditional farmers in developing nations. Examples include:

- *The Amazon.* Home gardens can contain dozens of trees and shrub species, and people harvest many more plant species from the wild.
- *Costa Rica.* Certain farmers employ more than fifty species of trees and shrubs in living fences that demarcate property lines and also provide firewood, vegetables, forage, and other products.
- *Java and Sri Lanka.* Traditional food gardens that combine trees, shrubs, groundcovers, and field crops may incorporate dozens of species per hectare.
- *Rwanda.* As many as fourteen varieties of beans can be found in a single field. Consumers like the variety in their meals, but the main value seems to be risk aversion; the mixture helps farmers overcome unreliable rains and other hazards.
- *The Andes.* More than forty types of potatoes, as well as other root crops such as oca and ulluco, can be found in the same field. Each has a separate culinary or social purpose.
- *Guatemalan highlands.* Maize, cowpea, and two types of field bean are commonly grown together in a mutually supporting combination that helps the soil and the farmer.
- *Syria.* Western specialists often disparage the untidy-looking wheat fields, but by planting three or more varieties, the farmers are better assured a profitable yield in that uncertain climate.
- *Mexico.* As many as 376 species of cultivated plants have been recorded in the home gardens of the Yucatán Peninsula.
- *Turkey.* Turkish wheat farmers still commonly employ age-old landraces, shunning the high-yield varieties because they need the long straw to feed their cows, goats, and horses.

Mixed plantings such as these are just one form of biodiversity-friendly farming. Others include crop rotation, low-input farming, and agroforestry in fields away from houses. All these forms of polyculture are garnering increased recognition and respect.

Endangered species. Until the 1960s Papua New Guinea was inundated with crocodiles, and hunting was a major industry. By 1969, however, hunters had eliminated the saltwater crocodile from much of the country. Yet demand for shoes, handbags, luggage, wallets, watchbands, and other luxury articles made from crocodile leather was insatiable, and more were being slaughtered. Then in the early 1970s wildlife officers came up with an answer: restore the population by banning the killing of mature crocodiles and farming their offspring instead (NRC 1983b).

Wildlife officers in Papua New Guinea now help build pens and teach the care of young reptiles that are so remarkably vulnerable and timid that they can literally die of fright. The villagers surround their ponds with a stockade and add crocodile hatchlings caught in nearby swamps.

This harmonious blend of agriculture and wildlife conservation has led to an organized industry somewhat like chicken rearing. Being a crocodile farmer is not as fearsome as might seem. Crocodiles that are kept fed remain so content they seldom move. Being cold-blooded, they waste no energy keeping warm. The combination of inaction and meager energy use means they grow fast on little feed. In fact 2 kilograms of fish are converted into 1 kilogram of young crocodile, a remarkable ratio. A specimen can reach 2 meters in length within two to three years, when it is worth more than $200.

Papua New Guinea's idea of relying on the wild for stocking the farms is now a model for saving other species elsewhere and is credited with helping save twenty-three of the twenty-four crocodilian species, most of which faced extinction just twenty years ago. Skins produced this way receive special dispensation and can be legally sold around the world.

Many countries are setting up similar programs. Venezuela, for example, issues special licenses to landowners and puts tamper-proof barcodes on every skin. Some 150,000 crocodile skins are now legally exported. As a result Venezuelan farmers have found wealth in their swamplands; the old pests now bring as much income per hectare as cattle. This creates an incentive both to keep the crocodiles breeding and to keep the swamps productive. In other words it blends biodiversity use with habitat protection.

Endangered habitats. As in the case of crocodiles any species that can prove its worth to people can stake a stronger claim to survival space in an increasingly crowded world. Papua New Guinea also has programs for the sustainable production of such wild animals as butterflies, deer, maleo (a strange bird with delicious eggs), and cassowaries, birds that can weigh 50 kilograms. These ranching systems are based on sustainably exploiting wild creatures, mainly by using traditional methods and incorporating the local people's long-term interests.

Indeed wildlife ranching is beginning to show that it can provide dozens of new farm resources while helping to save endangered species and, at least in some cases, their habitats. Butterflies were the first native livestock to be tried. In the 1970s a number of Papua New Guinea's beautiful birdwing butterflies were becoming scarce because of over-collecting. Through careful observation it was found that the birdwing larvae ate Dutchman's pipe vines and the adult butterflies liked hibiscus flowers. When those were planted together, the iridescent green and blue birdwings fluttered out of the forests and took up residence (NRC 1983a). Finding a sort of butterfly heaven with everything they needed for their lifecycle, the butterflies laid thousands of eggs—more than enough to provide the farmer a harvest as well as to repopulate the surrounding region (box 2.5).

For two decades villagers have been establishing the two plants, collecting the chrysalis crop, hatching the adults, injecting the undamaged ones with a little alcohol, and packing the fragile products for shipment. After mailing off the harvest, the farmer receives a check from the government. The process is catching on elsewhere and is being hailed as a way to help protect rainforests in more than a dozen nations.

Malaysia, too, is showing that protected areas can likely conserve biodiversity while becoming economically sustainable. Malaysians are breeding some of the world's smallest and largest rainforest ungulates. The mouse deer weighs only 1 kilogram and stands merely 30 centimeters high. Long hunted and enjoyed as a local delicacy, this rabbit-sized deer is being turned into livestock for the forest understory. A wild bovine called gaur is the biggest of all cattle—one bull has weighed in at one-and-a-half metric tons, or more than most compact cars. The gaur has been hunted to near extinction, mainly for its meat and its handsome trophy head. It too survives in the understory habitat and could become both a livestock animal and tourist attraction, added incentive to maintain forest cover.

Looking to Tomorrow

Programs are now needed to maintain and to build on projects that put agricultural development and biodiversity conservation in harmony.

Box 2.5 Biodiversity of butterflies

On a precipitous ridge in northern Papua New Guinea, Blu Rairi anxiously prowls his farm, checking his valuable livestock, noting new arrivals, deciding which to send to market, and, like conscientious ranchers everywhere, complaining about feed shortages. Rairi is a cheerful, prosperous rancher, but he does not own a big spread; it looks like a vegetable patch nestled next to the tropical forest behind his village. His livestock is unconventional, too. It has six legs. But don't be misled—gram-for-gram it is probably more valuable than any four-footed livestock in the world. It is certainly more beautiful. Rairi is a butterfly farmer.

In the 1970s the Port Moresby government established a Department of Insect Farming and Trading to regulate production and export of butterflies, moths, and beetles. The international demand for insects is greater than most people realize. Each year entomologists, collectors, and manufacturers of decorative items buy up to 20 million butterflies.

Foreigners pay well for Papua New Guinea butterflies—30 cents for common species, $5 for birdwings, $50 for mauve swallowtails. Because the insects weigh just a few grams each, that is better money than ranchers get from cattle. Moreover, cattlemen can't export their product via the post office.

Butterfly farming has proved especially good in remote areas such as Blu Rairi's village near Maprik because it needs no veterinarians, pesticides, artificial insemination, vaccines, fences, or morning milking.
Source: NRC 1983a.

Solving Global Problems

Hunger, malnutrition, deforestation, desertification, soil loss, and soil degradation are considered global problems, but they have to do mainly with plants and animals and soils in the hot regions of Africa, Asia, and Latin America. Species that can be tools for solving these global problems are to be found in the untapped wild and agricultural biodiversity of those regions. Among the now little-used species are the 2,000 native food plants of Africa that could be employed in feeding that hungry continent (box 2.6). There are also 3,000 fruits and more than 1,000 vegetables in the tropical zone, where malnutrition is rife. Moreover, 20,000 trees can be found in the tropics, where deforestation is so calamitous. And thousands of legumes that can combat soil degradation also exist.

Many species that are superbly suited for combating hunger, malnutrition, and deforestation are not being exploited. Additional examples of tools for solving global problems include:

- *Peach palm.* This tropical palm, known as *pejibaye* in Spanish-speaking countries and *pupunha* in Brazil, produces chestnut-like fruits containing carbohydrate, protein, oil, minerals, and vitamins in proportions nearly perfect for the human diet. Domesticated in the rainforests of western Amazonia, peach palm has been called probably the most nutritionally balanced of all foods, but it remains unknown in the chronically malnourished parts of the tropical world. Peach palm also provides a superb-tasting heart-of-palm (*palmito*) and is already being planted on a large scale for this purpose in parts of Brazil and Central America.

- *Moringa.* This is an extremely fast-growing woody species that produces pods that look like giant green beans and taste like asparagus. It also produces masses of very small leaflets that are boiled and eaten like spinach. Being so small, the leaflets dry quickly in the sun and can then be stored in a jar for the times when fresh vegetables are scarce. In

---

Box 2.6 Lost crops of Africa

Despite its seemingly never-ending hunger and malnutrition the area stretching from the Sahara to South Africa contains more than 2,000 native food plants. This vast region is the source of watermelon, melon, sesame, coffee, cola, okra, sorghum, pearl millet, finger millet, and black-eyed pea. But hundreds of more edible grains, fruits, vegetables, and oilseeds have yet to benefit from science. For those forgotten food plants there is no knowledge of what soils and conditions are preferred, what varieties yield the most nutritious foods, or how to control pests.

Africa has more native cereals than any other continent. It has its own species of rice, as well as finger millet, fonio, pearl millet, sorghum, teff, guinea millet, and several dozen wild grasses whose grains are eaten. This is a food heritage that has fed people for generations. It is also a local legacy of genetic wealth on which a sound food future might be built. But strangely it has largely been bypassed in modern times.

These lost plants have much to offer and not just to Africa. Indeed they represent an exceptional cluster of cereal biodiversity with particular promise for solving some of the greatest food-production problems that will arise in the next century. For example, Africa's native grains tend to tolerate extremes. They can thrive where introduced grains produce inconsistently. Some (teff, for instance) are adapted to cold; others such as

pearl millet tolerate heat; at least one sorghum withstands waterlogging; and many survive drought. Moreover, most can grow better than other cereals on relatively infertile soils. For thousands of years they have yielded grain even where land preparation was minimal and management poor. They combine well with other crops in mixed stands. Some types mature rapidly. They tend to be nutritious.

Of all the cereals finger millet is one of the most nutritious. Indeed some varieties appear to have high levels of methionine, an amino acid lacking in the diets of hundreds of millions of the poor who live on starchy foods such as cassava and plantain. Outsiders have long marveled at how people in Uganda and southern Sudan could develop such strapping physiques and work as hard as they do on just one meal a day. Finger millet seems to be the main reason.

Over large areas of Africa people once obtained their basic subsistence from wild grasses. In certain places the practice still continues, especially in drought years. One survey records more than sixty grass species known to be sources of food grains. Yet despite their widespread use and notable value for saving lives during times of distress, these wild cereals have been largely overlooked by both food and plant scientists.

Source: NRC 1995.

addition to providing these natural vitamin supplements, the moringa tree yields seeds that clarify turbid water. As mentioned before, compounds in its seeds make traces of silt and clay settle out as effectively as alum used in water departments. This species could be a powerful new weapon against two scourges, malnutrition and water-borne disease.

- *Velvet bean.* This weed-smothering, nitrogen-fixing herbaceous legume protects the land and helps crops yield well with few inputs. It seems likely to prove broadly applicable throughout the tropics and may well provide a way to retain and even restore fertility on vast areas of degraded farmland. In addition several dozen legume genera—including *Mucuna, Pueraria, Lotus, Lotononis,* and *Vicia*—offer likely successful groundcovers, including some for restoring seemingly impossibly degraded tropical soils.

- *Patauá.* Another native palm of Amazonia, patauá (pronounced *patawa*), bears large bunches of fruit containing an oil similar to olive oil in appearance, composition, and culinary quality. Although sold as an edible oil in Colombia, it is virtually unknown to the rest of the world. Given agronomic attention, it could become a major tropical crop. A century ago the Africa oil palm was obscure; now it is one of the world's major resources, although its oil is far inferior to patauá as food.

- *Vetiver.* Hedges of this grass are now being used to stop soil erosion in 106 countries, but vetiver has other vital uses for which it is still not being employed (NRC 1993). For one thing the hedges block rushing runoff from tropical storms, thereby reducing flooding and helping water penetrate the slopes. Under suitable conditions vetiver hedges are functional a few weeks after planting, so they offer the promise of instant working watersheds that improve year-round water availability as well as mitigating floods and mudslides. Vetiver is also a potential tool for claiming polluted sites because it can survive in soils contaminated with heavy metals or alkali as well as some salt. Tolerant of soluble aluminum and severe acidity (almost to pH3), it thrives in the so-called *laterite,* the infertile, aluminum-rich, very acidic soil that plagues much of the lowland tropics. Vetiver is thus a tool for bringing abandoned lands back into productive use.

World Heritage Gene Sites

Certain areas are especially important for the wild relatives and ancestral forms of major crops and should accordingly be conserved with as much diligence as sites protected for their scenic or cultural value. Most of the world's 8,500 national parks and other protected areas were set up solely for wildlife conservation; rarely if ever were they established to conserve plants of importance for agriculture. Now the roles of protected areas should be broadened to include reserves to protect the genetic diversity of the primitive ancestors and wild relatives of at least the major crops grown for food. These sites will also double as wildlife refuges because conserving crop biodiversity would also conserve habitats for wildlife.

Rapid Agrobiodiversity Assessment Teams

Future foreign assistance projects should include consideration of their effects on crop and livestock biodiversity on which succeeding generations will depend. This might include deploying rapid biodiversity assessment teams to identify high-priority biodiversity that needs collection or protection before the assistance project destroys it. These teams would highlight biodiversity implications of project interventions. Their goal would be to flag invaluable genetic materials and outline rescue plans before they are lost to the bulldozers.

Agrobiodiversity assessments might be done by skilled, independent organizations dedicated to the task and separate from the development agency. Team members would include a botanist, a crop generalist, and a biologist. Depending on the size of the area and the potential severity of biodiversity loss, teams would canvass a site over a period of hours, days, or weeks, assessing the presence of vulnerable crops, unique varieties, and wild relatives of important crops and livestock.

Diversified Marketing

As noted earlier, rising numbers of produce items are being marketed, and some are even being shipped around the world. New opportunities for developing countries with their wealth of fruits and other foods are therefore opening up. Indeed in some affluent countries research priorities and marketing trends are now shifting to focus on African, Asian, and Latin American resources.

The U.S. food industry, for instance, has sprouted a new breed of marketers and even a new branch of fresh food known as specialty produce, including hundreds of different fruit and vegetable products, from dried jackfruit to African horned melons.

These days people are realizing that small-scale produce marketing has a major role to play in some nations' development. Specialist niche markets that have recently been created or expanded include:

- Processed akee fruit from Jamaica
- Cloves from Zanzibar, which are used in India to pin together betel leaves in chewing *pan*
- Ngali nuts from the Solomon Islands, which are being processed for their oil in collaboration with an international chain of cosmetic shops
- Special cocoa from Grenada and Jamaica, which is in demand for blending with other cocoas
- Pimento and ugli fruit from Jamaica
- Tasteless paprika, for which Ethiopia has established a useful market as a food coloring.

Poor People's Crops and Animals

In all of this activity there is great potential for helping the needy. Possibilities include preserving genetic diversity used in traditional farming, developing traditional crops, and encouraging the use of traditional resources as well as traditional practices and knowledge. Many now neglected plants can lead to greater self-sufficiency for the poorest of the poor—the very ones usually missed by "green revolutions" (box 2.7). Finding more uses for neglected plants increases their chances of being saved from extinction. And the task of harnessing the neglected plants,

---

Box 2.7 Biodiversity that fed the Incas

The ancestors of the Incas tapped a wide array of plants to enrich their diets. They domesticated some eighty species of roots, tubers, grains, vegetables, fruits, and nuts. The Spanish, who conquered the Incas in the 1500s, brought the potato out of the Andes, but they left achira, ajipa, oca, arracacha, ulluco, and half a dozen other root crops the Incas had used in feeding their empire. The Incas knew these roots were valuable, but the outsiders' ignorance triumphed.

- Oca (*Oxalis tuberosa*). This exceptionally hardy plant is second only to the potato in importance as a root crop in the Andes. Its many varieties, which have never been collected systematically, include those with a high sugar content and others with a somewhat sour yet pleasing taste. Oca has become a commercial crop in New Zealand (under the misnomer yam) and would likely sweep through other parts of the world if given modern agronomic attention.
- Quinoa (*Chenopodium quinoa*). The Incas relied on quinoa's nutritious grain, an Andean equivalent of wheat although the plant is not a grass. An annual, broad-leaved herb, quinoa's abundance

of white or pink seeds occur in large sorghum-like clusters. The seeds contain 12 to 19 percent protein and are one of the richest sources of protein among grain crops. Moreover, their protein, like that of amaranth, possesses an exceptionally attractive amino acid balance for human nutrition because of its high levels of lysine and methionine. Quinoa has made its way into some health food stores and vegetarian restaurants but could become popular outside of highland South America with the right support and marketing effort.

- Lucuma (*Pouteria lucuma*). Fruits of this tree are sweet but dry and full of starch. They are suitable as a basic staple. A single tree, it is said, can feed a family year-round. Dried, the fruits store for years.

These are just three examples of more than twenty roots, legumes, grains, and fruits that are lost crops of the Incas. They can increase agricultural diversity throughout temperate zones because they are adapted to the highland tropics and therefore to cool temperatures and even frost.

Source: NRC 1989.

animals, and other natural resources will occupy all family members, including women and children, who are heavily involved in farming activities in developing countries.

Promising biodiversity and knowledge about little-known foods and other biological resources can often be found among ethnic minorities, nomads, and other societies with poorly developed links to markets. Many such plant resources are crops found mostly in home gardens that provide micronutrients for combating malnutrition, including the blindness caused by vitamin A deficiency.

Traditionalist farmers tend to manage a great deal of biodiversity, one of the reasons modern agriculture has passed them by. Many people continue to cultivate crops even if they obtain modest yields because such crops may be particularly well adapted to the area or because they are important for cultural reasons. Their persistence now needs to be promoted rather than patronized. The timing is right; because of scarce resources, there is good potential in enhancing lesser known crops. A quadrupling of yield is not uncommon when a researcher begins studying an underexploited crop. Such a leap in yield is difficult to achieve in wheat, maize, or rice, where a yield increase of just a few percentage points might be a worthy lifetime achievement.

Lending Specifically for Biodiversity Use

A special fund that recognizes the needs of biodiverse farming, especially one to provide loan guarantees, would be particularly helpful. Today much biodiversity goes unused even though relatively small grants could accomplish a great deal. A local fruit such as *araéa-boi* or *camu camu* in the Amazon may have more vitamin C than an orange and produce a delicious drink, but venture capital for creating commerce out of something like this is virtually nonexistent.

The commercial value of dozens of tropical fruits and other crops is hardly in doubt. Relatively small funding is all that is needed to jumpstart businesses geared to the neglected crops. And some of these tropical fruits could become big commercial successes, although perhaps not as big as coffee, oil palm, coconut,

chocolate, pineapple, kola, vanilla, and banana, the tropical fruits behind such corporate giants as Lever Brothers, Hershey, Nestlé, Dole, Chiquita, Coca-Cola, Pepsi, Del Monte, and Proctor and Gamble.

Saving Seeds and Rare Breeds

There are genetic adventures to be found in the industrial world too. An American botany student has been combing Hopi and Papago Indian reservations for seeds of old-time crops that survived in the Southwestern deserts before irrigation was available. He has been so successful in locating and propagating these plants that many Indian farmers have gone back to the half-forgotten foods of their childhoods. And those drought-tolerant ancient crops are beginning to excite more and more interest as water for irrigation becomes more costly (box 2.8). A similar process is under way with endangered breeds in North America and parts of Europe (box 2.9).

Diversifying Tropical Forestry

To meet predicted requirements for industrial timber, the world's tree-crop acreage will need to double. A major proportion of the additional area will likely be located in the tropics because of year-round growing conditions. Tropical nations therefore need to include forestry in their biodiversity activities. Immense biowealth is waiting to be tapped in the forests of tropical lands.

Some 20,000 species of trees alone are found in tropical forests. They include scores of legumes that have the potential to be great resources, quick-growing and soil-improving at the same time. These are not only useful in their own right, they are also natural shock troops for reclaiming degraded lands.

Conifers and eucalypts, which dominate tree plantings worldwide, also tend to be inimical to collateral biodiversity. Other plants grow poorly in their shade and wildlife shuns the forests, which are often likened to green deserts. In contrast many tropical trees foster biodiversity. Certain nitrogen-fixing species, such as mangium, leucaena, and alders, foster the growth of native

Box 2.8 Seed saver

In the harsh and meager land of the American Southwest, Apache, Havasupai, Hopi, Mojave, Navajo, Papago, Pima, Seri, and Yuma Indians developed an agricultural civilization that has been called one of the most remarkable of all. They had dozens of useful plants that were adapted to the harsh sun, difficult soils, and sporadic rains. On the wide, shining flat of the desert they grew crops with less direct rainfall than is used anywhere else.

But these cultures and crops are now on the verge of extinction. Hundreds of strains and species of desert plants that once were widely used Indian crops are passing into oblivion. The age-old techniques that kept them producing in one of the most difficult of all human habitats are being forgotten. Gary Nabhan and a growing number of colleagues are struggling to preserve this unique agricultural culture.

Fifty years ago when irrigated agriculture began trickling into the southwest, the old plants were discarded. Today only remnants exist. Only a few elders of the Hopi, Papago, and Pima still keep them from extinction. Nabhan estimates that the Papago tribe alone had some 5,600 hectares under traditional farming practices some sixty years ago; now only 120 hectares at most are still farmed in this way. Chiltepine, desert chia, canaigre, Papago onions, Papago peas, eighteen types of beans, and many others—crops that formed the basis of southwestern Indian diets for more than a thousand years—now survive only in a few villages, maybe in just one or two tiny plots.

Nabhan, however, has located nineteen domesticated plants that Papago farmers cultivated and thirty-three wild plants they encouraged or protected. In addition he knows that Papagos ate at least 275 different species of wild plants, forty of which were substantial food sources. His greatest find has been the tepary bean.

Once the most commonly cultivated bean in the Southwest, the tepary fed Indians for more than 5,000 years. The plant escapes drought by maturing rapidly and by sending roots as deep as 2 meters to find soil moisture. One Indian field that received only 80 millimeters of rainfall produced tepary plants that were strong and healthy, and nearly all were bearing seed by two months.

Box 2.9 Breed saver

Joe Henson's farm is a museum of life. Some of Britain's rarest farm animals—about forty breeds in all—roam his softly folded emerald hills near Guiting Power in the Cotswolds. Manx Loghtans, a sheep breed with four horns, are among Henson's heirloom livestock. Fewer than fifty Manx Loghtans remained in England when he started. Soay sheep also graze on this vignette farm, a breed unchanged since the Ice Ages. Brought to Britain by the Vikings, St. Kilda sheep with huge conical horns also grace the working farm.

Henson's cattle include placid brown West Highlands with such shaggy fur that you almost expect them to bark. And behind his stone fences are also small, black pigs with long snouts and white streaks down their hairy backs like the wild hogs of prehistoric days.

Not all endangered animals are wild. The Henson farm exemplifies a side of conservation that few people are aware of. Around the world hundreds of breeds of livestock, seemingly outdated by more productive or specialized cousins, are just being left to die out.

Henson and a small number of other British farmers and animal lovers were the first to grapple with the dangers of losing livestock genes. Now a growing number of landowners are beginning to acquire and protect antique animals. Many old and rare breeds have a hardiness and stamina not found in the standard animals used for commercial food production. Many of the traditional breeds were maintained because of their toughness under trying conditions. The Exmoor Horn sheep, for example, can lie for days beneath many feet of snow without suffering long-term effects.

Today, at the annual sale at Stoneleigh in Warwickshire, rare heifers often sell for twice the price of big-name heifers. Animal scientists, too, are slowly recognizing that potentially valuable genes may be found in the reject animals. In 1981, for instance, the British Meat and Livestock Centre ran some production tests on different breeds of beef cattle. For fun Henson offered a White Park bullcalf. The scientists laughed at his temerity; their animals had been bred for fast growth; White Parks have never been selected for anything. But when the beef production test results were tallied, the White Park bull had beaten all others in daily weight gain and carcass leanness.

understory vegetation. A four-and-a-half-year-old mangium forest in Sabah can be 15 meters tall with a lush ground cover of spontaneous native plants. In such cases mangium is literally restarting the rainforest in the shade beneath its canopy and the fertility supplied by its nitrogen-fixing roots (NRC 1983c). Mangium is thus one of many plant resources available for restoring priceless biodiversity to degraded lands in the tropics (box 2.10).

In addition there are species with promise to solve the twin problems of fuelwood shortages and land degradation related to deforestation. Both are important to pursue because indiscriminate firewood collecting and forest destruction are leading to great losses of biodiversity.

And the tropical zone contains trees that grow with such vigor in the year-round tropical warmth that they can absorb 15 kilograms of carbon dioxide annually. It is not difficult then to envisage future carbon dioxide absorption reserves laid out across some hillsides in developing countries, the only place carbon sequestration would be high. They might be established on today's degraded wastelands using legume trees adapted to the infertility. They would be financed by the main carbon dioxide emitters in more affluent nations. But in addition to being carbon sinks, such greenhouse forests could serve as biodiversity reserves.

Watersheds as Reserves

Watersheds that many cities rely on are also promising sites for on-site biodiversity preservation. The presence of trees and other plants will help rather than hinder the site's rainwater-harvesting function. In turn these locations are less likely to be invaded by land-hungry hordes because they are in a sense the lifeblood of nearby cities, towns, and villages. Millions of downstream urban dwellers depend on them for water. North Sulawesi in Indonesia and Sabah in Malaysia have already set up natural reserves on watersheds.

Policies

Policies should not force people to decide against biodiversity. Many policies now tie the hands of farmers, and great opportunities are being missed. For instance, a broad range of price supports, most focused on a few standard crops, favor monocropping and work against biodiversity.

Other policies determine whether a person exploits land with any consideration for the future. These include land tenure, breeding strategies for crop varieties, and extension and seed-supply systems.

Box 2.10 Mangium: The tree that nurtures biodiversity

In the 1960s foresters in Sabah, Malaysia, found that the little-known Australian rainforest tree called mangium matched the growth rates of fast-growing pine and eucalyptus species. Mangium has consequently risen to become one of the top four reforestation species in Asia. The Indonesian government is relying on it to reforest 4.4 million hectares because its foresters have found that, given a little help, mangium out-competes the vigorous and tenacious imperata grass, a curse of degraded tropical landscapes.

But mangium appears able to do even more than just grow well. Foresters have noted on Borneo that native vegetation springs up in the protection of a mangium forest. Plants belonging to the original rainforest complex sprout under the trees. Even dipterocarps, the crown jewels of Far Eastern forests, are reappearing spontaneously. This may at first seem illogical: How can a tree suppress bad plants and restore good ones? The answer is that the grasses and weedy scrub species need open sunlight and die in the shade, but many rainforest species thrive in the shade. And a mangium forest is more than just a good sunshade: it keeps out desiccating winds and lowers the ground temperature, both of which increase the humidity in the air and the moisture in the soil and thereby foster rainforest recovery. Adding to this is the fact that mangium is a legume, and the nitrogen its roots build up in the soil also benefit neighboring plants.

All in all this tree is a sort of vegetative nursemaid that nurtures plants that have trouble surviving on cut-over, degraded sites. As such it could be a major weapon for healing damaged tropical forests. Mangium will likely prove useful in reversing the loss of forest biodiversity and could provide a tool to restart rainforests in some areas.
Source: NRC 1983c.

Strategy

A strategy for harmonizing biodiversity conservation with agricultural development is a vital necessity if habitat protection is to transcend the needy and the greedy. Only when plants and animals are of local value will they and their habitats have a chance to survive. The fact that the protected lands of the tropics enclose the ever-evolving genes for the global future can breathe new immediacy and new energy into the funding, functions, and raison d'etre of protecting the environment. For the foreseeable future no other option is open if our complex and rapidly growing population is to be fed, clothed, and housed reasonably, inexpensively, pleasantly, and safely. In sum biodiversity holds the key to the future of world food production and to the long-term success of wildlife conservation.

References

NRC (National Research Council). 1983a. *Butterfly Farming in Papua New Guinea*. Washington, D.C.: National Academy of Sciences, NRC.

————.1983b. *Crocodiles as a Resource for the Tropics*. Washington, D.C.: National Academy of Sciences, NRC.

————.1983c. *Mangium and Other Fast-Growing Acacias*. Washington, D.C.: National Academy of Sciences, NRC.

————.1988. *Quality-Protein Maize*. Washington, D.C.: National Academy of Sciences, NRC.

————.1989. *Lost Crops of the Incas: Little-Known Plants of the Andes with Promise for Worldwide Cultivation*. Washington, D.C.: National Academy of Sciences, NRC.

————.1991. *Microlivestock: Little-Known Small Animals with a Promising Economic Future*. Washington, D.C.: National Academy of Sciences, NRC.

————.1992. *Neem: A Tree for Solving Global Problems*. Washington, D.C.: National Academy of Sciences, NRC.

————.1993. *Vetiver: A Thin Green Line against Erosion*. Washington, D.C.: National Academy of Sciences, NRC.

————.1995. *Lost Crops of Africa*. Vol. 1. Washington, D.C.: National Academy of Sciences, NRC.

Srivastava, J., N. Vietmeyer, and J. Lambert. 1996. *Medicinal Plants: An Expanding Role in Development*. World Bank Technical Paper 320. Washington, D.C.

Vietmeyer, N. D. 1986. "Lesser-Known Plants of Potential Use in Agricultural Forestry," *Science* 232 (June) 1, 379–84.

3. Policy Considerations along the Interface between Biodiversity and Agriculture

William Lesser and Steven Kyle

This chapter identifies the effect of international agreements and national economic policies on conservation and use of genetic resources in agriculture. Although institutions and policies can be evaluated from multiple perspectives, the approach taken here is predominately economic. From that perspective it is assumed that individuals and organizations operate in an economically rational manner within their cultural context. That is, the conservation loss or even destruction of biodiversity is presumed to be an economically rational response to incentives applied at the local level. Thus an understanding of incentive structures at the local level is essential if biodiversity is to be conserved and managed more wisely. For the most part it is assumed that biodiversity is best maintained locally. The emphasis is on understanding how national and multinational policies apply at the local level. That is not where all the decisions regarding biodiversity are made, but the fate of much biodiversity is ultimately decided there.

Policies and Regulatory Mechanisms for Agricultural Development

Agriculture is among the most heavily regulated economic activities on earth. Some regulations are specific to agriculture (such as price policies), some are economic (exchange rates), and some are legal (land tenure) or international (trade) policies.

Many policies determine the extent and form of a country's agriculture and hence its impact on biodiversity. In addition the form of agriculture influences genetic diversity within the system itself. Finally, policies have widely varying effects, depending on how they are understood and implemented at the farm level.

Such policies and the resource bases of all countries are quite diverse. The unifying theme of recent policy reform has been to open up economies to international markets; this trend, together with a consideration of the structure of developing economies, frames recommendations for agricultural policy reforms.

The imperative to intensify agriculture and the inevitability of environmental change underlie these recommendations. Indeed agricultural development may be considered desirable despite its altering the mosaic of habitats and its environmental consequences; the alternative is often to consign millions of people to a life of poverty and deprivation. Much can be done, however, to deflect some negative environmental effects.

The pressure for increased intensity of land use becomes still stronger when economic growth is biased toward agricultural production. Rising prices for agricultural exports will, according to well-known theorems of international trade, boost prices of agricultural inputs (Runge, Houck, and Halbach 1988). This implies that land prices will rise, which in turn will draw more marginal land into production and require more intensive use of already cultivated land to generate an adequate return.

The relationship among increased exports, land prices, and intensity of land use has been well documented in various studies. If the inevitability and desirability of accelerated agricultural development together with its unavoidable changes in the environment are recognized, the case for environmental protection must rest on the sustainability of the new land- and water-use patterns and the genetic diversity inherent in them.

Intensification of land use by definition means greater output per unit of area farmed. This may be accomplished by improved management or, more commonly, by increasing the level of inputs. Inputs in turn can be distinguished as more labor or "purchased inputs," such as improved seed, inorganic fertilizers, and chemical pesticides. In some areas where modern, short-season varieties have been deployed, multicropping is an option, thereby increasing demand for labor and purchased inputs (David and Otsuka 1994). However, purchased inputs are often independent of, or substitutes for, labor; the use of herbicides or tractors rather than manual weeding is a case in point. In the subsequent discussion the term *intensification* refers to increases in purchased inputs.

Farming systems and related operations can be envisaged across a continuum of intensification. Even under the least intensive mode, such as slash-and-burn farming in which a land parcel may be cropped only once or twice a generation, flora and fauna are altered when compared to uncultivated forest. Nevertheless, greater biodiversity would normally be encountered in slash-and-burn farming than in an intensively monocrop system (see chapter 4).

Macroeconomic Policies

In developing countries currency devaluation and removal of trade barriers are the two most common components of policy reform packages. This underscores the underlying trend: promoting a country's comparative advantage by reorienting the economy toward world markets rather than protecting domestic markets. It is this reorientation, often coinciding with agricultural intensification, which affects biodiversity, albeit indirectly.

A principal tool of the various policies designed to promote an outward-oriented strategy is devaluation of the real exchange rate. A devaluation provides incentives to expand exports while decreasing the consumption of imports.

Lowering of trade barriers and realignment of the exchange rate are also likely to affect agricultural imports, including the potential to import seed instead of sowing local varieties. In areas where imported varieties wholly or largely displace traditional varieties, agrobiodiversity declines. Such displacements have been noted following the introduction of high-yielding modern varieties in the 1960s and 1970s.

The loss of traditional varieties can also arise in areas where war or other disasters disrupt the normal cycle of planting, harvest, and seed retention. In Angola, for example, large areas are currently being resettled following a lengthy war. With virtually no local seed production remaining, resettled farmers are provided with agricultural input packages, including imported seed. Local varieties are rapidly disappearing because of this, a fact that will hamper future efforts to adapt imported seeds more closely to domestic agroclimatic conditions. Such events underscore the importance of *ex situ* seed collections, among other forms of preserving genetic material.

Agricultural Policies

The links between specific sector or crop-oriented policies are complex, with multiple routes of causality. Nonetheless, a discussion of common crop-specific policies will illustrate some of the roles policy reform can assume.

Border taxes. Border taxes on agricultural imports raise the prices of those commodities domestically and, other things being equal, increase incentives to produce these commodities internally. The impact on biodiversity depends on whether the land brought into production is new agricultural land, a shift from another crop, or intensification of areas already in production. An export tax works in reverse: to the extent that a commodity is taxed on export, the profitability of production is reduced, thereby discouraging planting of that crop.

Fixed prices. Like border taxes fixed prices affect markets through raising or depressing prices from the levels that would otherwise prevail. Fixed prices are an implicit tax on farmers, which discourages them from increasing production or investing in their operations. They are not exposed to the risk of price decreases during the growing season, but neither can they reap the benefit of price increases.

Input taxes and subsidies. Taxes on imports of agricultural inputs reduce the profitability of crops employing them, shifting incentives away from these crops. In the more common situation of subsidies for such imports (either through overvalued exchange rates or explicit subsidies) the effect is to promote use of purchased inputs.

The ecological effects of such shifts in the use of agricultural inputs vary considerably. When tractors or other machinery is subsidized, agricultural production generally expands because tractors typically allow an increase in cultivated area but not necessarily in yield. If chemical or biological inputs are used, such as fertilizers or pesticides, productivity per unit area usually increases (Hayami and Ruttan 1985). Subsidizing chemical inputs causes a more direct problem when pesticides, herbicides, or other inputs pollute or destroy habitats. DDT is but one of many chemicals that, once introduced into an ecosystem, enter the food chain and persist for long periods of time, often with unanticipated effects.

Supply restrictions. Policies to restrict supply, such as import quotas, have effects similar to those of an import tax. Less supply from abroad means higher prices domestically and a greater incentive to local production. Withdrawing land from cultivation also restricts supply. Fallow areas are generally more conducive to biodiversity than crop land. The economic effects, however, are less tangible because consumers benefit little from such actions, while producers and input suppliers lose to the extent that output is reduced. For this reason most countries avoid this type of policy, though some high-income countries have periodically adopted such measures, such as the payment-in-kind program in the United States.

Land-Use Policies

Large holdings, especially those devoted to production of plantation crops, such as bananas or sugarcane, are more likely to be farmed intensively as monocropped units. Crop diversity is thus reduced. Furthermore, long-term monocropping tends to increase pest and disease pressure, which often leads to larger applications of pesticides.

Land tenure. Smallholders typically deploy more diversified cropping patterns, especially if they are living close to subsistence levels. Such diversification makes sense as a risk-reduction strategy, given the extreme poverty of some smallholders. When large holdings occupy the best land, small farmers can be pushed onto more marginal or fragile lands, with consequent degradation. Inability to access inputs needed for maintenance of fertility can exacerbate such a situation.

Caution is warranted when generalizing about large and small farmers and risk aversion. Paddy farmers in Southeast Asia, for example, typically do not plant rice according to the size of their land holdings. Similarly, even small farmers in the Punjab grow wheat virtually to the exclusion of any other crop (for the environmental implications of this course see chapter 4). In favorable areas and when farmers have access to inputs, yield levels do not vary greatly by farm size.

Another generalization depicts small farmers as using sustainable practices, while commercial-scale producers employ unsustainable, high-input systems. Although there are many well-known examples of unsustainable large-scale methods—irrigation leading to salinization being but one—such problems are not limited to big operations. Many small, risk-avoiding farmers have contributed to land degradation because of overgrazing, poor erosion control on slopes, or inadequate organic matter returned to the soil. Nor are these problems always recent; one theory on the demise of the Mayan civilization before the arrival of the Spanish traces the cause to unsustainable farming practices.

The existence of a dualistic tenancy system can also affect the extent to which government policy influences farming practices. To the degree that smallholders are operating as diversified self-sustaining units, their lack of market links reduces the channels through which they can be affected by policy. But to the extent that large producers are able to exert political influence, they can prevent policies adverse to their interests or evade their application.

Resettlement. Countries resort to resettlement for different reasons. One common justification is to reduce population pressure, as on Java. Another motive is to gain access to natural resources and generate income, as in the Brazilian Amazon. In still other instances resettlement is less a policy and more an effort by impoverished peoples to survive. Often settlement follows in the wake of logging operations, thereby exacerbating the loss of biodiversity associated with undisturbed forest.

Much resettlement occurs on marginal agricultural land for the simple reason that better quality lands tend to be in production. The marginal nature of the land, poor access to necessary inputs, and the perception that land is abundant and hence has a low attributed value all tend to lead to a rapid degradation of the resource base. Inadequate training for the proper use of unfamiliar soil or in adapting farming patterns to novel climatic conditions often compounds the situation.

The term *resettlement* is also used to refer to land consolidation. This applies particularly to areas where inheritance traditions lead to farmers owning multiple but scattered pieces of land. Consolidation can improve efficiency by reducing travel time and by making mechanical plowing possible as opposed to tilling by hand. Consolidation affects already cultivated land. Thus environmental effects are quite different from the opening or permanent cultivation of new lands. For this discussion resettlement does not include consolidation programs.

Research Paradigm

Systematic international attention to the problems of raising agricultural productivity in developing countries began with the creation of the United Nations Food and Agriculture Organization (FAO) in the aftermath of World War II. At that time prevailing wisdom held that appropriate technologies existed; a mechanism was needed to introduce them to new environments. That assumption proved limited within a decade and led to the creation of the international agricultural research centers, starting in the 1960s. These centers are managed autonomously but belong to the Consultative Group on International Agricultural Research (CGIAR), which was cofounded by FAO, the United Nations Development Programme (UNDP), and the World Bank.

With an ongoing emphasis on plant breeding and related agronomic practices, the sixteen research centers have followed a Western-style approach of systematic scientific research. Most of the scientific staff received their training in Western universities. The national research programs through which research developments were to be delivered adopted the same model; the extension system from U.S. land grant universities was applied directly in a number of countries.

Criticisms. Reliance on the scientific experimental paradigm has often ignored local and indigenous agricultural knowledge (Busch and others 1991). If this knowledge were tapped, perhaps more balanced agricultural systems would develop. In particular the bias toward better-off operators at the expense of the smallest farmers, might be avoided, and fewer environmentally damaging fertilizers, pesticides, and herbicides would be required. Crop varieties would be less uniform, incorporating more genetic diversity, thereby providing greater assurance against widespread loss because of genetic vulnerability. And cropping systems would be more mixed, further contributing to pest control and genetic diversity. The Green Revolution is specifically identified with the standardization of varieties over wide areas.

Ruttan (1989) challenges such criticisms, noting that they are often "based on the crudest sort of casual empiricism." Moreover, he notes that biological technologies, which have been the focus of research at most international agricultural research centers, are "essentially scale-neutral"; they can be and are adopted by farmers of all scales when the technologies suit their needs. Others have substantiated that position empirically, particularly for irrigated rice (David and Otsuka 1994).

Other critics of the Green Revolution approach, such as Geisler and DuPuis (1989), attribute much to agricultural policies that encouraged new varieties. Such policies include the use of extension programs and the subsidization of fertilizer and pesticides that are especially well suited for use by improved varieties (Desai 1988). In recent years economic realignment has curtailed subsidies. Nevertheless, many farmers want to plant improved varieties, often at the expense of genetically diverse traditional varieties.

The institutional response has been an increased emphasis on farming-systems research, with particular attention to the needs of small, resource-poor farmers. One factor contributing to this new research thrust was the realization that increased production through intensification did not by itself necessarily enhance an equitable income distribution. The special requirements of small farmers obviously needed to be better understood, including the objectives (such as risk-aversion) of indigenous production systems. Warren (1989) identifies several factors that contribute to the marginalization of traditional practices including:

- Negative Euro-American attitudes about non-Western approaches
- Pressure by large, better organized farmer groups
- Training in Western countries, where large-scale farming practices dominate
- A research staff from urban areas who are unfamiliar with rural life.

As these constraints have eased for a number of reasons over the past two decades, farming-systems research has led to a greater diversity of research approaches, including more emphasis on minor crops and intercropping.

The farming-systems approach involves more sociological and extension work than biologically oriented research (Waugh, Hildebrand, and Andrew 1989). There is concern about the relative productivity of these efforts compared with varietal improvement, especially because most national research programs develop slowly (Ruttan 1989).

Research on minor and nonfood crops. Staple crops dominate the 1994 budget for the research

centers, which was $336.9 million, up slightly since the beginning of the decade (CGIAR 1995). Of that amount $70.5 million (about 21 percent) was spent on breeding and enhancement and $25.6 million (7.6 percent) on conserving biodiversity, which is up significantly in recent years.

More than half of total breeding expenditures at research centers is directed to the four major staples: rice, wheat, maize, and white potatoes (table 3.1). Focusing on the main "staffs of life" helped the largest number of people and allowed rapid progress because a backlog of basic research could be applied rapidly (Ruttan 1989). Even some minor crops such as cassava receive significant breeding support approaching that of the potato. But other regionally important crops such as banana receive only 1.4 percent of the total. Most of the world's crops fall outside research center mandates, at least as far as breeding is concerned.

Table 3.1 Expenditures at selected international agricultural research centers by crop, 1994 and 1996
(thousands of U.S. dollars)

Center	Year	Crop	Budget
International Center for Tropical Agriculture	1994	Beans	3,793
		Cassava	3,149
		Tropical forages	2,752
		Rice	1,748
International Center for Maize and Wheat Improvement	1996	Maize	6,340
		Wheat	5,733
		Triticale	368
		Barley	359
International Center for the Potato	1994	Potato[a]	4,760
		Sweet potato	2,040
International Center for Agricultural Research in the Dry Areas	1996	Barley	1,675
		Wheat	1,213
		Forage legumes	771
		Chickpea	728
		Lentil	670
		Dry peas	97
International Crops Research Institute for the Semi-Arid Tropics	1996	Peanuts	3,353
		Sorghum	2,763
		Millet	2,144
		Chickpea	1,027
		Pigeon pea	970
International Institute of Tropical Agriculture	1996	Cassava	1,065
		Banana	842
		Cowpea	339
International Rice Research Institute	1994	Rice	8,700
West African Rice Development Association	1994	Rice	2,100

a. Estimated division.
Source: CIAT 1994; CIMMYT 1996; CIP 1994; ICARDA 1996; ICRISAT 1996; IITA 1996; IRRI 1994; WARDA 1994.

Involvement of Local Communities in Policy Development

The need to understand the relationships between local peoples and their biological resources has long been recognized (NRC 1972). Gupta (1992) says he knows of no United Nations Environment Programme (UNEP) project being discussed in the local language of the people most likely to be affected. Far from being unique to UNEP, many projects limit or fail to involve residents, yet it is widely recognized that the actions of local peoples are critical for biodiversity conservation. Preserves that exclude local people, sometimes to the extent of ejecting long-established groups, are perceived as alien and are thus frequently degraded. In contrast reserves designed to provide benefits for local communities are often protected by them (McNeely 1988).

Hanna (1995) notes that environmental management ranges from a single entity enforcing absolute standards to more flexible, participatory approaches. Local participation improves the effectiveness of managing protected areas and enforcing environmental regulations because it reduces:

- Information costs by providing supplemental nontechnical knowledge
- Coordination costs by encouraging good representation
- Monitoring costs by making enforcement more legitimate
- Enforcement costs because local inputs lead to more appropriate regulations.

Projects related to biodiversity, in particular to agrobiodiversity, are numerous and diverse, making generalization difficult. Nonetheless, in traditional practice local communities have frequently developed considerable knowledge of factors affecting farming. For example, they have designated sacred groves and protected forests on mountain aquifers (Gupta 1992). Local participation thus can lead to management efficiencies. The difficulty of communicating with many diverse and often remote groups and the need to identify meaningful incentives are also limiting factors. Mascorenhas (1993) describes a participatory rural appraisal method that can be used to understand the relationships of rural people to their environment.

Nongovernmental organizations (NGOs) assist with contacts and information exchange at the local level, and their number is growing. CARE is one of the more established NGOs, with widespread local operations in developing countries. The Environmental Protection Society in Thailand is one example of a community-based NGO (McNeely 1988; Wellard 1993).

To establish reciprocity with indigenous groups, Shaman Pharmaceuticals asks communities in research sites about their particular needs. An Ecuadoran Quechua community was concerned about access to periodic and emergency health care. Shaman lengthened the local runway to handle emergency evacuations (King 1994). Such steps are instrumental in establishing appropriate incentives, but are neither quick nor inexpensive to implement.

Policy Issues and Knowledge Gaps

Differing policies and national and agroecological conditions make it difficult to generalize about the effects of economic policies on biodiversity. Nevertheless, some useful insights can be gained by evaluating the objectives of policies rather than their form. Agricultural intensification appears to be an essential response to increased population and demands for improved living standards. The issue then is the sustainability of improved agricultural systems, not their existence.

Policies to reduce trade barriers and devalue currencies in an effort to recapture comparative advantage can affect efforts to intensify crop production and conserve biodiversity, but internal and external economic factors are also involved. Imports of agricultural inputs are likely to increase, including imports of improved seed that may supplant local varieties. Wars and natural disasters also trigger the loss of local crops and varieties, underscoring the need for *ex situ* as well as *in situ* preservation.

Agricultural pricing policies often reflect changing exchange conditions. Policies such as subsidies that lower input prices generally increase production and intensity, but policies such as fixed prices that lower crop prices dampen production. Input subsidies increase the use of the subsidized products, which can have negative effects on the environment and biodiversity. Large holdings are in general relatively intensive monocultures, while small, risk-averse farms are generally more diverse.

Past national agricultural policies, combined with the research practices of international agricultural research centers, have often emphasized intensive farming practices that rely on purchased inputs. While production increases have often been impressive, agrobiodiversity has diminished for two interrelated reasons. First, the improved varieties substituted for local, genetically diverse traditional varieties. Second, small-farmer production practices have been largely ignored by mainstream agricultural research and development organizations. This situation is slowly changing, however, with the advent of farming systems research in the 1970s and an emerging concern for tapping indigenous knowledge and promoting more sustainable agricultural production among agricultural research and development centers.

It remains to be seen if the international agricultural research centers and national programs have the resources and skills to focus on the local issues implicit in farming-systems studies. If they can, a more genetically diversified agriculture will likely ensue. One way to reach this goal is greater reliance on local management, including locally relevant incentives, which could improve management efficiency. Establishing operable systems in local communities will require considerable effort, however.

Policy options should follow these guidelines:

- Restructuring of agricultural (and macroeconomic) policy should include awareness of implications for purchased inputs and the potential effects on crop diversity.
- Land-tenure restructuring programs should encourage the smallest farm size consistent with meeting target production goals.
- Research investment for locally important crops should increase to create more attractive alternatives to major staples. Net additions rather than reallocations within existing budgets should fund such research.
- Resettlement schemes should provide adequate training and access to inputs required for sustainable use of the new lands.
- Project guidelines should specify a compo-

nent for local management and incorporation of local knowledge.

In Situ and *Ex Situ* Conservation of Genetic Resources and Ownership Issues

Cost, sovereign rights, ownership, and knowledge gaps are some of the issues surrounding *in situ* and *ex situ* conservation of genetic resources.

In-Situ *Conservation and Incremental Costs*

In-situ conservation is essential for vegetatively propagated crops and cultivated plants with recalcitrant seeds. Crops with conventional seed such as traditional varieties of cereals in farmers' fields that can be easily dried and frozen may also be maintained *in situ* because this allows for ongoing evolution. Wild relatives can also be held. The definition of *in situ* used in the Biodiversity Convention (Article 2) applies specifically to preservation in natural habitats: "*In situ* conservation means conditions where genetic resources exist within ecosystems and natural habitats, and in the case of domesticated or cultivated species, in the surroundings where they developed their distinctive properties."

Brush (1994) identifies three arguments for conserving traditional varieties *in situ*:

- *Ex situ* collections are incomplete, and accessions are prone to genetic drift and loss of viability.
- *Ex situ* collections isolate plants from ongoing evolutionary processes.
- *In situ* conservation is an inexpensive complement to ex situ collections.

Wild material is poorly represented in most *ex situ* collections, and many accessions are not tested systematically to see if they need to be regenerated. The value of wild material as a source of commercially valuable genetic material has been well documented (Fowler and Mooney 1990). Even for important food crops wild populations and near-relatives are conspicuously absent or inadequately represented in seed gene banks; only 5 percent of the wild material of pearl millet and sorghum, for example, is housed in *ex situ* collections (Wilkes 1988). Only recently have gene banks begun assimilating wild materials (Blixt 1994). If only by default, *in situ* conservation is the prevailing means of preserving wild populations and near-relatives of crops.

Article 20(2) of the Convention on Biological Diversity calls on the industrial country parties to "provide new and additional financial resources to enable developing country parties to meet the agreed *full incremental costs*" of carrying out the convention (emphasis added). Incremental costs are not defined within the convention but have been given an operational definition by the Global Environment Facility (GEF) of the World Bank, the financial mechanism currently recognized under Article 21. The GEF (1995) defines incremental cost as "a measure of the future economic burden on the country that would result from its choosing the GEF-supported activity in preference to one that would have been sufficient in the national interest." Incremental costs would then be the costs for providing "global environmental benefits" that exceed baseline costs for satisfying national needs.

Presumably, *in situ* conservation that provided global benefits by structuring incentives for preserving potentially valuable germplasm, for example, would qualify for GEF funding. The phrase "global environmental benefits" is GEF, not Biodiversity Convention, terminology so that projects need not be limited to environmental benefits. Policies of GEF, or any possible successor organization, in this area have not yet been established.

Ex Situ *Conservation of Genetic Materials*

Gene banks exist at the international, regional, and national levels as well as in the working collections held by universities and private firms. Of these, the largest are the collections of international agricultural research centers. Wilkes (1988) estimates those collections contain 85 percent of the accessions worldwide. Clearly, the other gene banks duplicate some of their holdings, a valuable precautionary measure. The estimated proportion of cultivated gene pool remaining uncollected is in the 30–50 percent range for a number of crops, including millet, groundnuts, and beans. The majority of collected materials are at only the "passport level" (date and location of collection) and therefore are of limited value to breeding programs. Gene

banks at international agricultural research centers are part of core funding, and the legal status of and access to these materials have recently undergone some changes.

Regional gene banks range from the Nordic Gene Bank (Sweden) to the Southern Africa Research Council in Zambia, which was established in part with a grant from Norway. Because maintenance funding has been a problem for some of the regional and national gene banks, many of the materials are likely to have deteriorated. National gene banks are not well described in the literature. They range from major programs, such as India's new facility in New Delhi and the Fort Collins facility of the U.S. Department of Agriculture to small national collections. The authors have found that small collections are sometimes in very poor condition; many are in hot climates that lack refrigeration equipment. National systems depend largely on internal funding sources that are often inadequate and erratic. An international effort is now under way to support and replicate the Vavilov Center collections in St. Petersburg, which have fallen victim to the fluctuating political and economic situation in Russia.

Sovereign Rights to Genetic Resources *under the Biodiversity Convention*

Genetic resources as a common heritage came to the forefront of policy debate through the 1983 FAO *International Undertaking on Plant Genetic Resources*, which reiterated that genetic resources were a common heritage: "Recognizing that plant genetic resources are a heritage of [humankind] to be preserved, and to be freely available for use, for the benefit of present and future generations." The FAO also advanced the idea of establishing farmers' rights as a mechanism for compensating local farmers for the millennia of preserving and selecting traditional varieties subsequently used in plant breeding (Resolution 8/83).

This reflected an increasing frustration among farmers whose products were considered priceless but accorded no monetary value. Meanwhile, breeders and the companies they worked for were free to sell those products, in some cases selling materials back to the original innovators, albeit in modified form. Patents and plant breeders' rights provided legal mechanisms to protect the "improved" genetic products but ignored the materials on which those advances were based. With farmers' rights failing to provide any compensation, countries began to claim ownership, culminating in Articles 3 and 15 of the Convention on Biological Diversity. Resolution 3/91 of the FAO *International Undertaking* also recognized national sovereign rights but only within the reciprocal requirements.

Article 15(1) of the Biodiversity Convention reads as follows (emphasis added): "Recognizing the sovereign rights of States over their natural resources, the authority to determine access to genetic resources rests with the national governments and is subject to national legislation."

The authority of the Biodiversity Convention was not required for claiming these rights. Indeed the convention recognizes only existing rights, but it marked a turning point in the treatment of genetic resources. How property rights are to be apportioned domestically—between the government and individuals including landowners—is a matter outside the scope of the convention.

Requirements under Article 15. The convention regulates actions on biodiversity and genetic resources among countries. A country's sovereignty of use therefore ends at its borders: under Article 3 countries should "ensure that activities within their jurisdiction or control do not cause damage to the environment of other states." Two additional stipulations for use apply. First, both the materials and any associated research results must be accessible. Second, access and exchange must be done on "mutually agreeable terms" and subject to "informed consent" [Articles 15 (4) and (5)]. The full text is complex when considered within the convention as a whole, and interpretations differ on how policy recommendations should be applied.

Article 15(3) limits the scope of the convention to "parties that have acquired the genetic resources in accordance with this convention." This clause is generally interpreted to mean that the convention applies only to materials that are exchanged since the convention went into effect (Glowka, Burhenne-Guilmin, and Synge 1994).

As a general rule convention stipulations do not apply retroactively. Thus the large quantities of materials that were collected before December 29, 1993, are outside the scope of the convention. However, the Nairobi Final Act, a kind of addendum to the Biodiversity Convention, calls on the parties to resolve issues relevant to the rights to those materials. Because the previous plant genetic resources regime lacked any formal legal basis, those of the Biodiversity Convention are expected to take precedence (Witmeyer 1994).

Access legislation. The imposition of national sovereign rights on genetic resources is generally recognized to require some form of access legislation. Without specific legislation there is no prohibition, for example, on taking seeds from a squash purchased in a local market out of the country for use in breeding or other commercial activities. Some have argued that the wording of Article 15 of the Biodiversity Convention implies a general prohibition that applies until enabling legislation is adopted nationally. Yet under established legal interpretations a sovereign right is distinct from a property right over individual resources (FAO 1995). A national law is required for individual property rights.

Access legislation has taken two basic forms. The Philippines has a national proclamation (Executive Order 247, 1995) stating the conditions for access and the authorities responsible for granting access. That permission applies only for research purposes; a separate agreement is required for commercialization. Besides the Philippines only Queensland (Australia), Brazil, and Costa Rica have passed specific legislation on this matter, although the Andean Pact has for some months been in the process of drafting terminology, and in 1991 Argentina considered a draft law (Correa 1994).

Research permits provide the other major means of controlling access. These contractual agreements between two parties have been used for some time in exchanging materials for research purposes; they are known as material transfer agreements. A typical agreement stipulates that approved use is for research purposes only, commercialization requires separate approval, and materials could not be shared with third parties without permission. Material transfer agreements have been proposed for broader use. The U.S. Park Service has agreements for firms wishing to collect samples in Yellowstone and other national parks (Milstein 1994). Multilateral agreements, especially for agricultural resources, have also been proposed. A protocol under the Biodiversity Convention has also been suggested, possibly based on the 1993 FAO Code of Conduct for Plant Germplasm Collection and Transfer, a voluntary system.

Ownership and Access to Materials Collected before the Biodiversity Convention

With materials collected before the Biodiversity Convention excluded from its requirements, other mechanisms must be identified to regulate access, use, and compensation for that material. The Nairobi Final Act (Resolution 3) requires that countries make developing compensation and use policies for *ex situ* materials a priority, especially for agricultural and forestry uses. Two major ongoing efforts are involved: the recent and evolving policy for major international gene banks within the CGIAR system and the division of responsibilities between the Biodiversity Convention and the FAO Commission on Plant Genetic Resources.

The focus on CGIAR policies does not imply that the international agricultural research centers are the only institutions maintaining important collections. Regional and some national systems also maintain significant collections. However, the CGIAR collections are the major players in the international exchange of crop genetic resources.

CGIAR Policies. The bulk of acquisitions in the CGIAR collections appears to have been made under a frequently loose legal agreement with countries for *in trust* protection. In trust does not suggest ownership with its implicit privileges of control over use but rather a global reciprocal system of contributions and access that prevailed, later achieving some formal status under the FAO *International Undertaking.* Those underlying agreements shaped the context of subsequent arrangements for access and use (Witmeyer 1994).

In 1994 management of the CGIAR gene banks was placed under the auspices of FAO ("Consultative Group Signs Landmark Agreement" 1994). This new legal status stipulated that:

- Designated germplasm would be held in trust for the benefit of the international community (*designated germplasm* can be equated generally with collected materials that have no specific ownership or use agreements).
- Intellectual property rights would not be sought over designated germplasm or related information.
- Germplasm and related information would be available without restriction to users.
- The FAO Commission on Plant Genetic Resources would have authority to establish policy for the international network of *ex situ* collections.
- Recipients should be bound by the same restrictions as the international agricultural research centers for access and intellectual property protection.

For its part FAO is committed to operating the international network of gene banks within the tenets of the *International Undertaking on Plant Genetic Resources.* This involves assisting in policy establishment facilitating access and providing emergency support for genetic materials.

FAO Commission on Plant Genetic Resources. The commission is primarily responsible for formulating and carrying out policy. The notion of farmers' rights (Resolution 5/89), "rights arising from past, present, and future contributions of farmers in conserving, improving, and making available plant genetic resources," is a major focus of the commission's policy work. Subsequent resolutions have declared that farmers' rights are not incompatible with the Biodiversity Convention nor with plant breeders' rights. Some groups, such as the Rural Advancement Foundation International are critical of even indirect commercial use of materials held in trust (Mooney 1993).

Handling Materials Collected under the Biodiversity Convention

Treatment of materials collected under the auspices of the Biodiversity Convention is uncertain and contentious for several reasons. The convention has not been applied in these areas beyond a few tentative interpretations. Until actual practices begin to evolve, much of what can be said is speculative. Lack of clarity in defining the principal agent is also a problem. Legally, the parties of the Biodiversity Convention have authority, but FAO has proposed that it become the agent for crop (and more recently animal) genetic resources held both *in situ* and *ex situ*. That position has met with some skepticism by national governments (Biodiversity Coalition 1995), but formal action has yet to be taken.

FAO prefers a multilateral system based on farmers' rights. Underlying the farmers' rights approach is creation of a multinational fund for compensating farmers. The fund would likely be mandatory because experiences with a voluntary fund under the nonbinding *International Undertaking* indicate that approach is not effective. Financial requirements for the fund have been estimated $300 million annually (Keystone Center 1991). The bulk of those monies would be directed to maintaining the current *ex situ* system. *In situ* conservation will require additional resources (FAO 1995; Brush 1994). The final basis for the calculations has yet to be established.

As applied to *in situ* materials (funding of *ex situ* collections is a separate topic), the fund has been described as more of a moral obligation than an incentive system such as intellectual property rights (Lesser 1994). FAO (1995), however, proposes that farmers' rights also refer to future contributions and that funds used for future *in situ* conservation would satisfy the need for incentives. Those types of incentives would, however, differ from intellectual property rights because they would lack the direct connection between an individual's actions and the expectations of market rewards. They would parallel more closely the practice in some countries of applying a royalty to recording tapes to compensate musicians and others for expected lost sales when consumers make private recordings. The recording tape system must operate by assuming some relationship between, say, the level of compact disc sales and private taping. Yet there remains a direct connection between commercial success and compensation. For genetic resources for which commercial use may

not occur for decades, if ever, the direct market connection is nonexistent. In effect, farmers would be subsidized for maintaining particular farming practices rather than for responding to an incentive.

For traditional farmers using landraces, one form of incentive could be payment for continuance of those farming practices. That would perhaps be better described as a payment or subsidy for a service rather than an incentive involving market risk. In the self-monitoring role of intellectual property right incentives all returns come from the market. For subsidies external monitoring would be required to determine if agreed practices were indeed being followed. Worede and Mekbib (1993) describe a composite local community and plant breeders program that has been effective in maintaining the use of landraces in Ethiopia.

Policy Issues and Knowledge Gaps

Science, politics, and economics are involved in conservation of genetic resources. This discussion is limited to politics and economics. The major economic issue is the funding of both *in situ* and *ex situ* conservation. The CGIAR collections are supported by annual pledges from donors, and while there are no indications those sources are not secure, continuity of funding is nonetheless an issue. Funding for regional and national gene banks is far more variable.

Long-term support for *in situ* conservation is even less clear for several reasons. While the general benefits of *in situ* conservation are widely appreciated, they are not quantified by crop. For crops that can also be held in *ex situ* collections, allocation of funds to *in situ* programs is uncertain. Additional resources will be required to determine the relative benefits of *in situ* and *ex situ* conservation. Furthermore, when *in situ* conservation is necessary or beneficial, relatively few examples exist of how to manage compensation programs for traditional farmers to continue farming practices that would otherwise become obsolete.

The political issues are even more complex. At one level is the division of responsibility between FAO and the Parties of the Biodiversity Convention. At the national level countries are now determining how to protect and claim value for genetic resources through access legislation. Although a bilateral approach such as contracting seems appropriate for high-value material, a multilateral system would be more effective at maintaining free exchange. But a mutually acceptable compensation system that would provide the needed incentives is lacking. Country skepticism means that alternatives to the farmers' rights-based proposal from FAO should also be considered. FAO is developing a multilateral approach. Before an international compensation system can be established, the needs and uses of funds should be identified more precisely.

Policy issues include:

• Establishing a secure funding source for *ex situ* germplasm collections, especially at the international centers

• Allowing more specific discussion of the use of intellectual property rights for the CGIAR collections, including control and negotiating exchanges with the private sector

• Clarifying the division of responsibility for agricultural genetic resources between the parties of the Biodiversity Convention and FAO

• Establishing a program for estimating the value of *in situ* genetic resource conservation as a basis for allocating limited funds

• Developing model access legislation for national consideration, possibly including a multilateral system for agricultural resources and a bilateral system for other uses

• Evaluating alternatives to a farmers' rights system for agricultural genetic resources because the private sector and some governments view such rights skeptically.

Trade Agreements

Major international trade agreements are a recent phenomenon dating to the end of World War II when the first (Geneva) Round of the General Agreement on Tariffs and Trade (GATT) was adopted. GATT grew out of the conviction, particularly that of the United States, that trade would be economically advantageous, if only to avoid repetitions of the escalation of tariffs widely believed to have precipitated worldwide depression in the 1930s.

GATT operates on a few basic principles, the most significant of which are:

• *National treatment.* Foreign products must be treated the same as nationally produced ones (Article I).

• *General most-favored-nation treatment.* Opportunities granted to one trading partner must be granted to all (Article I).

• *Noninvolvement with domestic affairs.* Agreements relate to activities between countries, not within them (Article I).

• *Preferences for developing countries.* Developing countries receive certain exemptions such as conservation of foreign exchange and are accorded delays in implementation and tariff concessions not allowed to industrial countries (Article XVIII).

• *Tariffs.* Over time, policies function by transmuting all trade barriers to tariffs that decrease according to an established schedule.

• *Trading partners.* The establishment of regional trading groups such as the European Union (EU) and the North American Free Trade Agreement (NAFTA) are permitted under GATT as long as GATT requirements are honored (Article XXIV).

Before the Uruguay Round agricultural trade issues had been granted special treatment under GATT. Although export subsidizes were prohibited for other commodities, they were permissible for agricultural products as long as a country did not gain more than an equitable share of the world market [Article XVI(3)]. Environment and trade issues were significantly expanded in the current round. This section addresses the relationships between these two areas and biodiversity use and conservation.

Agricultural Issues

GATT. Restricting agricultural subsidies to an equitable share of the world market proved unworkable, so there has been no effective control over agricultural trade. Within the Uruguay Round the United States was the major proponent of liberalization, joined by a mix of industrial and developing countries. The European Union has been a major opponent of liberalizing trade in agricultural commodities. Developing countries saw domestic subsidies as limiting their direct access to protected agricultural markets and their indirect access to third-country markets where surplus commodities from domestic price supports were sold below cost. True reform would reduce or eliminate those domestic subsidies, thereby drawing GATT into national affairs.

Agreed-to reforms involved an immediate conversion from nontariff barriers to tariffs, which were to be reduced an average of 36 percent over six years (ten for developing countries). Developing countries were allowed additional preferential treatment, including tariff reductions as low as two-thirds that of developed countries and exemptions for export subsidies incorporated in development programs. Despite these impressive-sounding agreements, projected import prices in Organisation for Economic Co-operation and Development (OECD) countries will change little, with the exception of Japan and the high-income Asian countries, and import prices in nearly all developing countries will be largely unaffected (Hathaway and Ingco 1995).

The explanation for this seeming anomaly of significant tariff reductions yet stable import prices is the base period selected by which reductions would be measured. The chosen base, 1986–88, represents a period of below-average world prices. Because the *tariff equivalent* is computed as the difference between domestic and world prices, the effect was to begin with very high tariff levels from which to calculate reductions. In some cases actual tariffs have been lower than required by GATT.

Other factors affected this outcome. Provisions were included for offsetting tariff reductions; large-percentage reductions on one commodity could compensate for no reductions on another ("dirty tariffication"). However, as has often been the case, large reductions were made for commodities with low levels of protection, limiting absolute liberalization. For domestic subsidies the United States and the EU negotiated absolute expenditure caps but no requirement for reductions on particular commodities. Hence no major relocations of agricultural production should be expected at least through the year 2002.

Overall, world welfare gains are estimated at roughly $48 billion annually. The agricultural agreement can be credited with providing a firm basis for future reductions and holding U.S. and EU domestic subsidies at a constant level. Food-importing countries should also escape major price increases attributable to GATT, at least over the short term. In the case of wheat, for example, prices are unlikely to rise by more than 3.8 percent by 2002 thanks to trade agreements (Goldin and van der Mensbrugghe 1995).

NAFTA. NAFTA's specifications are far more explicit than those of GATT. NAFTA calls for eliminating barriers to the movement of agricultural goods within ten years. Various agricultural producers, particularly Mexico and Canada, are making changes to enhance efficiency. Without significant improvements in efficiency production of potatoes in Mexico, for example, will decline substantially. Some informal projections suggest that maize production in Mexico will fall because of competition from the U.S. corn belt. Some of that slack would likely be taken up by vegetable production, for which Mexico has a climatic and labor-cost advantage.

Concerns have been expressed that small farmers will be forced out of maize production, leading to the loss of traditional varieties and wild relatives associated with their production methods. Teosinte, a close-relative of maize, grows on the verges of small fields, cross-pollinating with cultivated varieties (Wilkes 1993). The loss of maize production would mean the loss of teosinte germplasm. The limited contact many traditional farmers have with market crops suggests that this is unlikely to occur, however.

The small-scale forest product industry may be changed dramatically, leading to biodiversity loss. Mexico has significant forest land that is managed cooperatively with long-term landowners. Management is not market-oriented as in the United States and Canada, meaning that wood products in Mexico are priced differently. This has led to concerns that import competition will lead to more rapid exploitation and hence loss of biodiversity in old-growth forest. Landowners may respond by accepting lower returns on their land investment, but the likelihood is for rapid change in the Mexican forest sector (Soberon, personal communication).

Environmental Issues under GATT and NAFTA

Environmental issues have long been incorporated under GATT but have been limited to two aspects of Article XX, which states that:

> ...nothing in this Agreement shall be construed to prevent the adoption or enforcement by any contracting party of measures:
>
>   (b) necessary to protect human, animal, or plant life or health; ...
>
>   (g) relating to the conservation of exhaustible natural resources if such measures are made effective in conjunction with restrictions on domestic production or consumption.

More and more of society is paying increased attention to environmental matters. As other trade loopholes are closed, environmental concerns could be used increasingly as a nontariff barrier. And countries with stricter controls over discharges have expressed concerns of becoming uncompetitive with countries with laxer requirements. This is a major justification for NAFTA's detailed environmental requirements, particularly on the treatment of effluents. Many trade economists discount this concern, noting that pollution abatement adds an average of only 3 percent to the cost of production, although the amount can be considerably greater for some industries, especially when costs are added for the production of inputs, such as electricity (Runge 1994). On the other hand concerns have been registered that countries with less strenuous antipollution regulations will attract dirty industries.

Liberalized trade is intended to enhance economic growth, which unless regulated is often associated with environmental degradation. It is therefore appropriate to include environmental safeguards in GATT. Two such safeguards are specifically addressed in the Uruguay Round:

- Agreement on sanitary and phytosanitary measures (such as quarantine)
- Agreement on technical barriers to trade (for example, lifecycle packaging).

In addition, Article I prohibits discrimination against "like products," which has become enmeshed in the "production process" debate.

Sanitary and phytosanitary measures. In addition to quarantine, sanitary and phytosanitary measures control health and safety standards, such as livestock slaughter requirements and fumigation of plant materials. Under the Uruguay Round regulations the following conditions apply:

- Regulations are to be in harmony with international standards.
- When no international standards exists, regulations may be based temporarily on available scientific information.
- Higher standards can be employed only if there is scientific justification.
- Risk assessments must fit the circumstances and may include economic risks such as the spread of a new pest or disease.

Provided that these requirements allow for a reasonable level of protection against the international movement of pests and diseases, the connection with biodiversity is limited.

Packaging. Packaging issues have been associated with GATT because Germany and other countries have adopted package recycling requirements (Esty 1994). Manufacturers are required to make provisions for reuse of their packaging materials, even if no economical recycling technology exists. This is seen as a special burden for firms shipping products into those countries. While this can be a matter of significant economic importance, its connection with severe environmental degradation is limited. Landfills, the prevailing disposal system for packaging materials, do not generally trigger serious pollution, at least beyond the immediate area of the fill.

Process or product. The fundamental environmental issue in production methods is this: Can identical finished products be differentiated by production method? In particular if a product is produced in two countries (or even two plants within a single country), one more polluting than the other, are they like or dissimilar products under GATT? Several environmental groups such as the World Wildlife Fund argue that they would be different products, thus permitting exclusions under the conservation of natural resources provisions of Article XX(g) (WWF 1993).

A partial interpretation was provided in the Mexican Yellowfin Tuna Case (Report of the Panel, GATT doc. No. DS21/R). The United States banned canned tuna imports from Mexico because the fishing practices violated the Federal Marine Mammal Protection Act. In particular Mexican purse-seining techniques were blamed for the incidental drowning of an unacceptably large number of dolphins. Mexican canned tuna was not acceptable in the United States because of the production method, not because of safety concerns about the tuna itself.

The panel decided against the United States, ruling the import ban a violation of GATT. That ruling stirred environmental groups to decry the GATT. They lamented the loss of a means to check environmental degradation elsewhere in the world, especially in developing countries. In reality the decision was a technical one related to the specific means by which the United States established the incidental tuna take and not a sweeping rebuke of the product-by-process concept. The allowable dolphin take was based on that of the U.S. tuna fleet rather than some absolute standard. For the panel that meant that the United States could indirectly determine allowable Mexican imports. Moreover, the United States was found not to have exhausted less trade-restrictive approaches (Runge 1994).

Perhaps more pertinent was the first major environmental ruling of the appeals body of the World Trade Organization (WTO), GATT's successor. In that ruling a provision of the U.S. Clean Air Act was judged as discriminating against foreign gasoline refiners. Although the technical issues were quite distinct from the tuna case, they shared a standard based on the performance of U.S. firms rather than an absolute scale related to environmental considerations. This case thus also fails to set a clear standard for environmental considerations under the WTO.

Stronger NAFTA action. NAFTA has moved much further than GATT to standardize internal pollution regulations among member countries in response to protests from the environmental community before the U.S. ratification agreement; green issues were handled through an environmental side agreement administered by a trilateral Commission on Environmental Cooperation. As a result Mexico is investing considerable sums in public water and air treatment projects in spite of a severe economic crisis. Because of this different approach to harmonization, many of the environmental issues raised under GATT do not apply to NAFTA.

Policy Options and Knowledge Gaps

Global agriculture will be little affected by GATT, at least until after 2002, when tariff levels are revisited. For the initial period the high baseline levels from which reductions are computed and other technical matters will minimize the effect on agrobiodiversity. For the foreseeable future many national tariffs will be at low levels so that further reductions will not have major implications. However, U.S. and EU freezes on domestic subsidy levels will reduce the intensity of production in some areas, thereby benefiting the environment.

Only recently have environmental issues been highlighted in trade agreements. NAFTA is attempting to harmonize environmental standards among the United States, Canada, and Mexico. However, many developing countries are opposed to the upward harmonization of environmental regulations.

The environmental safeguards in GATT are more limited. The principal issue is to determine when environmental restrictions are legitimate and when they act as undue impediments to trade. A product-versus-process controversy has emerged in environmentally related trade restrictions. At issue is whether an identical product can be discriminated against in trade if it is produced in a manner importing countries deem damaging to the environment. Definitive rulings must await additional decisions by GATT's successor, the WTO. The initial relevant rulings have been narrow.

The main policy options include:
- Recognizing the uncertainty of WTO rulings and establishing additional environmental regulations as appropriate for World Bank projects
- Establishing biodiversity as one of the "exhaustible natural resources" that can be invoked under GATT Article XX(g)

- Further limiting farm subsidies whenever possible because they are often associated with loss of biodiversity
- Pressing the WTO to adopt a broad interpretation of resource-related trade limitations.

Effects of Patents and Plant Breeders' Rights on Biodiversity Conservation

Patents have been granted since the fifteenth century, evolving into their modern form after the Industrial Revolution. Explicit protection for living organisms is more recent. Major steps in patenting biological material include establishment of the International Convention for the Protection of New Varieties of Plants in 1960, also referred to as plant breeders' rights, and initial patenting in the United States of microorganisms (1980), plants (1985), and animals (1987). Several countries followed the U.S. example. Historically, agricultural applications for intellectual property protection have lagged behind industrial products for both technical and policy reasons.

Objectives of Intellectual Property Rights

Of the five traditional forms of intellectual property rights—patents, plant breeders' rights, copyrights, trademarks, and trade secrets—patents, plant breeders' rights, and trade secrets are most applicable to crop genetic resources (Lesser 1994; Correa 1994). Their principal objective is to provide investment incentives in creative enterprises by preventing direct copying or, in the case of trade secrets, improper acquisition of protected information. Without a legal prohibition an investor has little opportunity to recover his or her investment because of direct competition with copiers. Stated another way, intellectual property rights protect intangible goods such as knowledge within the definition of technology as applied knowledge. Intellectual property rights seem to increase investment in research and development, especially for easily copied inventions like plants and pharmaceutical products, although the evidence is not as firm as required by some skeptics (Lesser 1991).

A secondary role of intellectual property rights is to facilitate access to and transfer of eas-ily copied technologies. This has proven particularly useful in the case of plant varieties (Biodiversity Secretariat 1995), as figures in three of the five sections of Article 16 of the Biodiversity Convention show. Critics disparage intellectual property rights for a number of reasons, including a bias toward the more technologically advanced countries and a turning of life forms into commodities ("UPOV Sells Out" 1990; Singh Nijar and Ling 1994). And these rights work through market mechanisms, meaning that they have no application for noncommercial products, such as varieties for resource-poor farmers.

Today approximately forty-four countries explicitly exclude patents for plants and animals, but twenty-eight others (four of which are developing countries) are members of the International Convention for the Protection of New Varieties of Plants. Intellectual property rights are territorial; they apply only in countries in which protection has been sought and granted. Several countries are currently adopting plant breeders'-rights legislation, many by joining the International Convention as mandated by the trade-related intellectual property rights amendments to the GATT Uruguay Round agreement (Biodiversity Secretariat 1995). Technically, plant breeders' rights or plant patents or both would satisfy the commitments, but most countries are opting for breeders' rights alone. All GATT signatories must also adopt some trade-secret protection; currently there is no international compilation of the extent of availability.

Conservation Link

A conceptual connection can be made between intellectual property rights and conservation. A common application is the charging of royalties for use, meaning that genetic resources have perceived value, providing an incentive to conserve them. This would help reverse one of the leading causes of resource loss—the higher value realized through exploitation, such as logging as currently practiced in most parts of the tropics, than through sustainable use (McNeely 1988).

Two factors must be considered, however; first, experience is limited. Second, questions have been raised about the applicability of intellectual property rights to the protection of genetic resources (Correa 1994; Lesser 1995). The reasons are technical but can be explained succinctly: intellectual property rights are designed to encourage production of commercial products. U.S. patent law, for example, requires that at least one use for an invention must be identified in the application. The invention must also be described so that a person skilled in the subject matter can recreate it (the disclosure requirement). Genetic resources, which are collected on the expectation that they may be found to have future value, satisfy neither requirement. Plant breeders' rights are intended for agricultural applications only and would not apply to genetic resources in general. Even crop resources such as traditional varieties would not satisfy the stability and uniformity requirements of plant breeders' rights (Lesser 1995).

Such concerns have focused attention on alternatives such as expressions of folklore and appellations of origin. Neither applies generally to genetic resources either, leading to calls for a new, specific form of intellectual property rights for genetic resources (Biodiversity Secretariat 1995; Correa 1994; Posey 1994). Until such a time contracts or multilateral agreements will likely suffice. (Subsequent discussion treats contracts as a form of intellectual property rights even though they are technically distinct.)

Limited information exists about agreements for genetic prospecting, especially for pharmaceuticals and natural pesticides. The best publicized has been the Merck-INBio agreement in Costa Rica (Reid and others 1993). INBio is said to have made subsequent arrangements valued in the millions of dollars. In general agricultural applications are not as valuable as human pharmaceuticals but could be expected to provide some royalties. Strains of *Bacillus thuringiensis* and extracts from the neem tree are examples of agricultural uses but not necessarily of payments. The issue for conservation therefore becomes how those monies are used, especially at the local level. Shaman Pharmaceuticals and Andes Pharmaceuticals are making a business of using indigenous medicinal knowledge and returning a share of the value to the local communities (Finesilver 1995). This approach takes considerable attention in its own right, including

an understanding of how local communities perceive and manage their natural environments (Warren, Slikkerveer, and Brokensha 1995).

Genetic Uniformity Issue

Modern, intensive agriculture is highly efficient and uniform. Some of this genetic uniformity has been associated with intellectual property rights, with plant breeders' rights in particular because they require uniformity and stability. Mechanization and the market also demand uniformity.

Much of the global narrowing of crops has occurred in the absence of intellectual property rights. This is not to deny that genetic uniformity is a problem or that such rights may contribute to the declining use of traditional varieties, but intellectual property rights are not likely a major factor.

Exchange of Genetic Materials

There are two major policy questions about intellectual property rights and restrictions on the flow of genetic resources: Is the result specific to intellectual property rights, and what is actually happening in the field?

On the first question the value of genetic resources that can be captured through biotechnology has apparently affected the open exchange of materials. Indeed it is becoming common for exchanges among all parties, including among university researchers, to be accompanied by a material transfer agreement. Economic considerations have affected the form of transfer but not necessarily their extent.

A systematic 1980s U.S. survey of crop material exchanges determined that plant breeders' rights have had no major effect (Butler and Marion 1985; Plucknett and others 1987). Business and universities recognized their mutual dependence and maintained near-constant levels of exchange. The same situation seems to apply today but has not been documented. Access might be a problem with breeders or researchers not associated with major institutions because it is the potential for reciprocity in exchange that largely maintains the informal access system.

The exchange of materials has undoubtedly been affected in cases in which difficulties have been encountered in obtaining permits for biological prospecting. The absence of legislation, combined with uncertainty within governments about the value of materials and hesitation over negotiations, has sharply curtailed access to genetic resources in many countries, probably more a consequence of the Biodiversity Convention and reported commercial arrangements such as the Merck-INBio deal than of intellectual property rights as such. Lesser and Krattiger (1994) have proposed a "facilitator mechanism" for assisting countries in voluntarily overcoming these limitations, but whatever approach is used, some systematic effort seems to be required before access is restored in many countries.

Rights and Options of Local Communities

Access to intellectual property rights is technically independent of the status of individuals; rights are available to all natural and legal persons (a technical term for businesses). As a practical matter intellectual property rights are both complex and expensive to secure, placing them beyond the means of most communities not operating through an established partner. A new system for genetic resources should be simple and low cost. A rotating patent fund has been suggested for India (Gupta 1992).

Another problem is the lack of clarity on the property rights of local and indigenous peoples. Until land-tenure issues are resolved, there seems little point in securing intellectual property rights. Numerous countries have separated mineral rights from title to the land. The same could be done for genetic resources. Access legislation could clarify these issues.

It is conceptually possible to separate ownership of genetic resources from indigenous knowledge of their use. Ownership of the knowledge as community property is not contested, so even now communities can arrange for the commercialization of their knowledge (Laird 1995; Pinel and Evans 1995). It is often impossible to protect knowledge except through secrecy, which accounts for reports of ethnobotanists occasionally encountering difficulties in obtaining information about traditional herbal medicine and agricultural practices.

Policy Issues and Knowledge Gaps

In general intellectual property rights are not suited for the protection of genetic resources. Countries therefore need to adopt access legislation. The available but dated information on the effect of such rights on the exchange of genetic materials has identified no major limitations. Those surveys need to be updated. Although the exchange of genetic materials does not appear to have slowed with the adoption of intellectual property rights, the mechanisms have changed and rely heavily on material transfer agreements. However, individuals or entities not associated with a major institution may be losing access to genetic resources of crops and livestock. This possibility should be explored further and, if necessary, alternative mechanisms identified.

Attaching ownership to intangible goods to make them salable with less threat of losing control could be used to enhance the value of biodiversity and provide an incentive for conservation. In practice such ownership is not broadly applicable to genetic resources, so the incentive effect will be small. Generating value, however, is but the first step, one for which material transfer agreements could be used. Also needed is an understanding of how to use the funds to create the greatest conservation incentive. At a minimum revenues must be directed to both the national and local levels. Directing allocations at the local level requires further study.

Mechanisms are needed for local communities to claim part of the value of genetic resources they have identified and protected. In part this will necessitate clearer national policies for the rights of traditional communities to their ancestral lands, a highly political issue in some countries. But at a minimum countries need to specify what genetic resource rights are claimed by the government and what are available for landowners and other claimants. Systems also need to be identified that will allow local communities to claim rights over traditional knowledge, separate from the resources themselves. Such rights would enhance the exchange of information that is now restricted.

Policy changes are required to provide incentives for conservation and to maintain open exchange systems. The issues are to:

- Identify and implement a new system along the lines of international property rights applicable to traditional varieties and breeds, wild populations, and near-relatives of crops and livestock.
- Clarify access and ownership issues for genetic resources on the land use by local communities.
- Clarify ownership of findings and applicable exchange conditions for research supported by bi- and multilateral funds.
- Establish mechanisms to assist small research entities lacking reciprocal capacity for access to materials.

References

Binswanger, H., and P. Pingali. 1986. "Resource Endowments, Farming Systems and Technology Priorities for Sub-Saharan Africa." Unpublished paper, World Bank, Agriculture and Natural Resources Department, Washington, D.C.

Biodiversity Coalition. 1995. "Genetic Resources—The Battle Rages On," *Biodiversity Coalition Newsletter* No. 11, September.

Biodiversity Secretariat. 1995. "Intellectual Property Rights and Transfer of Technologies Which Make Use of Genetic Resources." UNEP/CBD/COP/2/17. United Nations Environment Programme, 6 October 1995, Nairobi.

Blixt, S. 1994. "The Role of Gene Banks in Plant Genetic Resource Conservation under the Convention on Biological Diversity. In A. F. Krattiger, W. H. Lesser, K. R. Miller, Y. St. Hillard, and R. Senanayake, eds., *Widening Perspectives in Biodiversity.* Geneva and Gland, Switzerland: International Academy of the Environment and International Union for the Conservation of Nature.

Brush, S. B. 1994. "Providing Farmers' Rights through In Situ Conservation of Crop Genetic Resources." Food and Agriculture Organization (FAO) Background Study Paper 3. Rome.

Busch, L., W. B. Lacy, J. Burkhardt, and L. R. Lacy. 1991. *Plants, Power, and Profit: Social, Economic, and Ethical Consequences of the New Biotechnologies.* Oxford: Basil Blackwell.

Butler, L. J., and B. M. Marion. 1985. *Impacts of Patent Protection in the U.S. Seed Industry and Public Plant Breeders.* NC-117, Monograph 16. Madison: University of Wisconsin.

CGIAR (Consultative Group on International Agricultural Research). 1995. *CGIAR 1994 Financial Report.* Washington, D.C.: CGIAR.

CIAT (International Center for Tropical Agriculture). 1994. "Annual Program and Budget Report." CIAT, Cali, Colombia.

CIMMYT (International Center for Maize and Wheat Improvement). 1996. "Annual Program and Budget Report." CIMMYT, Mexico City, Mexico.

CIP (International Center for the Potato). 1994. "Annual Program and Budget Report." CIP, Lima, Peru.

"Consultative Group Signs Landmark Agreement to Place CGIAR Gene Banks under FAO Trusteeship," 1994. *Diversity* 10 (4): 4–5.

Correa, C.M. 1994. "Sovereign and Property Rights over Plant Genetic Resources." FAO Background Study Paper 2. Rome.

David, C. C., and K. Otsuka, eds. 1994. *Modern Rice Technology and Income Distribution in Asia.* Boulder: Lynne Rienner Publishers.

Desai, G. M. 1988. "Policy for Rapid Growth in the Use of Modern Agricultural Inputs." In J. W. Mellor and R. Ahmed, eds., *Agricultural Price Policy for Developing Countries.* Baltimore: Johns Hopkins University Press.

Esty, D. C. 1994. *Greening the GATT: Trade, Environment, and the Future.* Washington, D.C.: Institute for International Economics.

FAO. 1995. *Revision of the International Undertaking on Plant Genetic Resources Analysis of Some Technical, Economic and Legal Aspects for Consideration in Stage II: Access to Plant Genetic Resources and Farmers' Rights.* Commission on Plant Genetic Resources. CPGR-6/95/8 Supp. June. Rome: FAO.

Finesilver, J. M. 1995. "Biodiversity Prospecting: Prospects and Realities." In A. H. Zakri, ed., *Prospects in Biodiversity Prospecting.* Kuala Lumpur: Genetics Society of Malaysia.

Fowler, C. 1980. "Statement at Plant Variety Protection Act Hearings of the Committee on Agriculture, Nutrition, and Forestry," U.S. Senate, 17–18 July, Washington, D.C.

Fowler, C., and D. Mooney. 1990. *Shattering: Food, Politics, and the Loss of Genetic Diversity.* Tucson: University of Arizona Press.

GEF (Global Environment Facility). 1995. "Incremental Costs and Financing Modalities," GEF/C-2/6/Rev. 2, May. World Bank Counsel Paper. Washington, D.C.

Geisler, C. C., and E. M. DuPuis. 1989. "From Green Revolution to Gene Revolution: Common Concerns about Agricultural Biotechnology in the First and Third Worlds." In J. J. Molnar and H. Kinnucan, eds., *Biotechnology and the New Agricultural Revolution.* AAAS Selected Symposium 108. Boulder: Westview Press.

Glowka, L., L. Burhenne-Guilmin, and H. Synge. 1994. *A Guide to the Convention on Biological Diversity.* Environmental Policy and Law Paper 30. Gland, Switzerland: International Union for the Conservation of Nature.

Goldin, I., and D. van der Mensbrugghe. 1995. "The Uruguay Round: An Assessment of Economywide and Agricultural Reforms." In W. Martin and L. A. Winters, eds., *The Uruguay Round and the Developing Economies.* World Bank Discussion Paper 307. Washington, D.C.

Gupta, A. K. 1992. "Biodiversity, Poverty and Intellectual Property Rights of Third World Peasants: A Case of Renegotiating Global Understanding." In M. S. Swaminathan and S. Jana, eds., *Biodiversity Implications for Global Food Security.* Madras: Macmillan India Press.

Hanna, S. 1995. "Efficiencies of User Participation in Natural Resource Management." In S. Hanna and M. Munasinghe, eds., *Property Rights and the Environment: Social and Ecological Issues.* Stockholm and Washington, D.C.: The Beijer International Institute of Ecological Economics and the World Bank.

Hathaway, D. E., and M. D. Ingco. 1995. "Agricultural Liberalization and the Uruguay Round." In W. Martin and L.A. Winters, eds., *The Uruguay Round and the Developing Economies.* World Bank Discussion Paper 307. Washington, D.C.

Hayami, Y., and V. Ruttan. 1985. *Agricultural Development: An International Perspective.* Baltimore: Johns Hopkins University Press.

ICARDA (International Center for Agricultural Research in the Dry Areas). 1996. "Annual Program and Budget Report." ICARDA, Aleppo, Syria.

ICRISAT (International Crops Research Institute for the Semi-Arid Tropics). 1996. "Annual Program and Budget Report." ICRISAT, Hyderabad, India.

IITA (International Institute of Tropical Agriculture). 1996. "Annual Program and Budget Report." IITA, Ibadan, Nigeria.

IRRI (International Rice Research Institute). 1994. "Annual Program and Budget Report." IRRI, Manila, Philippines.

Keystone Center. 1991. "Final Consensus Report of the Keystone International Dialogue Series on Plant Genetic Resources." Third Plenary Session. Keystone Center, Oslo, Norway.

King, S. R. 1994. "Establishing Reciprocity: Biodiversity, Conservation, and New Models for Cooperation between Forest-Dwelling Peoples and the Pharmaceutical Industry." In T. Greaves, ed., *Intellectual Property Rights to Indigenous Peoples: A Source Book.* Oklahoma City: Society for Applied Anthropology.

Krueger, A. 1983. *Trade and Employment in Developing Countries: Synthesis and Conclusions.* Cambridge, Mass.: National Bureau of Economic Research.

Laird, S. 1995. "Natural Products and Commercialization of Traditional Knowledge." In T. Greaves, ed., *Intellectual Property Rights for Indigenous Peoples: A Source Book.* Oklahoma City: Society for Applied Anthropology.

Lesser, W. 1991. *Equitable Patent Protection in the Developing World: Issues and Approaches.* Tsukuba:

Eubios Ethics Institute.

———.1994. "Institutional Mechanisms Supporting Trade in Genetic Materials: Issues Under the Biodiversity Convention and GATT/TRIPs." United Nations Environment Programme, Environment and Trade 4, Nairobi, Kenya.

———.1995. "Attributes of an IPR System for Land-races." In M. S. Swaminathan, ed., *Farmers' Rights and Plant Genetic Resources.* Madras: Macmillan India Press.

Lesser, W., and A. F. Krattiger. 1994. "Marketing Genetic Technologies in South-North and South-South Exchanges: The Proposed Role of a New Facilitations Organization." In A. F. Krattiger, W. H. Lesser, K. R. Miller, Y. St. Hillard, and R. Senanayake, eds., *Widening Perspectives on Biodiversity.* Geneva and Gland, Switzerland: IAE and International Union for the Conservation of Nature.

Mascorenhas, J. 1993. "Participatory Approaches to Management of Local Resources in South India." In W. deBoef, K. Amanor, K. Wellard, and A. Bebbington, eds., *Cultivating Knowledge: Genetic Diversity, Farmer Experimentation and Crop Research.* London: Intermediate Technology Publications.

McNeely, J. A. 1988. *Economics and Biological Diversity: Developing and Using Economic Incentives to Conserve Biological Resources.* Gland, Switzerland: International Union for the Conservation of Nature.

Milstein, M. 1994. "Yellowstone Managers Eye Profits from Hot Microbes," *Science* (264): 655.

Mooney, R. P. 1993. "Exploiting Local Knowledge: International Policy Implications." In W. deBoef, K. Amanor, K. Wellard, and A. Bebbington, eds., *Cultivating Knowledge: Genetic Diversity, Farmer Experimentation and Crop Research.* London: Intermediate Technology Publications.

NRC (National Research Council). 1972. *Genetic Vulnerability of Major Crops.* Washington, D.C.: National Academy of Sciences, NRC.

———.1992. *Conserving Biodiversity: A Research Agenda for Development Agencies.* Washington, D.C.: National Academy Press, NRC.

Pinel, S. L., and M. J. Evans. 1995. "Tribal Sovereignty and the Center of Knowledge." In T. Greaves, ed., *Intellectual Property Rights for Indigenous Peoples: A Source Book.* Oklahoma City: Society for Applied Anthropology.

Plucknett, D. L., N. J. H. Smith, J. T. Williams, and N. Murthi Anishetty. 1987. *Gene Banks and the World's Food.* Princeton: Princeton University Press.

Posey, D. 1994. "International Agreements and Intellectual Property Rights for Indigenous Peoples." In T. Greaves, ed., *Intellectual Property Rights for Indigenous Peoples: A Source Book.* Oklahoma City: Society for Applied Anthropology.

Reid, W. V., S. A. Laird, C. A. Meyer, R. Gómez, A. Sittenfield, D. H. Janzen, M. A. Gollin, and C. Juma, eds. 1993. *Biodiversity Prospecting Using Genetic Resources for Sustainable Development.* Washington,

D.C.: World Resources Institute.

Runge, C. F. 1994. *Freer Trade, Protected Environment.* New York: Council on Foreign Relations Press.

Runge, C. F., J. Houck, and D. Halbach. 1988. "Implications of Environmental Regulations for Competitiveness in Agricultural Trade." In J. Sutton, ed., *Agricultural Trade and Natural Resources.* Boulder: Lynne-Reiner Publishers.

Ruttan V. W. 1989. "The International Agricultural Research System." In J. L. Compton, ed., *The Transformation of International Agricultural Research and Development.* Boulder: Lynne Rienner Publishers.

Singh Nijar, G., and C. Y. Ling. 1994. "The Implications of the Intellectual Property Rights Regime of the Convention on Biological Diversity and GATT on Biodiversity Conservation: A Third World Perspective." In A. K. Krattiger, W. H. Lesser, K.R. Miller, Y. St. Hillard, and R. Senanayake, eds., *Widening Perspectives on Biodiversity.* Geneva and Gland, Switzerland: IAE and International Union for the Conservation of Nature.

Soberon, J. n.d. Personal communication. Executive Secretary, Comisión Nacional para el Conocimiento y Uso de la Biodiversidad.

Swaminathan, M. S., and S. Jana. 1992. "The Impact of Plant Variety Protection on Genetic Conservation." In M. S. Swaminathan and S. Jana, eds., *Biodiversity Implications for Global Food Security.* Madras: Macmillan India Press.

"UPOV Sells Out." 1990. *Grain* no. 2, December.

WARDA (West African Rice Department Association). 1994. "Annual Program and Budget Report." WARDA, Bouaké, Côte d'Ivoire.

Warren, D. M. 1989. "Linking Scientific and Indigenous Agricultural Systems." In J. L. Compton, ed., *The Transformation of International Agricultural Research and Development.* Boulder: Lynne Rienner Publishers.

Warren, D. M., L. J. Slikkerveer, and D. Brokensha, eds. 1995. *The Cultural Dimension of Development: Indigenous Knowledge Systems.* London: Intermediate Technology Publications.

Waugh, R. K., P. E. Hildebrand, and C.O. Andrew. 1989. "Farming Systems, Research and Extension." In J. L. Compton, ed., *The Transformation of International Agricultural Research and Development.* Boulder: Lynne Rienner Publishers.

Wellard, K. 1993. "Linking Local Knowledge Systems and Agricultural Research: The Role of NGOs." In W. deBoef, K. Amanor, K. Wellard, and A. Bebbington, eds., *Cultivating Knowledge: Genetic Diversity, Farmer Experimentation and Crop Research.* London: Intermediate Technology Publications.

Wilkes, H. G. 1988. "Plant Genetic Resources over Ten Thousand Years: From a Handful of Seed to the Crop-Specific Mega-Gene Banks." In J. R. Kloppenburg, Jr., ed., *Seeds and Sovereignty.* Durham: Duke University Press.

————.1993. "In Situ Conservation in Guatemala of Teosinte, the Closest Relative of Maize." Personal communication.

Witmeyer, D. 1994. "The Convention on Biological Diversity Changes Rules of the Game for International Plant Genetic Resources Reserve," *Diversity* 10 (3): 28–31.

WIPO (World International Property Organization). 1990. "Exclusions from Patent Protection." HL/CM/INF/1 Rev., May. WIPO, Geneva, Switzerland.

Worede, M., and H. Mekbib. 1993. "Linking Genetic Resource Conservation to Farmers in Ethiopia." In W. deBoef, K. Amanor, K. Wellard, and A. Bebbington, eds., *Cultivating Knowledge: Genetic Diversity, Farmer Experimentation and Crop Research.* London: Intermediate Technology Publications.

WWF (World Wildlife Fund). 1993. *The Uruguay Round's Technical Barriers to Trade Agreement.* World Wildlife Fund Research Report. Gland, Switzerland.

4. Effects of Land-Use Systems on the Use and Conservation of Biodiversity

Nigel J. H. Smith

Agriculture is arguably the principal cause of habitat destruction and biodiversity loss around the world. The expansion of farming and livestock raising into forest and other environments often destroys habitats for wildlife and native plants (Altieri 1991). Because of the often overwhelming impact of agriculture on the world's ecosystems, it is often perceived as the enemy of biodiversity. But some land-use systems devoted to raising crops or livestock maintain surprisingly high levels of biodiversity. In the Yucatán, for example, home gardens contain 387 plant species (Herrera 1994), and other forms of agroforestry can mimic some of the complexity of rainforests. This chapter identifies some of the principal effects of agriculture and livestock raising on biodiversity, explores ways in which biodiversity is enhanced within agricultural production systems, and suggests some policy options, especially incentives, that might arrest or slow the loss of habitats rich in species or endemics.

An underlying premise is that agriculture and livestock raising must be intensified and degraded areas must be restored to help safeguard remaining habitats that have been little disturbed by humans. Agricultural intensification is not a straightforward procedure, and it can lead to its own set of environmental problems. To some it means deploying an arsenal of purchased agrochemicals and machinery that can pollute the environment, degrade the soil, and lead to rural unemployment. Agricultural intensification that draws on the strengths of traditional systems while adopting some modern, scientific approaches is stressed here.

The alternative to intensification, agricultural *extensification*, exacerbates habitat decline and species loss. Agricultural extensification entails expansion of cultivated areas, which inevitably leads to habitat loss for wildlife. The world's population is expected to double before it stabilizes sometime in the middle of the next century, and much of increased food production will have to come from areas that have already been brought into cultivation—otherwise a great deal of the remaining biodiversity heritage of the world will be irretrievably lost. How to boost the productivity of agriculture without causing irreversible damage to the natural resource base is a major challenge confronting society.

Another major theme of this chapter is that the protection and better management of biodiversity are essential to the process of agricultural intensification across a broad range of managed environments. How agricultural intensification is playing out in various land-management systems will be analyzed. In some instances intensification has triggered biodiversity losses and other collateral damage to the environment. Particular attention is paid to ways to render the intensification process both productive and environmentally friendly.

A concern for the encroachment of agriculture on habitats with little or no human interference must consider the shifting mosaic of land-use systems. Market forces, fiscal policies, land tenure, and other factors often propel the expansion of one relatively homogeneous land-use system, such as monocropping with modern varieties or cattle ranching, at the expense of polycultural systems that contain a great deal of infraspecific variation, as well as a rich mixture of species. But some agricultural production systems, such as agroforestry and plantations, can help rehabilitate degraded areas so that they are economically productive again while helping to regain at least some of the biodiversity that has been lost. Most of the earth's surface has been modified by human activities, so an understanding of land-use systems and their associated practices are vital to efforts to conserve and manage biodiversity.

Before discussing major agricultural production systems, this chapter lays out a conceptual framework to guide analysis of the interrelationships between biodiversity and agricultural production systems. The conceptual compass adopted here focuses on several policy-related questions, including: How do agricultural production systems and agricultural sector policies, institutions, and programs including technology choices affect biodiversity? How does the conservation of biodiversity help improve the sustainability of agriculture? How can agricultural development policies enhance biodiversity?

Conceptual Approach

Four perspectives underpin the conceptual framework used here to explore issues related to agricultural production systems and biodiversity. First, the notion of *cultural landscapes* is introduced to alert policymakers concerned with conservation and agricultural development to the fact that virtually all ecosystems on earth have been modified to some extent by human activities. Second, the importance of understanding *land-use dynamics* is highlighted to make policymakers more aware of how shifts in the mix of agricultural production systems in a given area can enhance or destroy biodiversity. Third, a case is made for appreciating the *driving forces* behind land-use changes—such as shifts in market opportunities or fiscal incentives—so that appropriate policies can be identified to help mitigate some of the more environmentally damaging land-use changes. Fourth, the relationship between *intensification*

and *resiliency* is explored to underscore the importance of biodiversity for sustainable agriculture.

Cultural Landscapes

The majority of the earth's land surface is now covered by habitats that have been modified in varying degrees by human activities. The intensity of human interventions in landscapes ranges along a spectrum from little if any human use, such as in wilderness reserves, to highly managed environments, such as paddy rice farms (figure 4.1). Most of the earth is therefore dominated by cultural landscapes (Parsons 1986). How biological resources are used or abused in such habitats will determine the fate of much of the world's biodiversity.

What should be considered "natural" and what is "man-made" therefore is somewhat blurred. Conservationists often talk about saving biodiversity in natural habitats. The notion that some areas are natural while all others have been upset or even defiled by humans has underpinned much of the thinking about setting aside nature reserves (Hecht 1992a). Two problems arise from such an approach. The first is philosophical: people are considered unnatural, even offenders on the landscape. On a more practical note so-called natural habitats may have been altered by human actions such as slash-and-burn farming, grazing by livestock, or gathering of plant products. Many of the forests of tropical America, for example, are actually regrowth from previous cycles of farming by indigenous people, many of whom disappeared after the arrival of Europeans (Cook 1921; Coomes 1995; Siskind 1973). When individuals or organizations stress the need to save nature or natural biodiversity, it is not always clear what they are talking about. Programs to safeguard pristine environments are chimerical.

Only in rare instances can landscapes be identified that are truly virgin. It is therefore more helpful to envisage landscapes along a spectrum of disturbance rather than to attempt to separate natural areas from those dominated by humans. Significant concentrations of biodiversity are encountered at many points along this spectrum. Conservation strategies need to be developed for safeguarding biodiversity

Figure 4.1 The relationship between the degree of human intervention (management intensity) and biodiversity loss

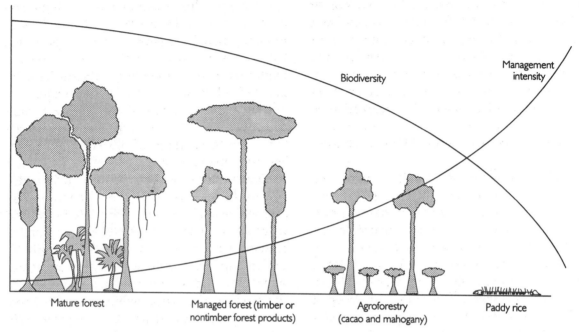

| Mature forest | Managed forest (timber or nontimber forest products) | Agroforestry (cacao and mahogany) | Paddy rice |

Source: Author's rendering. Prepared by Mark McLean.

along the entire spectrum, ranging from habitats with little human disturbance to agricultural production systems.

Selective replacement of species in the environment has been carried out deliberately or unconsciously by humans for a long time (Sauer 1988). Intelligent and responsible intervention in evolution is warranted and can be considered part of the natural order (Leavitt 1992). Human interventions in the landscape can create a mosaic of habitats that increases biodiversity, much of it of direct use to people (Toledo, Ortiz, and Medellín 1994). Biodiversity that is linked to agricultural production thus warrants conservation and wise management.

In fact a great deal of biodiversity that is currently or of potential importance to agriculture requires habitat disturbance to survive. Thus protecting some wild plants from periodic fire or grazing can actually lead to their local disappearance or even extinction. I am not referring to the suppression of natural fires such as those triggered by lightening; a vast literature has accumulated on the disastrous consequences of such policies for some temperate forests and dryland chaparral communities in California. Many plants that are of interest to crop breeders occur in weedy communities, habitats that depend on

periodic disturbance by humans for survival (Wood 1993). Examples of such weedy plants that have already contributed to improving crops or that promise to do so include *Oryza nivara* in India, which provides the only known source of resistance to grassy stunt virus; various near relatives of wheat in southwest Asia; and a near relative of maize, *Zea diploperennis*, in Mexico.

Land-Use Dynamics

A land-use perspective on the relationships between biodiversity and agriculture has two main dimensions:
1. The changing mosaic of land-use systems, such as cattle ranching encroaching on crop farming or forest extraction
2. The internal dynamics of land-use systems, such as a shift to more damaging or environmentally benign agricultural practices.

No attempt is made here to suggest that one land-use system is better for biodiversity than another. True, one can identify some agricultural production systems that generally contain more biodiversity than others. But it does not necessarily follow that the more biodiverse systems should be promoted to the exclusion of other agricultural production systems. Benefit-cost analysis of competing demands for the land is needed, even though data and meaningful valuation of biodiversity are often difficult (Montgomery and Pollack 1996). Extraction of nontimber forest products generally causes the least disruption of habitats, but in most cases extractive activities are a supplement to income generation rather than the main source of livelihood. Little quantitative work has been done on comparing the economic and environmental costs of different land-use systems in the tropics.

A mixture of land uses usually provides the optimal use of natural resources in a given area. A variety of managed and natural habitats provides a range of resources for local people to tap, as well as havens for insects that serve as biological control agents on crops (Waage 1991). It is the balance between the land-use systems, including reserves, that is critical. The issue of the appropriate mix of land-use systems applies both at farm and at watershed and regional scales.

Agricultural development policies should therefore avoid promoting one agricultural production system at the expense of others, some of which may also be appropriate for the target area or region. For example, further increases of rice yields in intensive paddy systems will be to little avail if the rural and urban poor do not have wood or charcoal to cook their meals. Agroforestry systems are more biodiverse than monocropping with cereals, but if agroindustries are not in place to process fruits, nuts, and essential oils or sufficiently large markets cannot be found for the perennial crops, agroforestry will not be commercially sustainable.

Practices can be identified within each land-use system that enhance biodiversity. Again, increasing biodiversity at all costs is not a realistic goal. Potential losses in yield or income to farmers need to be considered. Tradeoffs are clearly involved in deciding which agricultural practices within each land-use system merit support.

Driving Forces behind Land-Use Changes

To promote the conservation and better use of biodiversity, driving forces that shape the mix of agricultural production systems and other land uses on a given landscape need to be understood. If agricultural activities are impinging on parks or reserves, factors that motivate the surrounding people to enter nominally protected habitats must be identified (Flint 1991). How can biodiversity in surrounding habitats be safeguarded while attending to the aspirations of the surrounding populations? Policy recommendations in this area can come only from a better understanding of the driving forces behind human activities.

Driving forces can be grouped into *direct* driving forces (such as colonists pouring into a pioneer settlement zone and cutting into forest) and *underlying* or *indirect* forces (such as population growth, land tenure, and fiscal incentives). Underlying forces include a range of measures amenable to policy intervention, from fiscal policies that may promote unnecessary deforestation, as happened in the Brazilian Amazon in the 1970s with the expansion of cattle ranching, to farm credit that favors modern varieties at the expense of traditional ones. Other driving forces that may or may not be linked to the fiscal or regulatory environment include changing markets, such as the increasing consumer demand for organically grown produce. For the most part the indirect or underlying aspects of driving forces deserve the most attention from policymakers.

Migration can trigger rapid loss of biodiversity, as when settlers arrive in forest environments and adopt farming practices alien to the fine-tuned land-use systems practiced by local populations. Migration can result from several causes ranging from skewed land distribution in source areas to civil strife, rapid population growth, or degradation of the natural resource base in the source areas, thereby creating ecological refuges. Each one of these driving forces behind migration has its own set of remedial measures, some of which are more difficult to carry out than others. Population growth in Central America, for example, has been pinpointed as one of the major driving forces behind habitat destruction and biodiversity loss (Gámez 1989). Issues related to slowing or containing population growth are complex and beyond the scope of this chapter. Suffice it to say, however, that land use and biodiversity are linked to other economic sectors.

Resiliency and Intensification

For intensification to be successful in thwarting further assaults on little-disturbed habitats, it must be sustainable. It is clearly important to ensure that yield gains need to be durable, otherwise productivity will collapse, forcing farmers to seek other options including abandoning their land and seeking new frontiers. The resiliency of land-use systems is the key to their sustainability.

Biodiversity is essential to resiliency because it provides greater options for alternative approaches to agricultural production as well as diversification of the existing mix of crops and varieties. Resilient agricultural systems are more sustainable, and sustainable agricultural systems tend to reduce pressure on surrounding habitats.

Although many definitions of sustainable agriculture have been offered, it is easier to identify systems that are unsustainable: when agricultural systems collapse because of degradation of the natural resource base or other factors, agricultural extensification usually ensues with further encroachment on remaining forest and other habitats.

Agricultural production systems need to be resilient so that they can adjust more readily to changes in the biophysical or socioeconomic environment. Many of the changes that occur in systems are nonlinear and unpredictable (Holling 1987); thus ecosystems, including those managed by people, must be sufficiently resilient so that they do not disintegrate and enter a downward ecological spiral when confronted with surprises (Arrow and others 1995; Holling 1976; Holling and Bocking 1990). The resiliency of an agricultural production system rests to a large degree on how natural resources are managed, particularly biodiversity (Claridge 1991).

Three points are pertinent to a discussion on the relevance of resiliency of agricultural systems to biodiversity. First, sustainable systems can be low or high input. Sustainable agriculture has been equated with low-input farming (Castro 1991), but low-input systems are not always sustainable, as will be discussed in the case of slash-and-burn farming in the face of population pressure. Second, high species diversity is not always the optimal use of soil, light, and water resources for agriculture. Relatively species-poor ecosystems can be stable over long periods (Pimm 1984, 1991), a principle borne out with the experience of some farmers engaged in intensive cereal monocropping and ranchers with well-managed pastures. In more simplified systems the risks can be higher, and research and careful management are critical to maintaining productivity.

Biodiversity in agricultural systems occurs at two levels: spatial and temporal (Pimm and Gittleman 1992). Spatial diversity is the most common image of biodiversity. Agricultural systems are often thought to be more sustainable if they contain a relatively large number of species, preferably with significant genetic variation within each of the crops. Traditional agroforestry systems typically fit that bill. But agricultural systems can also achieve biodiversity through time with a changeover of crops or varieties; some intensively managed agricultural systems have thus achieved stability over centuries or even millennia (Smale and others 1995). But monocropping generally relies on a constant supply of new crops or varieties to replace obsolete crops or cultivars that have succumbed to shifts in markets or other challenges such as pest outbreaks.

Related to the importance of novel crops and varieties is the need to maintain open systems to help their resiliency (Holling 1994; Wilbanks 1994). Sustainability cannot be achieved by relying solely on indigenous crops and varieties. The history of agricultural improvement is replete with examples of how the introduction of new technologies, including exotic crops and varieties, has raised productivity and the income of rural and urban populations. The solution to a production bottleneck in one region may be found among farmers and researchers on the other side of the globe.

Land-Use Systems and Biodiversity

Any discussion of the impact of farming on the environment, and more specifically biodiversity, needs a template of land-use systems. A number of different classifications of agricultural systems have been proposed, each the product of varying interests, regional experiences, and expertise of their authors. The classification adopted here is drawn from several sources and is tailored more to tropical and subtropical regions, where most of the world's biodiversity is found. The land-use categories provide a starting point for analyzing specific policy issues. It is not the intention to establish hard and fast categories because production systems often overlap.

Although this classification may not capture all agricultural production systems, it nevertheless encompasses most of the important food and cash-crop farming systems. Furthermore, many variations and subsystems are found within each category. The broad categories to be considered include:

- Intensive cropping with short-cycle crops
- Shifting agriculture
- Agropastoral systems
- Agroforestry
- Plantation systems
- Forest extraction.

To the extent possible the following topics are explored for each land-use system:

- Negative effects on biodiversity
- Examples in which biodiversity has been enhanced both by reducing pressure on surrounding habitats and incorporating greater biodiversity within the land-use system
- The role of indigenous or traditional knowledge
- The role of scientific research
- Policies that promote the destruction or enhancement of biodiversity, including property rights.

An important dimension to consider in the interactions between land use and biodiversity is the on-farm and off-site effects. Modern, intensive agricultural production systems tend to have more impact off-site because of the potential for contamination of water supplies with agrochemicals. Furthermore, irrigation sometimes entails large engineering projects such as dams that can flood habitats important for wildlife as well as agrobiodiversity. Sometimes agricultural intensification calls for controlling floods, and such measures can disrupt fisheries.

In the case of irrigation and flood control, off-site impact can be envisaged as both upstream and downstream. Water diversion for agriculture can adversely affect fisheries and other

wildlife. Downstream effects would include altered water quality below dams and water polluted with agrochemicals. Dams change water quality by trapping sediment, changing water temperature, and in some cases altering chemical properties because of increased rates of plant decomposition in reservoirs.

Rain-fed agriculture can also have unintended off-site impact on biodiversity. In the case of the Masai Mara Park in Kenya, wheat farms at its borders are allegedly interfering with long-established migration routes of wildlife. And the Masai, traditionally pastoralists in Kenya, are increasingly turning to crop production for food and income generation, a trend that will likely further squeeze wildlife habitats, especially for the large, migratory ungulates (Baskin 1994a).

Intensive Cropping with Short-Cycle Crops

Intensive farming with annual crops is the most important source of food for humanity and accounts for much of the earth's surface in agricultural production. It encompasses a broad variety of production systems, from highly mechanized operations to those that rely primarily on human labor and animal traction. The purpose in lumping them together here is to make a critical point: agricultural intensification is not simply the process of adopting modern approaches to farming.

Intensive cropping systems span traditional farming operations such as paddy rice and raised-bed agriculture that rely primarily on manual labor and mulching to modern systems that depend heavily on mechanization and purchased inputs such as in Iowa (see chapter 5). Intensive agriculture is essential to raise food production further and relieve pressure on other habitats, but it can lead to resource degradation. A substantial portion of humanity depends on cereals and short-cycle root crops as basic staples—particularly rice, wheat, maize, potato, and sweet potato—so how production systems based on these staffs of life can be made even more productive is critical to the world's food equation.

Although the expansion of modern farming has brought many benefits, the long-term effects of high-input agriculture have hardly been accounted for. High-input modern farming with its reliance on monoculture, mechanization, and deployment of potent agrochemicals diminishes biodiversity and destroys many beneficial insects and soil microorganisms. Also heavy reliance on chemicals can lead to significant water pollution, destroying fisheries and paddy systems (Roger, Heong, and Teng 1991).

In some regions high-input, modern agriculture is taking an unacceptable toll on the environment and biodiversity. The erosion of the natural resource base is eventually reflected in declining yields. The case of the Punjab, where the Green Revolution in wheat started in the 1960s, is a case in point. Wheat yields are beginning to decline in Punjab because of soil degradation. Few farmers practice crop rotation with legumes anymore, preferring instead to plant wheat every year.

Such intensive monocropping has reduced organic matter in the soil, thereby impairing its capacity to retain moisture and to provide a habitat for soil microorganisms. Furthermore, the decline in organic matter in arable soils of the Punjab reduces their capacity to store nutrients and renders the soils less friable for root penetration. In response to the decline in wheat yields in the Punjab, some farmers are diversifying their operations with silviculture for pulp production. A similar pattern prevails with rice farmers in parts of Bangladesh who are experiencing stagnant or declining productivity in spite of increased applications of fertilizer and other inputs (Ali 1987). The fall in productivity of rice in Bangladesh is attributed to changes in soil organic matter and nutrient imbalances, among other factors (Pagiola 1995).

A relatively rapid turnover of varieties characterizes modern, high-input agriculture based on grain and pulse crops. Some heterogeneity is thus achieved over time. This genetic relay race works as long as there are plenty of proto-varieties waiting in the wings and soil and water resources are not degraded. If the flow of new varieties slows or ceases, farmers become even more vulnerable to pest and disease attacks, among other environmental challenges (NRC 1993a). Historically, modern cereals have depended on agrochemical protection. As the cost of pesticide mounts and concerns about environmental damage grow,

farmers and consumers are seeking alternative ways to achieve high yields.

The true costs of some modern, intensive cropping systems—the loss of topsoil and soil organic matter or the displacement of traditional varieties—have not been assessed. As the twentieth century draws to a close, we are on the threshold of new types of intensive agricultural production systems in which management levels ratchet up and the need to conserve and use biodiversity more wisely is ever more urgent. To face the challenge of boosting yields in more intensively managed agricultural systems, it will be necessary to stretch the yield potential of an ever-wider variety of crops by dipping much deeper into their respective gene pools.

Both indigenous knowledge and scientific research will be needed in this worldwide effort to further boost crop and livestock yields. In traditional, high-input systems farmers generally deploy several varieties to reduce risks and employ less-destructive pest control measures such as crop rotation (Goldman 1995). In the Andes of southern Peru, for example, farmers maintain an average of twenty-one potato cultivars per field (Zimmerer 1991). This is in stark contrast to a modern potato farm where only one cultivar may be grown, such as Russet Burbank for the french-fry trade. Spatial biodiversity characterizes traditional, high-input systems.

An inverse relationship often exists between the genetic variation of crops and the economic resources of farmers. Rural people with limited financial resources typically maintain a greater diversity of crops and varieties than more market-oriented operators, as in the case of bean growers in the state of Aguascaliente in Mexico (Hernández 1993). One cannot argue that farmers should be prevented from adopting modern varieties for the sake of conserving agrobiodiversity. The important policy questions here are: Does adoption of modern varieties inevitably lead to genetic erosion on the landscape? How can more intensive, high-yielding agriculture retain greater levels of biodiversity?

The tradeoff issue emerges here. Some farmers in more well-off areas may be able to improve yields and achieve relatively stable operations by purchasing hybrids and agrochemicals. Even under less than optimal conditions, modern varieties sometimes displace traditional varieties because of their superior performance. In the case of hybrid maize in parts of eastern and southern Africa, for example, many small farmers have found that hybrid maize produces higher yields than traditional varieties even without fertilizer, and this greater yield capacity holds even in unusually dry years (Heisey and Smale 1995). Little wonder then that hybrids in Kenya accounted for approximately two-thirds of the area planted to maize in 1988, up from a third in the early 1970s (Byerlee and Heisey 1993).

The robust performance of hybrid maize in Africa illustrates a point worth emphasizing again: biodiversity is not an end in itself. Agricultural development should not promote greater biodiversity at all cost. In some cases the erosion of traditional varieties in the face of superior modern varieties is arguably warranted, especially in regions facing rapid population growth and a deteriorating food production per capita. The replacement of traditional varieties by modern, high-yielding cultivars is potentially serious, however, when the obsolete varieties have not been saved elsewhere, either in gene banks or in farmers' fields in other areas, and there is not even an awareness among policymakers and development planners that a trade off is involved. In the past, genetic erosion has proceeded in many regions at an alarming pace with few or inadequate measures to assess its implications or to rescue the doomed varieties.

Another strategy adopted by some farmers offers a compromise between modern and traditional varieties, thereby helping to maintain some of the agrobiodiversity that may otherwise be lost. Farmers occasionally opt for more modest production levels by maintaining a mix of modern and traditional varieties, as in the case of maize growers in parts of Central America, potato growers in the Andes, and some rice growers in Southeast Asia (Bellon and Brush 1994; Brush, Taylor, and Bellon 1992). And in Italy a few farmers still maintain two species of wheat that have long since been abandoned by most cereal growers because the protective covering of the seeds of primitive wheats is persistent and is fed to livestock and because the strong stems of the archaic wheats are useful for thatching (Qualset and others, in press).

Agricultural intensification therefore does not always lead to a complete homogenization of croplands. Farmers should have options available to them to choose which path to intensification they want to adopt, and the research and development community has an obligation to come up with technologies for high-input agriculture that reduce negative effects on the environment and biodiversity. Farmers exposed to the opportunity of adopting modern varieties sometimes retain at least some of the traditional varieties for reasons ranging from superior taste of the traditional varieties to uses for livestock and construction, importance in rituals, and better adaptation to certain soils. Risk aversion is undoubtedly another reason why market-oriented farmers are motivated to maintain a diversity of varieties and crops in their operations.

An understanding of the historical antecedents to attempts at devising sustainable agriculture can teach us much about how to make agriculture more compatible with biodiversity conservation. Agricultural production was intensified long ago in several parts of the world in response to the need to increase food production. Agricultural intensification in remote times has helped relieve pressure on other habitats and has also minimized environmental damage and biodiversity loss because higher yields were achieved without the use of toxic or otherwise polluting agrochemicals. Three examples will be briefly reviewed here: raised-bed agriculture in tropical America, extensive irrigation systems in highland South America, and paddy rice systems in Southeast Asia.

Both raised fields and terracing with irrigation were devised by farmers in many parts of the tropics thousands of years ago. In some cases these systems are still in use, but in others they have been largely abandoned. Sophisticated irrigation systems using canals have been operational in parts of the Andes since 350 A.D. (Zimmerer 1995). Encouragingly, attempts are being made to rehabilitate terraces and raised fields in some areas to improve the resiliency and productivity of agriculture. Several features of such systems could be emulated more widely in agricultural development programs for both the highland and lowland tropics.

In highland areas scientists are taking a closer look at the potential of such systems for improving agricultural production while mitigating damage to the environment. Around Lake Titicaca in the Andes, for example, farmers are reviving raised beds because they confer several advantages such as greater soil fertility, better water control, and reduced frost damage. Furthermore, nutrients are largely trapped in channels between the raised beds, thus reducing downstream pollution (Carney and others 1993). The raised beds around Lake Titicaca were originally constructed between 1000 B.C. and 400 A.D.; The beds are about 1 meter high, 4–10 meters wide, and 10–100 meters long (Bray 1990). Pollen analysis shows that they were used primarily for potato and quinoa production. Water in the channels provides a heat sink by raising temperatures about two degrees Celsius, thereby helping to protect crops from frost damage. About 122,000 hectares of raised beds have been located in the vicinity of Lake Titicaca, which once supported a population of about 1 million people (Denevan 1995).

Environmental archaeology can thus highlight adaptive farming strategies of the past with the promise for raising agricultural productivity in the future (Erickson 1992a). Unfortunately most agronomists and development institutions working in the Andes and other developing areas tend to view traditional systems of landscape management as primitive and thus not worthy of their attention. Nevertheless some progress is being made to resuscitate intensive agriculture using raised fields in the vicinity of Lake Titicaca. Between 1981 and 1986 several indigenous communities in northern Lake Titicaca were collaborating with government and nongovernmental agencies to diffuse information on raised-bed technologies, and by 1989 some 200 hectares of such fields had been brought back into production (Erickson 1992b).

In highland Mexico the *chinampa* agriculture around the shores of Lake Texcoco offers promise for intensive food production to help feed growing Mexico City and surrounding communities. Developed extensively by the Aztecs approximately 500 years ago, some chinampas have been in continuous production for centuries (Stakman, Bradfield, and Mangelsdorf 1967).

Chinampas are raised platforms ranging from 2.5 to 10 meters in width and up to 100 meters long that were built up with lake sediments and organic matter. They protrude like fingers from the lake shore and are peninsulas of agrobiodiversity in an increasingly urbanized world. The Aztecs built 9,000 hectares of these specialized raised fields, which are thought to have fed at least 171,000 people a year (Sluyter 1994).

The remaining chinampas are currently used mainly for growing vegetables and flowers and are threatened by urban sprawl and dropping water levels in the lake. Only a few hundred hectares remain, but they could foster increased biodiversity in agricultural settings if they were promoted. On one chinampa, for example, a 0.2-hectare-plot contained twenty domesticated and thirty wild plants. At least forty different kinds of vegetables are grown on the remaining chinampas (Torres-Lima, Canabal-Cristiani, and Burela-Rueda 1994).

Other raised-bed agricultural systems in Central America can be found in the vicinity of Tlaxcala, Mexico (Wilken 1969), and around Lake Atitlán in Guatemala. Such often ignored agricultural production systems warrant further examination to assess whether they can be rehabilitated and expanded. Some of the most threatened habitats in Central America are mountain forests. More intensive cultivation around lake margins could deflect crop production from highly erodable slopes that may be currently cloaked in natural vegetation.

In the last few decades extensive areas of abandoned raised fields have been found in lowland parts of Latin America, many of which were masked by forest until recently. As forest clearing proceeds, many of the areas once dedicated to raised-field agriculture are destined for cattle ranching rather than intensive crop production (Erickson 1995). The potential of such areas for high-yield cropping to supply the burgeoning urban centers of Latin America warrants scrutiny. Ancient raised fields in lowland Central and South America have been found in such widely scattered locations as the Guayas valley in Ecuador (Denevan and Mathewson 1983; Parsons 1969); the San Jorge River floodplain in Colombia (Parsons and Bowen 1966); the Gulf coast of Mexico (Siemens 1983, 1995); poorly drained savanna of South America (Denevan 1970; Denevan and Bergman 1975; Denevan and Schwerin 1978); and the Yucatán (Nations and Komer 1983; Turner 1974). The Maya alone built some 22,900 hectares of raised fields in lowland Central America (Sluyter 1994), most of which are no longer in intensive crop production.

Several paddy rice systems in Southeast Asia attain impressive yields while maintaining relatively high levels of agrobiodiversity. The Ifugao, who long ago built an impressive system of aqueducts and terraces in the northern Philippines, classify at least seventy-eight varieties of rice. In less steep terrain near Chang Mai in Thailand, farmers cultivate more than forty rice varieties in paddies (Brush 1986).

After the release of high-yielding rices many traditional varieties were abandoned, and semidwarf types often dominate the landscape in paddy rice areas. In the early 1980s, IR36 alone was grown on more than 10 million hectares in tropical Asia (IRRI 1983). Genetically homogeneous rice paddies can be more vulnerable to pests and disease outbreaks, even with increased applications of pesticides.

The pesticide treadmill prompted the Indonesian government to adopt integrated pest management to try and cope with rising pest problems in rice fields. In 1986 Indonesia officially adopted integrated pest management as a national policy aimed particularly at rice production. By 1991 pesticide use had dropped nationally by 70 percent and by 90 percent in some locations, yet national rice yields increased by 10 percent during 1986–91 (Barfield and Swisher 1994). Increased rice productivity is attributed mainly to encouragement of biocontrol agents and to the deployment of pest- and disease-resistant varieties. Profits achieved by rice farmers in Indonesia increased even more, and doomsday predictions that a rapid weaning from dependence on commercial insecticides would lead to a collapse of rice production did not materialize. Parts or all of integrated pest management packages have also been adopted by some commercial vegetable growers in Central America (Thrupp, Bergeron, and Waters 1995).

The significance of integrated pest management to biodiversity is clear: relatively undisturbed habitats should be safeguarded as reservoirs of biocontrol agents for future deployment. Integrated pest management strategies enhance rather than destroy biodiversity. But if biodiversity continues to be destroyed, future options for deploying integrated pest management will be curtailed.

Preservation of biodiversity and habitat conservation can contribute to sustaining intensive crop production in other ways. Management of watersheds is critical to maintaining adequate supplies of irrigation water and setting aside substantial areas of forest is usually necessary to prevent premature siltation of reservoirs, flash flooding, and prolonged periods of reduced water flow. In some countries such as El Salvador it has proved necessary to reforest cutover areas with exotic, fast-growing conifers that have limited value for conserving biodiversity. It would be preferable to avoid wholesale destruction of forests in the first place. Forests act as sponges for moisture, thereby conserving water and releasing it more gradually than in denuded landscapes. Reservoirs are usually built for a variety of purposes, including generation of hydroelectric power, irrigation, and water supplies for urban and industrial use. In Tegucigalpa, the largest city in Honduras, insufficient water supplies prompted government authorities to safeguard nearby La Tigra National Park, which was being invaded by loggers and farmers (Smith and others 1992).

For the highly managed landscapes of modern cereal farms research on genetically diverse populations of crops and animals warrants support. It is not a question of reverting to traditional systems and abandoning the "failed" Green Revolution. There is no turning back. Rather, research should focus on ways to incorporate some of the best-adapted features of traditional high- and low-input systems with modern, science-based technologies so that agricultural systems remain highly productive while maintaining more biodiversity (McNeely 1993).

Shifting Agriculture

Shifting agriculture, sometimes referred to as slash-and-burn agriculture, is often indicted as one of the principal causes of deforestation and biodiversity loss (Lanly 1982; Lima 1958).

Shifting agricultural systems are confined mostly to tropical forest regions, usually mega-centers for biodiversity. In shifting agriculture farmers clear a patch of forest or brush, burn the debris, and cultivate the resulting plot for a few years before abandoning it. Fires set by shifting cultivators sometimes burn out of control and encroach on surrounding forest. This is mainly a problem in transitional or monsoon forests, where conditions are drier and more favorable to the spread of fire.

Small farmers are the main practitioners of shifting agriculture and are held responsible for much of the deforestation in the tropics (Ehui 1993; Myers 1986). It is not uncommon to see policy recommendations that call for arresting or stamping out shifting agriculture because of its perceived low yield and danger to the environment (Kellman 1974; Valverde 1971). Shifting agriculture is practiced on close to a third of the world's arable land and supports some 300 million people, so trends and developments in this major land-use system will have major implications both for biodiversity and the well-being of a sizable portion of the world's population (NRC 1993b).

In spite of the many misconceptions about shifting agriculture, a number of production systems are involved, and some of them are environmentally sound. A major distinction needs to be made between shifting agriculture as practiced in pioneer zones where primary forest is being destroyed, often by people from other regions with different technologies and land management practices, and longer-settled areas where a wide assortment of agroforestry configurations are deployed, many of which mimic the forest ecosystem albeit on a simpler scale (Denevan 1980). In older settlements shifting agriculture can actually increase the biodiversity of an area because a patchwork quilt of different habitats is created, thereby allowing a mixture of plant and animal species that are adapted to plant communities at various stages of succession. Fields in shifting agricultural systems are often ephemeral and small; they soon revert to forest or some semblance of forest, thereby protecting the soil and water supplies. Moderate levels of disturbance in most habitats generally enhances ecological complexity, landscape het-erogeneity, and species diversity (Wilcox and Duin 1995).

A further distinction needs to be made between shifting cultivation to supply the needs of the farmers and burning forest to plant a few crops mainly to demonstrate ownership of a piece of land. Taxation policies provoke forest clearing, particularly in Latin America. In parts of Central America, for example, land left in forest is taxed at a higher rate than farmland. Landowners thus have an incentive to clear land when it might otherwise be left in forest.

Such practices are ancient in Latin America and other parts of the world. In 1699, for example, the king of Portugal decreed that all uncultivated lands in Brazil were to be expropriated (Burns 1993). And in the Ottoman Empire the destruction of tree cover was virtually complete by the early nineteenth century, spurred in part by a tax on every tree (Douglas and Hart 1985). Goat herds delivered the death blow to the remaining woods.

Shifting agriculture is particularly well suited for fragile environments such as tropical forests with poor soils or in hilly country that without terracing would suffer severe soil erosion under continuous cropping (Jodha and Partap 1993; Weischet and Caviedes 1993). Also shifting agriculture is sometimes an ephemeral phase before some other land use takes over. In Latin America slash-and-burn agriculture is often a transition to cattle raising (Hecht 1992b; Hecht and Cockburn 1989; Hiraoka 1980; Hiraoka and Yamamoto 1980; Smith 1982; Stewart 1994). In other cases abandoned fields may remain productive with planted trees and bushes, thereby following a trajectory toward agroforestry.

Rather than start from the premise that shifting agriculture needs to be fixed, a wiser course would be to better appreciate its role in providing the needs of local people while assessing its environmental impact. The many intricacies and nuances of such systems need to be understood because they can offer hints about their adaptive features, and in a given area such systems should be evaluated for their ability to cope with changing environmental conditions.

One of the first prejudices that needs to be put to rest is that against the use of fire. Fire is typically viewed as a destructive agent, but it is an essential management tool for resource-poor farmers who use it to control weeds and release nutrients bound in the vegetation (Peters and Neuenschwander 1988). Another widespread image of slash-and-burn agriculture is that it is constantly assaulting primary forest. In many areas farmers are clearing second growth—vegetation at various stages along a recuperation path back to forest—rather than mature forest. In the case of Rondônia in the Brazilian Amazon, for example, 42 percent of land brought into agricultural production between 1988 and 1989 was cleared from second growth (Skole and others 1994). In the Philippines the Hanunó prefer second growth, especially bamboo, for their swidden plots because it burns well (Conklin 1954). In some areas little primary forest is left, so people are forced to make do with clearing second growth, such as on the Kanela reservation in Brazil (Flowers and others 1982).

Another widespread myth is that swidden agriculture is capable of supporting only sparse populations. During the heyday of the Classic Maya the population density of the Yucatán was roughly equivalent to that of Europe today, and much of it was supported by shifting agriculture. Swidden agriculture based on maize in the limestone-rich Petén region of Guatemala is capable of supporting up to seventy-seven people per square kilometer (Cowgill 1962).

Shifting agricultural systems tend to break down and cause a net reduction in biodiversity when fallow periods become too short. This usually occurs when the carrying capacity of the environment is exceeded because of population growth or the influx of migrants. Although shifting agriculture can support relatively dense populations, this generally occurs in areas with better soils or in places where cultures have fine-tuned adaptive relationships with the forest. A rapid population increase may tip swidden systems on a downward trajectory. In Panama, for example, yields in shifting cultivation areas have been dropping since 1950 because fallow periods have become too short to allow soils to recuperate (Croat 1972).

When the resiliency of shifting agricultural systems snaps or is about to collapse, intensification is called for (Watters 1971). To some that immediately conjures up an image of mecha-

nization and fertilizers (Verdade 1974). While such measures may be appropriate in some cases, other less-intrusive, environment-friendly options for modifying swidden systems are available. Intensification can follow many different trajectories, depending on soil conditions, access to credit and other inputs, and market conditions. In the Brazilian Amazon some swidden systems are evolving into more or less permanent agroforestry plots.

One option to consider before transforming shifting agriculture into some other form of land use such as pasture is to tap indigenous knowledge systems to see if traditional practices can be adapted for market-oriented growers. Many indigenous swidden fields are remarkably rich in crops. The Hanunó of Mindoro Island in the Philippines, for example, interplant as many as forty crops in a single field (Conklin 1954). The Bine of New Guinea and the Andoke and Witoto in the Colombian Amazon average close to a dozen crops in their swidden fields (Eden 1980, 1988). The varietal array of each crop represents another level of agrobiodiversity in many indigenous swidden plots. Among Tukanoan groups in the northwest Amazon, for example, between seventeen and forty-eight varieties of their basic staple, manioc, are typically found in swidden plots (Dufour 1990).

When such biologically diverse indigenous agricultural systems become linked to markets, species richness tends to decline (Ruddle 1974). Nevertheless, a closer scrutiny of indigenous swidden systems with a focus on the crops and varieties deployed, planting patterns, and pest control strategies would provide a rich information base for devising more productive and sustainable swidden systems for marginal areas.

Some swidden systems trigger excessive loss of biodiversity, but others are environmentally sound. Shifting agriculture thus warrants analysis from a balanced perspective. An analysis of driving forces is critical when assessing the merits or drawbacks of shifting agriculture for a practical area. In many parts of Latin America, for example, insecure land tenure is a major reason people clear forests (Revkin 1990; Westoby 1989). In 1987 unusually large areas of forest in the Brazilian Amazon were cut and torched because of the impending new constitution in

Brazil, which stated that "unproductive" lands could be expropriated (Hecht 1992b; Nepstad, Uhl, and Serrão 1991). Slash-and-burn agriculture in such cases is practiced more to claim property, than to produce food or goods for the market.

Agropastoral Systems

Cattle ranching in the humid tropics is often pinpointed as the main cause of habitat destruction and biodiversity loss, particularly in Latin America. In the second half of the twentieth century cattle raising has encroached on tropical forests especially rapidly (Eden, McGregor, and Vieira 1990; Parsons 1989). In the Brazilian Amazon fiscal incentives in the 1960s and much of the 1970s fueled the "grass rush" to the Amazon (Hecht 1992b; Mahar 1989; Sternberg 1973). Fiscal incentives were responsible for converting at least 20 million hectares of rain forest to pasture, triggering the loss of valuable gene pools of such economically important trees as rubber, cacao, and Brazil nut (Dwyer 1990).

The conversion of forest for cattle production can have major off-site effects on biodiversity. In the Amazon floodplain, where large tracts of forest are being cleared to raise cattle and water buffalo, the loss of such seasonally available habitat for fish is undercutting the productivity of many fisheries important for subsistence and commerce (Goulding, Smith, and Mahar 1995). As the river level rises each year, many Amazon fish species penetrate the forest along the banks of the river and lake margins, where they feed and breed. The relentless cutting and permanent removal of such habitat is thus destroying an important environment that underpins the single most important natural resource of the Amazon River: its fish.

The hamburger connection was also raised as a driving force in the grassing-over of rainforests: consumers in North America were accused of contributing to deforestation when they purchased fast-food hamburgers. Even at their heyday, though, beef exports from tropical forest regions of Latin America were minimal. In many cases countries such as Costa Rica are hard pressed to meet internal demand for meat and dairy products. Amazonia is a net importer of beef. The continued expansion of cattle operations in the Amazon basin is being driven primarily by domestic markets for beef.

But the news on the cattle front is not all gloomy for biodiversity. In Latin America cattle are incorporated on many small farms, some of which are developing diverse agroforestry systems. Agricultural development policies that ignore the role of livestock in sustaining small farms may render farmers more vulnerable to inclement weather or other environmental surprises. Cattle contribute to the sustainability of small farms by providing emergency cash, diverse income sources, transportation for agricultural products, and manure for some crops (Rudel and Horowitz 1993; Seré and Jarvis 1992).

Furthermore, cattle operators of all scales in the Brazilian Amazon are recuperating degraded pastures rather than clearing more forest (Smith and others 1995). One way that farmers and ranchers upgrade pastures is to sow more productive and disease-resistant grasses. The sustainability of cattle operations, as in crop production, thus hinges on a continued flow of new plant materials to remain productive. With proper management, including the judicious use of fire, pastures can remain reasonably productive in rainforest environments.

Several factors have influenced the decision of farmers and ranchers to improve their pastures rather than cut down forest. An increase in land prices in many areas of Amazonia has made it worthwhile to invest more on farms and ranches (Serrão 1989). A reduction in new road construction has been partly responsible for the upward trend in land prices in the region. Cost-effective pasture recuperation technologies are now available, developed in many cases by partnerships between the private and public sectors.

While it would be unwise to promote the clearing of more forests for cattle ranching, plenty of scope exists for boosting beef and milk production from existing pastures, both large and small. Approximately half the pastures in the Brazilian Amazon have been degraded by weed invasion (Nepstad, Uhl, and Serrão 1991). Beef and dairy production could be increased substantially without cutting down a single tree. Furthermore, extensive savannas occur in parts of the Amazon that could be more effectively managed to increase productivity of free-range cattle. One way to prevent further assaults on the forest therefore is to offer credit and more technical support for farmers and ranchers interested in upgrading their pastures.

The biodiversity of pastures in Amazonia and many other parts of the tropics could be increased by intercropping with other plants. In parts of Asia and the Pacific, for example, intercropping of pastures with trees, especially coconut, is well developed (Grossman 1984; Plucknett 1979). More than fifty shrub and tree species are employed as living fences around pastures and fields in Costa Rica (Sauer 1979). Some ranchers in the Brazilian Amazon are experimenting with various legumes in pastures to help suppress weeds and improve soil fertility. But the common practice of burning pasture to control weeds and release nutrients is a current impediment to more widespread adoption of this practice. Many ranchers are reluctant to diversify their operations to include tree crops in pastures because of fire and other management considerations. Smallholders who raise both livestock and crops are likely to be the main vanguard of this innovation, and their practices warrant further study.

A wide variety of agricultural productions systems that rely heavily on livestock are found in drier parts of the tropics and subtropics, especially in Africa and tropical Asia. As in shifting cultivation, such systems are often particularly appropriate for areas with poor infrastructure or otherwise difficult environments (World Bank 1991). In the central Andes, the Himalayas, and the drier parts of India herding is an essential supplement to crop farming, which is especially risky because of cold or drought (Guillet 1983; Jodha 1992).

Agricultural development policies sometimes promote overgrazing and the loss of biodiversity because the complex cultural and ecological dimensions of pastoral activities are poorly understood (NRC 1990). The needs of stockmen for seasonal grazing lands are sometimes ignored. When agricultural development converts areas formerly used for extensive grazing, stockmen are denied access to forage for their herds. Unable to practice transhumance,

they may restrict livestock to more confined areas, thereby increasing pressure on forage resources. In eastern Africa herd mobility as practiced by pastoralists such as the Masai increases grazing capacity of the land by some 50 percent (NRC 1990). Pastoralists and farmers tap forage biodiversity of several areas seasonally, especially in Africa and the drier parts of Asia. When such ancient land-use systems are altered by development policies, destruction of biodiversity and impoverishment of pastoralists many ensue.

Fuelwood gatherers degrade the land for both pastoralists and farmers in some of the drier parts of Africa (NRC 1990). Increasing demand for fuelwood in urban areas has spurred wider wood-gathering efforts to sell wood directly or convert it to charcoal. The pruning and sometimes outright destruction of small trees and shrubs by fuelwood gatherers reduces forage for livestock and accelerates soil erosion. The fuelwood crisis, which is not being met by adequate plantings of quick-growing trees, illustrates again the link between agriculture, biodiversity, and other economic sectors.

The animal side of agropastoral systems also has implications for biodiversity. As modern crop farming has generally reduced the biodiversity of farmland, so to has the livestock industry (see chapter 6). Many traditional breeds have disappeared as farmers focus on highly productive cattle, pigs, sheep, and chickens (Alderson 1994; Crosby 1986, 181; Plucknett and Horne 1992; Smith 1990). Of the 3,831 breeds of cattle, water buffalo, goat, pig, sheep, horse, and donkey believed to have existed in this century, 16 percent have become extinct, and a further 15 percent are rare (Hall and Ruane 1993).

More than eighty distinct breeds of cattle are found in Africa, and some of them are currently being replaced by exotic breeds (Rege 1994). Loss of such biodiversity is more than just an academic concern. Several breeds of cattle and goats in West Africa have been helpful in research on resistance to trypanosomiasis, a widespread livestock disease in Africa. The Kuri breed of cattle around Lake Chad has the unusual ability to feed underwater but is in danger of genetic swamping from imported zebu cattle (Myers 1991).

Traditional breeds are vital for cross-breeding work to increase hardiness and other traits (Maule 1990; Salazar 1973). In many cases traditional breeds are more robust in difficult environments than the more widespread super breeds. The deployment of traditional breeds such as heat-tolerant Bali cattle may make more sense than promoting other tropical breeds such as the zebu. Too often agricultural development projects promote exotic or introduced breeds rather than assessing the potential of local breeds. Although it may not always be feasible to use local breeds, the fate of unique livestock should be considered in any development project.

Safekeeping traditional breeds poses several challenges. Unlike seed gene banks, it is not easy to store livestock germplasm in off-site collections. Frozen sperm is used mostly for spreading the genes of elite bulls rather than more localized breeds. Frozen embryos are an expensive way to try and save endangered livestock breeds. The best way is to maintain herds and flocks in their natural settings—the farm and ranch. The experience of various rare breed societies and organizations is worth reviewing for this reason.

In the United Kingdom the Rare Breeds Survival Trust has made impressive strides in reversing the loss of some traditional breeds of livestock, particularly sheep, pigs, and cattle. The trust lobbies for fiscal incentives for farmers to safeguard rare breeds, holds annual shows to display rare breeds and generate interest in them, and helps conduct surveys on the status of breeds. Similar efforts are under way in some other parts of the industrial world. In the United States the American Livestock Breeds Conservancy works to protect close to 100 threatened breeds. The conservancy was founded in 1977, and such efforts should be encouraged in the tropics and subtropics as well, where the greatest concentration of traditional breeds is often found. Developing regions have widely differing infrastructure and institutional endowments, but much of the initiative for conserving threatened breeds has come from the private sector. The Rare Breeds Survival Trust is a nongovernmental organization (NGO), and NGOs and livestock associations clearly have an important role to play here.

More research is warranted on the domestication of wild animals for meat, high-value leather, and other goods. Such efforts are now under way with only a handful of species, including crocodiles in New Guinea, iguanas in Central America, and ostriches in the United States. Little research and development have gone into the potential of wild animals that are hunted for food such as the pig-like babirusa for domestication (Fitzhugh and Wilhelm 1991). As with crops, research and development focus on staple animals. Virtually all research on livestock has focused on cattle, sheep, pigs, and chickens; some other animals could be domesticated that are better adapted to challenging environments.

One example will serve to illustrate this point. Along the Amazon floodplain much of the remaining forest is being felled, primarily to make way for cattle and water buffalo production. The loss of forests is undercutting fisheries because many of the fish species important for commerce and subsistence depend directly or indirectly on floodplain forests for their sustenance. A prolific native rodent, the capybara produces succulent meat that is highly regarded. The capybara feeds on herbs and floating grasses and does not require land clearing to create food resources for it. Some farmers are already domesticating the animal for meat production but are doing so in a clandestine manner because federal law prohibits raising wild animals in captivity and sale of their products. If wildlife regulations were amended to allow the marketing of game animals and their products if they are raised in captivity, capybara farms might proliferate and reduce the area devoted to cattle ranching.

Agroforestry

Agroforestry is often touted as one of the more sustainable land-use systems for the tropics, especially in degraded areas. *Agroforestry* is a relatively new word for an ancient practice that involves the intercropping of shrub or tree species with other crops including annuals. Many different agroforestry systems have evolved over the millennia, ranging from home gardens to multilayered tree crops in fields (Nair 1991). Spatial designs vary considerably from an occasional tree in a field to carefully planned mixtures of perennial trees and shrubs with annual crops in between.

Agroforestry offers numerous environmental benefits when compared to intensive short-cycle cropping. Mixed tree crop farms protect the soil better and use water and soil nutrients more efficiently (Fernandes and Matos 1995). The greater floristic diversity of agroforestry systems opens up more niches for wildlife, particularly birds, and the microclimate created by planted trees and shrubs protects soil microorganisms (Holloway 1991). Some agroforestry plots are extremely rich in species, thereby providing multiple tiers and a suitable environment for wildlife. In the vicinity of just one village in the uplands of the Peruvian Amazon, some sixty species are deployed in agroforestry systems (Hiraoka 1986).

Agroforestry is one of the trajectories of slash-and-burn agriculture. Instead of completely abandoning a field after annual cropping, many indigenous groups and other small-scale farmers return periodically to harvest fruits, nuts, and other useful products from fields that are being slowly engulfed by the forest (Sponsel 1986). By planting perennials in swidden plots, farmers can extend the useful life of managed fallows for decades (Denevan and Treacy 1987; Harris 1971; Padoch and others 1985).

In some cases swidden systems evolve into more or less permanent agroforestry systems. People in various parts of the tropics have transformed significant patches of the landscape into cultural forests. On the floodplain of the Amazon estuary and sections of the Ucayali in Peru, farmers have enriched the forest over the years with economically important tree species that now provide the main livelihood (Anderson 1988, 1990; Anderson and Ioris 1992; Hiraoka 1985a, 1985b, 1989; Padoch 1988; Padoch and de Jong 1991; Padoch and others 1985). Extractive activities in these cultural forests are based mainly on a medley of fruits, nuts, heart of palm, and cacao. Relatively permanent agroforestry systems appear to be best developed near sizable urban markets, but such specialized agroforestry systems could possibly be modified for more widespread adoption along the floodplains of tropical rivers. Cultural forests full of useful plants have also been created over extended periods of time

in other parts of the tropics, including the Yucatán Peninsula (Gómez-Pompa, Salvador, and Sosa 1987) and the humid zone of West Africa (Harris 1976).

Although agroforestry is more environment-friendly than most annual cropping systems, market forces constrain both the number of species deployed and the extent of mixed cropping systems. In the Brazilian Amazon, for example, most agroforestry systems in fields contain from two to four species (Smith and others 1995). A similar pattern of a limited number of intercropped species prevails in northern India, where tarai poplars are interplanted with either wheat or sugarcane and later with either turmeric or ginger. Throughout the eight-year rotation with poplars, farmers also choose from a wide variety of vegetables for planting during the winter.

Some farms contain agroforestry plots with dozens of intercropped annuals and perennials, but excessive diversity of crops can actually be counterproductive. In the tropics average annual productivity in ecosystems becomes saturated in the range of ten to forty species (Baskin 1994b). In some parts of the tropics agroforestry is still essentially confined to home gardens. Finding economically viable crop combinations that contain between two and ten species would thus be a high priority for agricultural research and development in the tropics.

The further development of agroforestry hinges on incorporating local people in the design of new agroforestry configurations. Farmers throughout the tropics are experimenting with a wide range of crop combinations, and their experiences need to be incorporated in agricultural research and development programs (Uquillas, Ramírez, and Seré 1992). Farmers are also domesticating a wide range of wild forest plants in their home gardens, some of which are later adopted for field agriculture. Local knowledge is critical in identifying which plants are useful in surrounding forest and other habitats. One of the best ways to conserve biodiversity is to find uses for it. If its value is not appreciated, it can slip into oblivion.

The full potential of agroforestry is also linked to the conservation of forests, both in humid areas and the more open, scrubby woodlands of the drier tropics. In the Amazon, for example, people are domesticating a wide assortment of perennial plants in home gardens for a variety of purposes, ranging from fish bait to medicines and construction materials. Seeds and seedlings are gathered in the forest and planted in home gardens. Or wild species sometimes arise spontaneously in home gardens and are protected. Home gardens are a largely untapped reservoir of plant genetic resources.

Given the heterogeneity of agroforestry in most areas, it would be unwise to promote a single technology package for farmers to adopt. Rather, a flexible basket of species and agronomy practices would better suit the wide range of farming conditions where agroforestry is appropriate (Current, Lutz, and Scherr 1995). Another important lesson from studies of agroforestry adoption is that candidate trees and shrubs must help meet the needs of farmers, not just improve the environment. Although much needs to be learned about constraints to agroforestry adoption in many areas, it is clear that unless the trees generate income or otherwise provide goods or services to local people, they will not adopt or maintain mixed perennial cropping systems.

Plantation Systems

Establishing monocultures based on perennial crops is a high priority for many agricultural research and development programs. Some commercial plantations focus on fruit production such as mango and citrus and others are set up for industrial purposes such as latex for rubber. Other plantation systems are devoted to the confectionery and beverage trade, such as cacao and tea, and still others are geared toward vegetable oil, timber, or pulp production.

Commercial plantations are a major land use in the tropics and subtropics. Plantation forestry geared to timber and pulp production alone covers some 11 million hectares. Plantation systems of all kinds are expanding by about 3 million hectares a year (FAO 1995). Given their widespread impact on biodiversity, finding ways to mitigate the negative environmental effects of plantations deserves high priority.

In some cases promoting commercial tree crops—particularly rubber, oil palm, and cacao—

has accelerated tropical deforestation and the loss of biodiversity. Plantation expansion, particularly of rubber and oil palm, is the leading cause of tropical deforestation in peninsular Malaysia (Vincent and Hadi 1993). As of 1988, perennial tree crops occupied 4.16 million hectares there, mostly at the expense of forest. The impressive increase in area planted to rubber and oil palm in Malaysia is driven by their inherent economic feasibility not misguided by fiscal incentives.

While benefiting Malaysia's economy, such expansion of commercial plantations has inflicted appreciable if still unmeasured losses of biodiversity. Only a small number of forest-dwelling animals survive in tree plantations in Malaysia, as is probably the case in most other tropical regions. No monocultural system supports a breeding population of forest-dwelling birds in the Malay Peninsula (Vincent and Hadi 1993). Only a few birds adapted to disturbed sites can make a home in monocrop tree plantations.

The large size of plantations tends to magnify their environmental impact; some plantations for cellulose production, for example, exceed 100,000 hectares. Furthermore, commercial plantation systems are often heavy users of inorganic fertilizers, herbicides, fungicides, and insecticides. As in intensive short-cycle cropping, deployment of these agrochemicals can trigger collateral damage, such as water pollution and destruction of beneficial insects and animals.

One strategy to reduce damage to the environment while improving production is to incorporate greater biodiversity in plantations. Greater genetic variation of perennial species deployed in plantation systems should help reduce dependence on chemicals to control pests. Steps have already been taken in this direction:

• The deployment of several clones for each of the three species of eucalyptus in the Jari pulp operation in the Brazilian Amazon. Eucalyptus plantations cover some 50,000 hectares at Jari, but they are not genetically uniform. The idea behind planting more than one high-yielding clone is to reduce the risk of severe disease or pest outbreaks.

• At Jari stream banks and steep slopes are left in their original vegetation, thereby creating wildlife corridors and habitats for native species of plants and animals.

- Half a dozen coconut varieties have been planted on a 12,000 hectare plantation operated by Sócôco in the Brazilian state of Pará.
- In Malaysia several high-yielding clones have been released to diversify plantations, and researchers are working on developing high-yielding clones that resist South American leaf blight in case the fungal disease reaches Southeast Asia. Such clones will be held in reserve in case they are needed.
- Several companies in the Brazilian Amazon use kudzu vine, a fast-growing leguminous ground cover, to suppress weeds in oil palm plantations rather than applying herbicides. Kudzu also enriches the soil with nitrogen.
- A plant pathologist working for an oil palm plantation in the Brazilian state of Pará has anecdotal evidence that caterpillar damage is less severe on oil palm when strips of forest are left standing nearby, possibly because of biocontrol agents that survive in the original vegetation.
- Near Ariquemes, Rondônia, in the Brazilian Amazon, a cattle rancher who is diversifying his operation with citrus groves has noted that pest and disease problems on his orange trees are less severe near a large stand of bamboo. The bamboo is not native but may shelter some biocontrol agents. The alleged biocontrol value of native and even planted woods warrants further elucidation because it appears that ecological complexity is likely to benefit both the environment and agricultural production.
- In Brazil companies establishing extensive plantations are required by law to plant a proportion of their land with indigenous species, thereby expanding natural biodiversity (Brown and Lugo 1994; Lugo, Parrotta, and Brown 1993; Parrotta 1993).
- In Colombia regional development agencies and the national federation of coffee growers are promoting the interplanting of coffee with other perennials, including a native bamboo (Parsons 1991). Although such steps may appear modest, they increase biodiversity of normally monocropped areas and diversify products for growers.

The stakes are much higher in perennial systems than with annuals. With cereal or pulse crops, varieties that no longer perform well can be quickly pulled and replaced with other material at the next planting cycle. Perennial crop growers have a much greater initial investment and cannot switch so easily to different clones or varieties. The difficulty is finding appropriate mixes of perennials or varieties that can make a profit for growers. Also, hard data are rarely available to show that diversification of plantation systems is a cost-effective measure. Diversification is usually undertaken as insurance against disease and pest epidemics.

Another important strategy to mitigate destruction of biodiversity is to target already cleared areas for establishing plantations. Substantial parts of the tropics and subtropics are covered with vegetation at various stages of succession. In some cases the forest is unlikely to return because of soil degradation or because seed sources have been eliminated by wanton deforestation. In India and Puerto Rico, for example, tree plantations can rehabilitate degraded areas by helping to accelerate succession since they provide a favorable microclimate for the spontaneous establishment of native species (Lugo, Parrotta, and Brown 1993). In this manner they enhance biodiversity, and when the planted trees are ready for harvest, they generate income for land managers.

Finally, plantations make good buffers around protected areas because they provide shade and windbreaks. Plantations are superior to fields in annual crops in this regard. With good fire control measures typical of tree plantations, they can also help prevent fires from penetrating remaining tracts of forest. When shifting cultivators become more concentrated in an area, particularly in transitional zones, remaining forest is often confined to narrow strips and small islands, both of which are more vulnerable to fires escaping from slash-and-burn fields. For example, a fire in Chiapas, Mexico, destroyed 600,000 hectares of forest in 1982 (Gómez-Pompa and others 1993). Chiapas is one of the richest centers of biodiversity in Central America.

Managed Forests

The remaining forests represent an extensive pool of largely unexploited biodiversity, but most woodlands in the tropics and subtropics are under severe pressure from farmers, ranchers, or loggers. In some areas all three are involved in deforestation. Pressures on forests are increasing as farmers press up against their margins and timber extraction accelerates. In temperate lands the forest area has increased in this century because some crops have been taken out of production, thereby allowing the land to revert to forest, and because of silviculture programs that have promoted the widespread planting of trees, particularly conifers. In the tropics forests are still shrinking. How such forests are used and managed therefore has major implications for biodiversity.

A historical perspective may prove helpful. Before World War II vast areas of mature forest could be found in tropical areas. In many countries forest agencies and research institutes had established permanent sample plots in virgin forest. Subsequent research has demonstrated that extensive tracts of primary forest have experienced varying degrees of human disturbance. These permanent forest plots along with other floristic surveys were used to gather data on the composition and structure of plant associations. Such studies underscore how little is known about the vast genetic variation of plants and animals in tropical forests and their economic potential. Whole ecological communities, species, and subspecies are being destroyed before humanity can even document many of them, let alone appreciate their value.

Several forest management strategies have been devised to exploit timber and non-wood products without seriously impairing the ecosystems involved, but such plans usually work only when harvesting rates are modest. As human populations have increased around the margins of forests and the tempo of logging rates has quickened, products from many tropical forests are no longer being harvested on a sustainable basis. Furthermore, roads cut through the forest to gain access to minerals and other resources have allowed waves of settlers to follow in their wake, leading to whole-scale destruction of the forest, as in Kalimantan, Indonesia (Brookfield, Potter, and Byron 1995).

The police-based system of forest protection and management that functioned in the past is less feasible today. Loggers and farmers need to be involved in the design and implementation of forest management. Community-based management is increasingly promoted as the best way to proceed with rural development, particularly for nontimber forest products, but it is no panacea. Many forests are being mismanaged by individual landowners and companies rather than communities. Like individual entrepreneurs, communities may be overzealous in extracting forest products if the market is strong, thereby depleting natural resources and biodiversity. Local participation in the decisionmaking process is not enough; investments in research and technology development are still needed to help manage forests sustainably.

In some areas of the humid tropics, particularly the Brazilian Amazon, extractive reserves have been set up so that local people can derive a viable income from the forest without cutting it down. For the most part forest management for nontimber forest products should be envisaged as a supplement to the diet and income of rural populations, rather than the mainstay. Excessive reliance on forest extraction alone to gain a livelihood may actually backfire. To help extractive reserves become more sustainable, people that live in them will need to diversify their operations by growing cash crops and raising livestock, which will involve some clearing.

Tropical forests are highly heterogeneous, so a model for sustainable timber cutting or fruit extraction in one area may not be appropriate for another. Issues that warrant special attention for that reason are the role of traditional knowledge of economic plants in the forest; the minimum critical size for healthy ecosystem functioning; and devising rotations between cutting or harvesting so that they are sufficiently long to allow the resource to recuperate.

If forests can be managed sustainably for lumber or nontimber forest products or both, appreciable biodiversity will be safeguarded. Forests will eventually be able to pay for themselves. The rich reservoirs of plants in tropical forests, about which little is known, are needed for future botanical prospecting. Tropical forests contain wild populations of more than 200 crops, and these gene pools have hardly been tapped to upgrade such crops as rubber, mango, avocado, and coffee.

The agricultural value of conserving forests underscores the inadequacies of the current system of protecting natural areas. A significant, unresolved issue in conservation practice is deciding what exactly is supposed to be preserved. The scientific underpinnings for selecting areas for preservation are weak in many cases. Many of the nominally protected areas have tenuous political support locally, regionally, and nationally. Setting aside forest for nature reserves and managed harvesting of products often means reducing the area available for more profitable land uses, at least in the short term. Forest management for timber and non-wood products thus needs to be placed on as firm an economic foundation as possible.

Much will depend on the value of products subject to some form of management and protection. Where such products fetch high prices—sandalwood in India, camphor in Indonesia, greenheart in Guyana, or ebony in West Africa—the danger for overexploitation looms. In many cases adequate management plans cannot be devised because of gaps in scientific research. Further investigation into the breeding systems and genetic variation of numerous species of actual or potential importance for forest management is therefore urgently needed.

Policy Implications

Policies specific to each land-use system are examined in the previous section. Overriding policy issues are broached here, some of which are also dealt with in chapter 8.

New Agricultural Research and Development Model

A new research paradigm is needed that systematically incorporates agrobiodiversity concerns. While work is under way at various institutions to further this goal, the pace is uneven and biodiversity has not yet been effectively mainstreamed into agricultural research and development. The world is looking for new models for high-productivity agriculture, models that retain the benefits of ever-improving yields and the potential to raise incomes while being more environment-friendly.

Policymakers and stakeholders must understand that conserving and managing biodiversity for agricultural development are linked. Conservation and natural resource management are not separate issues. Conservation is one of the strategies for the wise use of natural resources.

Genetically diverse (heterozygous) populations of crops and animals on managed landscapes warrant more research. Hybrids and modern varieties may have a comparative advantage in certain privileged farming areas where irrigation, fertile soils, and good socioeconomic infrastructures are in place, but they have a much more limited role in more marginal environments where population growth is rapid.

More farmers and livestock owners must be involved in establishing research priorities and in testing new technologies (Dusseldorp and Box 1993). A greater appreciation for local knowledge is justified to develop appropriate technologies and natural resource management strategies for safeguarding and enhancing biodiversity.

A fuller assessment of undervalued plants and animals of potential economic value should be a high priority, including locally important crops, some traditional breeds, and wild plants and animals that could be domesticated. This research would help diversify agricultural production systems and increase options for farmers. Biodiversity and resiliency of land-use systems would increase.

Greater support is also justified for studies of paleoagricultural systems and environmental archaeology for clues about how highly productive and biodiverse agricultural systems were honed long ago, particularly in challenging environments. Such studies can point the way to promising natural resource management strategies.

Accelerated work on the systematics of plants and animals is urgently needed so that scientists, gene bank curators, and managers of conservation units will have a better idea of the numbers and variation of species they are dealing with (Miller, Rossman, and Kirkbridge 1989). When evolutionary relationships are better sorted out, the work of crop and livestock breeders is facilitated.

Socioeconomic Infrastructure and Property Rights

Assuming that landowners are more likely to invest in upgrading and intensifying their operations if land values increase, it would be unwise to promote the building of new roads in pioneer areas. One of the greatest obstacles to a more rational management of tropical forest for timber and other products is the availability of forest that can be more cheaply mined because of extensive road networks (Schneider 1994).

Existing transportation routes should be improved rather than building new roads. This will increase land values, and farmers and livestock owners will have an easier time getting their produce to markets. It could be argued that paving existing roads is likely to accelerate deforestation and the loss of biodiversity. This may be true in some cases but may not hold in all. Landowners along improved roads may be more likely to manage areas currently in production more intensively because of better market links.

Other components of an improved socioeconomic infrastructure would include rural electrification for agroindustry and credit that promotes agrobiodiversity and is delivered in a timely manner. Credit is often available only for technologies that tend to undermine biodiversity. A revamping of credit priorities in many regions is in order.

Land tenure is also relevant to policies to promote protection and enhancement of biodiversity in agricultural settings. Land tenure seems to be a perennial issue in rural development in many regions, particularly in Latin America. Lack of well-defined property rights has been identified as a major constraint to more responsible management of natural resources (Garrity, Kummer, and Guiang 1993; World Bank 1991).

Several points about property rights are worth emphasizing as they relate to land tenure and biodiversity. Land tenure is relevant to biodiversity conservation and the enhancement of agrobiodiversity because it can be a driving force for environmental destruction and because it can also provide an incentive to invest in more rational management of natural resources:

- People will generally not be motivated to invest in tree crop farming such as agroforestry unless they feel secure in their rights to work on the land (Current, Lutz, and Scherr

1995). Official land titles may not be necessary as long as the rights of people who have traditionally occupied the area are respected. If it is not feasible to provide official land titles, other mechanisms for security to the land and access to credit deserve investigation.

- Where natural resources are managed by communities rather than individual homesteads, such common property resources warrant protection under the law. Indigenous groups can develop market-oriented, environmentally sound strategies for managing agrobiodiversity and for protecting habitats only if their land ownership is not violated. Communities need to be assured they have the right to control access to resources on their land so that chances will improve that resources will be managed wisely and biodiversity protected.

- Where land is farmed by individual smallholders who do not have official documentation, legalization of their holdings should be accelerated or at least traditionally recognized land ownership patterns should not be undermined by development projects.

Agricultural Development Projects

Biodiversity performance indicators need to be applied to land-use systems pertinent to a rural development or agricultural project. The set of biodiversity indicators would alert policymakers and development project task managers about potentially negative repercussions of agricultural practices. Although work on the set of indicators is still at an early stage (table 4.1), it is designed to provide an analytical tool to guide thinking on how to assess whether certain agricultural and forest extraction practices are more or less likely to impair biodiversity.

To mitigate biodiversity loss and to enhance the use of biological riches, a rapid agrobiodiversity survey is needed before any rural development project is undertaken. Such relatively inexpensive surveys would document the current mix of land-use systems, appreciate the driving forces that shape them, identify major players in conserving and managing biodiversity at the local level, and assess the richness and uniqueness of crops and livestock.

A multidisciplinary agrobiodiversity survey team would visit the proposed development site to:

- Assess the current extent and richness of agriculturally related biodiversity (for example, traditional varieties or landraces in use; wild or weedy populations and near relatives; types of livestock and breeds)
- Explore the impact of the proposed development project on existing biodiversity, both agricultural and wild
- Examine whether proposed agricultural development activities have paid sufficient attention to local needs, natural resource management strategies, and ways to enhance biodiversity within proposed agricultural systems.

Agricultural development projects need to be screened for their off-site impact. For example, all projects involving irrigation should have a component for watershed management that includes safeguarding mature vegetation communities, especially forest. In floodplain areas tree farming, particularly with native fruit and nut species that are also consumed by fish at high water, should be promoted rather than beef production. In this manner synergies may be obtained between biodiversity conservation and agricultural development.

Biodiversity Conservation Projects

The importance of safeguarding relatively undisturbed habitats as reservoirs of wild populations of crop plants and their near relatives as well as economically important wildlife needs to be incorporated in more biodiversity protection plans. In Guatemala, for example, a small park near Purulha, Baja Verapaz, was set up to preserve the endangered quetzal, Guatemala's national bird, but the park also contains several near relatives of avocado that could eventually prove useful in breeding efforts (Smith and others 1992). Most nature reserves are established to protect endangered ecosystems and showcase animals or for ecotourism. Only a handful of *gene parks* have been set aside specifically to conserve genetic resources of crop plants. Conserving genetic resources of plants important for agriculture and industry could provide

Table 4.1 Preliminary performance indicators on biodiversity conservation and management in various agricultural production and forest extraction systems

Indicator	Cause(s)	Proposed mitigating action(s)
Natural habitat loss	Encroachment by agricultural production systems	• Intensify systems to increase productivity and income-generating options
Habitat fragmentation	Encroachment of agriculture in an uncoordinated manner	• Minimize fragmentation, gene flow interruption, and species loss because remnants are too small to support them by providing wildlife corridors along bridges of natural habitat
Species loss even when natural habitat is still intact	Air or water pollution; excessive sedimentation of water courses; excessive hunting, fishing, collecting, or logging	• Decrease agrochemical use by shifting to integrated pest management • Incorporate crop rotation or more perennials • Promote environment-friendly (green) production systems • Devise plans for harvesting wild plant and animal resources
Decline of biodiversity of crop species on farms	Adoption of new farming practices, such as monocropping with a cereal crop, possibly propelled by fiscal incentives	• Eliminate fiscal or regulatory measures that promote homogeneity • Explore traditional, polycultural systems that can be rehabilitated while raising yields and income
Decline in biodiversity within species	Release of modern varieties and application of agrochemicals to protect them, possibly propelled by fiscal incentives; adoption of intellectual property rights	• Support research on traditional varieties that can achieve higher yields and on modern varieties less dependent on agrochemicals • Promote heterogeneous crop varieties over genetically pure ones • Provide incentives for both modern and traditional varieties and ecolabeling of products certifying that they come from traditional varieties

Source: Author.

a powerful rationale for further efforts to preserve wilderness.

Links to Ecotourism

Efforts to enhance agrobiodiversity could be enhanced if they were linked to ecotourism. Ecotourism can help bolster efforts to promote *in situ* conservation of traditional crop varieties (Wilkes 1989). Ecotourism is currently geared to introducing visitors to natural areas with showcase birds and mammals or vegetation with aesthetic appeal such as rainforests or some semiarid landscapes. But there is also a market for showing tourists traditional breeds of livestock and heirloom crop varieties.

Vignette farms are already functioning in various parts of the industrial world such as the United Kingdom and the United States. The challenge will be to promote similar operations in developing countries, especially in megacenters for agrobiodiversity. Some promising steps have already been taken in this direction. Near Mérida in the Yucatán Peninsula of Mexico, for example, a functioning farm run by a Mayan family has been set up near an archaeological site to attract tourists. Such enterprises educate nationals about the importance of indigenous agrobiodiversity as well as capturing foreign exchange.

References

Alderson, L. 1994. *The Chance to Survive.* Yelvertof, U.K.: Pilkington Press.

Ali, A. M. S. 1987. "Intensive Paddy Agriculture in Shyampur, Bangladesh." In B. L. Turner II and S. B. Brush, eds., *Comparative Farming Systems.* New York: Guilford Press.

Altieri, M. A. 1991. "Increasing Biodiversity to Improve Insect Pest Management in Agro-Ecosystems." In D. L. Hawksworth, ed., *The Biodiversity of Microorganisms and Invertebrates: Its Role in Sustainable Agriculture.* Wallingford, U.K.: C.A.B. International.

Anderson, A. B. 1988. "Use and Management of Native Forests Dominated by Açaí Palm (Euterpe oleracea Mart.) in the Amazon Estuary," *Advances in Economic Botany* 6: 144–54.

———.1990. "Extraction and Forest Management by Rural Inhabitants in the Amazon Estuary." In A. B. Anderson, ed., *Alternatives to Deforestation: Steps Toward Sustainable Use of the Amazon Rain Forest.* New York: Columbia University Press.

Anderson, A. B., and E. M. Ioris. 1992. "Valuing the Rain Forest: Economic Strategies by Small-Scale Forest Extractivists in the Amazon Estuary," *Human Ecology* 20 (3): 337–69.

Arrow, K., B. Bolin, R. Costanza, P. Dasgupta, C. Folke, C. S. Holling, B. Jansson, S. Levin, K. Mäler, C. Perrings, and D. Pimentel. 1995. "Economic Growth, Carrying Capacity, and the Environment," *Science* 268: 520–21.

Barfield, C. S., and M. E. Swisher. 1994. "Integrated Pest Management: Ready For Export? Historical Context and Internationalization of IPM," *Food Reviews International* 10 (2): 215–67.

Baskin, Y. 1994a. "There's a New Wildlife Policy in Kenya: Use It or Lose It," *Science* 265: 733–34.

———.1994b. "Ecologists Dare to Ask: How Much Does Diversity Matter?" *Science* 264: 202–03.

Bellon, M. R., and S. B. Brush. 1994. "Keepers of Maize in Chiapas, Mexico," *Economic Botany* 48 (2): 196–209.

Bray, W. 1990. "Agricultural Renascence in the High Andes," *Nature* 345: 385.

Brookfield, H., L. Potter, and Y. Byron. 1995. *In Place of the Forest: Environmental and Socio-economic Transformation in Borneo and the Eastern Malay Peninsula.* Tokyo: United Nations University Press.

Brown, S., and A. E. Lugo. 1994. "Rehabilitation of Tropical Lands: A Key to Sustaining Development," *Restoration Ecology* 2: 97–111.

Brush, S. B. 1986. "Genetic Diversity and Conservation in Traditional Farming Systems," *Journal of Ethnobiology* 6 (1): 151–67.

Brush, S. B., J. E. Taylor, and M. R. Bellon. 1992. "Technology Adoption and Biological Diversity in Andean Potato Agriculture," *Journal of Development Economics* 39: 365–87.

Burns, E. B. 1993. *A History of Brazil.* New York: Columbia University Press.

Byerlee, D., and P. Heisey. 1993. "Performance of Hybrids under Low-input Conditions in Eastern and Southern Africa." Unpublished paper. Economics Department, International Center for Maize and Wheat Improvement, Mexico City, Mexico.

Carney, H. J., M. W. Binford, A. L. Kolata, R. R. Marin, and C. R. Goldman. 1993. "Nutrient and Sediment Retention in Andean Raised-Field Agriculture," *Nature* 364: 131–33.

Castro, G. 1991. "Extractive Reserves," *Bioscience* 41: 284.

Claridge, M. F. 1991. "Genetic and Biological Diversity of Insect Pests and Their Natural Enemies." In D. L. Hawksworth, ed., *The Biodiversity of Microorganisms and Invertebrates: Its Role in Sustainable Agriculture.* Wallingford, U.K.: C.A.B. International.

Conklin, H. C. 1954. "An Ethnoecological Approach to Shifting Agriculture," *Transactions of the New York Academy of Sciences* 17 (2): 133–42.

Cook, O. F. 1921. "Milpa Agriculture, A Primitive Tropical System." In *Annual Report of the Board of*

Regents. Washington, D.C.: Smithsonian Institution.

Coomes, O. T. 1995. "A Century of Rain Forest Use in Western Amazonia: Lessons for Extraction-based Conservation of Tropical Forest Resources," *Forest and Conservation History* 39: 108–20.

Cowgill, U. M. 1962. "An Agricultural Study of the Southern Maya Lowlands," *American Anthropologist* 64 (2): 273–86.

Croat, T. B. 1972. "The Role of Overpopulation and Agricultural Methods in the Destruction of Tropical Ecosystems," *Science* 22: 465–67.

Crosby, A. W. 1986. *Ecological Imperialism: The Biological Expansion of Europe, 900–1900.* Cambridge: Cambridge University Press.

Current, D., E. Lutz, and S. J. Scherr. 1995. *Costs, Benefits, and Farmer Adoption of Agroforestry: Project Experience in Central America and the Caribbean.* World Bank Environment Paper 14. Washington, D.C.

Denevan, W. M. 1970. "Aboriginal Drained-Field Cultivation in the Americas," *Science* 169: 647–54.

——.1980. "Latin America." In G. A. Klee, ed., *World Systems of Traditional Resource Management.* New York: Halsted Press.

——.1995. "Prehistoric Agricultural Methods as Models for Sustainability," *Advances in Plant Pathology* 11: 21–43.

Denevan, W. M., and J. M. Treacy. 1987. "Young Managed Fallows at Brillo Nuevo," *Advances in Economic Botany* 5:8-46.

Denevan, W. M., and K. H. Schwerin. 1978. "Adaptive Strategies in Karinya Subsistence, Venezuelan Llanos," *Antropológica* 50: 3–91.

Denevan, W. M., and K. Mathewson. 1983. "Preliminary Results of the Samborondon Raised-field Project, Guayas Basin, Ecuador." In J. P. Darch, ed., *Drained Field Agriculture in Central and South America.* Oxford: BAR International Series 189.

Denevan, W. M., and R. W. Bergman. 1975. "Karinya Indian Swamp Cultivation in The Venezuelan Llanos," *Yearbook of the Association of Pacific Coast Geographers* 37: 23–37.

Douglas, J. S., and R. A. J. Hart. 1985. *Forest Farming: Towards a Solution to Problems of World Hunger and Conservation.* London: Intermediate Technology Publications.

Dufour, D. L. 1990. "Use of Tropical Rainforests by Native Amazonians," *Bioscience* 40: 652–59.

Dusseldorp, D., and L. Box. 1993. "Local and Scientific Knowledge: Developing a Dialogue." In W. Boef, K. Wellard, and A. Bebbington, eds., *Cultivating Knowledge: Genetic Diversity, Farmer Experimentation and Crop Research.* London: Intermediate Technology Publications.

Dwyer, Augusta. 1990. *Into the Amazon: The Struggle for the Rain Forest.* San Francisco: Sierra Club Books.

Eden, M. J. 1980. "A Traditional Agro-System in the Amazon Region of Colombia," *Tropical Ecology and Development* 1: 509–14.

——.1988. "Crop Diversity in Tropical Swidden Cultivation: Comparative Data from Colombia and Papua New Guinea," *Agriculture, Ecosystems, and Environment* 20: 127–36.

Eden, M. J., D. F. M. McGregor, and N.A.Q. Vieira. 1990. "Pasture Development on Cleared Forest Land in Northern Amazonia," *Geographical Journal* 156 (3): 283–96.

Ehui, S. K. 1993. "Côte d'Ivoire." In *Sustainable Agriculture and the Environment in the Humid Tropics.* Washington, D.C.: National Academy of Sciences, National Research Council.

Erickson, C. L. 1992a. "Applied Archaeology and Rural Development: Archaeology's Potential Contribution to the Future," *Journal of the Steward Anthropological Society* 20 (1–2): 1–16.

——.1992b. "Prehistoric Landscape Management in the Andean Highlands: Raised-field Agriculture and Its Environmental Impact," *Population and Environment* 13 (4): 285–330.

——.1995. "Archaeological Methods for the Study of Ancient Landscapes of the Llanos de Mojos in the Bolivian Amazon." In P. W. Stahl, ed., *Archaeology in the Lowland American Tropics: Current Analytical Methods and Applications.* Cambridge: Cambridge University Press.

FAO (Food and Agriculture Organization). 1995. *Forest Resources Assessment 1990—Global Synthesis.* Forestry Paper 124. Food and Agriculture Organization. Rome.

Fernandes, E. C. M., and J. C. S. Matos. 1995. "Agroforestry Strategies for Alleviating Soil Chemical Constraints to Food and Fiber Production in the Brazilian Amazon." In P. R. Seidl, O. R. Gottlieb, and M. A. C. Kaplan, eds., *Chemistry of the Amazon: Biodiversity, Natural Products, and Environmental Issues.* Washington, D.C.: American Chemical Society.

Fitzhugh, H., and A. E. Wilhelm. 1991. "Value and Uses of Indigenous Livestock Breeds in Developing Nations." In M. L. Oldfield and J. B. Alcorn, eds., *Biodiversity: Culture, Conservation, and Ecodevelopment.* Boulder, Colo.: Westview Press.

Flint, M. 1991. *Biological Diversity and Developing Countries, Issues and Options: A Synthesis Paper.* London: Overseas Development Administration.

Flowers, N. M., D. R. Gross, M. L. Ritter, and D. W. Werner. 1982. "Variation in Swidden Practices in Four Central Brazilian Indian Societies," *Human Ecology* 10 (2): 203–17.

Gámez, R. 1989. "Threatened Habitats and Germplasm Preservation: A Central American Perspective." In L. Knutson and A. K. Stoner, eds., *Biotic Diversity and Germplasm Preservation, Global Imperatives.* Dordrecht: Kluwer.

Garrity, D. P., D. M. Kummer, and E. S. Guiang. 1993. "The Philippines." In *Sustainable Agriculture and the Environment in the Humid Tropics.* Washington, D.C.: National Research Council, National Academy Press.

Goldman, A. 1995. "Threats to Sustainability in African Agriculture: Searching for Appropriate Paradigms," *Human Ecology* 23 (3): 291–332.

Gómez-Pompa, A., J. Salvador, and V. Sosa. 1987. "The 'Pet Kot': a Man-Made Tropical Forest of the Maya," *Interciencia* 12 (1): 10–15.

Gómez-Pompa, A. Kaus, J. Jiménez-Osornio, D. Bainbridge, and V. M. Rorive. 1993. "Mexico." In *Sustainable Agriculture and the Environment in the Humid Tropics*. Washington, D.C.: National Academy Press, National Research Council.

Goulding, M., N. J. H. Smith, and D. Mahar. 1995. *Floods of Fortune: Ecology and Economy along the Amazon.* New York: Columbia University Press.

Grossman, L. S. 1984. *Peasants, Subsistence Ecology, and Development in the Highlands of Papua New Guinea.* Princeton: Princeton University Press.

Guillet, D. 1983. "Toward a Cultural Ecology of Mountains: the Central Andes and the Himalayas Compared," *Current Anthropology* 24 (5): 561–74.

Hall, S. J. G., and J. Ruane. 1993. "Livestock Breeds and Their Conservation: a Global Overview," *Conservation Biology* 7 (4): 815–25.

Harris, D. R. 1971. "The Ecology of Swidden Cultivation in the Upper Orinoco Rain Forest, Venezuela," *Geographical Review* 61 (4): 475–95.

———.1976. "Traditional Systems of Plant Food Production and the Origins of Agriculture in West Africa." In J. R. Harlan, J. M. J. De Wet, and A. B. L. Stemmler, eds., *Origins of African Plant Domestication.* The Hague: Mouton.

Hecht, S. B. 1992a. "Extractive Communities, Biodiversity and Gender Issues in Amazonia." In L. M. Borkenhagen and J. N. Abromovitz, eds., *Proceedings of the International Conference on Women and Biodiversity.* Cambridge, Mass.: Harvard University, Kennedy School of Government.

———.1992b. "Logics of Livestock and Deforestation: The Case of Amazonia." In T. E. Downing, S. B. Hecht, H. A. Pearson, and C. Garcia-Downing, eds., *Development or Destruction: The Conversion of Tropical Forest to Pasture in Latin America.* Boulder, Colo.: Westview Press.

Hecht, S. B., and A. Cockburn. 1989. *The Fate of the Forest: Developers, Destroyers, and Defenders of the Amazon.* London: Verso.

Heisey, P. W., and M. Smale. 1995. "Maize Technology in Malawi: A Green Revolution in the Making?" CIMMYT Research Report 4. Mexico City, Mexico.

Hernández, E. 1993. "Aspects of Plant Domestication in Mexico: A Personal View." In T. P. Ramamoorthy, R. Bye, Jr., A. Lot, and J. Fa, eds., *Biological Diversity of Mexico: Origins and Distribution.* New York: Oxford University Press.

Herrera, N. D. 1994. *Los Huertos Familiares Mayas en El Oriente de Yucatán.* Mérida: Universidad Autónoma de Yucatán.

Hiraoka, M. 1980. "Settlement and Development of the Upper Amazon: The East Bolivian Example," *Journal of Developing Areas* 14: 327–47.

———.1985a. "Changing Floodplain Livelihood Patterns in the Peruvian Amazon," *Tsukuba Studies in Human Geography* 9: 243–75.

———.1985b. "Floodplain Farming in the Peruvian Amazon," *Geographical Review of Japan* 58 (ser. B, no. 1): 1–23.

———.1986. "Zonation of Mestizo Riverine Farming Systems in Northeast Peru," *National Geographic Research* 2 (3): 354–71.

———.1989. "Agricultural Systems on the Floodplains of the Peruvian Amazon." In John O. Browder, ed., *Fragile Lands of Latin America: Strategies for Sustainable Development.* Boulder, Colo.: Westview Press.

Hiraoka, M., and S. Yamamoto. 1980. "Agricultural Development in the Upper Amazon of Ecuador," *Geographical Review* 70: 423–45.

Holling, C. S. 1976. "Resiliency and Stability of Ecosystems." In E. Jantsch and C. H. Waddington, eds., *Evolution and Consciousness: Human Systems in Transition.* Reading, Mass.: Addison-Wesley.

———.1987. "Simplifying the Complex: The Paradigms of Ecological Function and Structure," *European Journal of Operational Research* 30: 139–46.

———.1994. "An Ecologist View of the Malthusian Conflict." In K. Lindahl-Kiessing and H. Landberg, eds., *Population, Economic Development, and the Environment.* New York: Oxford University Press.

Holling, C. S., and S. Bocking. 1990. "Surprise and Opportunity: in Evolution, in Ecosystems, in Society." In C. Mungall and D. J. McLaren, eds., *Planet under Stress.* Toronto: Oxford University Press.

Holloway, J. 1991. "Biodiversity and Tropical Agriculture: A Biogeographic View," *Outlook on Agriculture* 20 (1): 9–13.

IRRI (International Rice Research Institute). 1983. *Research Highlights for 1982.* Los Baños: IRRI.

Jodha, N. S. 1992. *Common Property Resources: A Missing Dimension of Development Strategies.* World Bank Discussion Paper 169. Washington, D.C.

Jodha, N. S., and T. Partap. 1993. "Folk Agronomy in the Himalayas: Implications for Agricultural Research and Extension," *International Institute for Environment and Development Research Series* 1 (3): 15–37.

Kellman, M. C. 1974. "Some Implications of Biotic Interactions for Sustained Tropical Agriculture," *Proceedings of the Association of American Geographers* 6: 142–45.

Lanly, J. P. 1982. *Tropical Forest Resources.* Forestry Paper 30. Rome: FAO.

Leavitt, F. J. 1992. "The Case for Conservation," *Nature* 360: 100.

Lima, R. R. 1958. "Os efeitos das queimadas sôbre a vegetação dos solos arenosos da região da estrada de ferro de Bragança," *Boletim da Inspetoría Regional de Fomento Agrícola no Pará* 8: 23–25.

Lugo, A. E., J. A. Parrotta, and S. Brown. 1993. "Loss of Species Caused by Deforestation and Their Recovery through Management," *AMBIO* 22: 106–09.

Mahar, D. J. 1989. *Government Policies and Deforestation in Brazil's Amazon Region*. Washington, D.C.: World Bank.

Maule, J. P. 1990. *The Cattle of the Tropics*. Edinburgh: Centre for Tropical Veterinary Medicine.

McNeely, J. A. 1993. "Agricultural Development and the Conservation of Biodiversity: Issues, Policies, and Programmes for the World Bank." Paper presented at a World Bank in-house seminar on Biodiversity Conservation and Agricultural Development, 14 January, Washington, D.C.

Miller, D. R., A.Y. Rossman, and J. Kirkbridge. 1989. "Systematics, Diversity, and Germplasm." In L. Knutson and A. K. Stoner, eds., *Biotic Diversity and Germplasm Preservation, Global Imperatives*. See Gámez 1989.

Montgomery, C. A., and R. A. Pollack. 1996. "Economics and Biodiversity: Weighing Benefits and Costs of Conservation," *Journal of Forestry* 94 (2): 34–8.

Myers, N. 1986. "Forestland Farming in Western Amazonia: Stable and Sustainable," *Forest Ecology and Management* 15: 81–93.

———.1991. "Man's Future Needs the Beasts." In M. H. Robinson and L. Tiger, eds., *Man and Beast Revisited*. Washington, D.C.: Smithsonian Institution Press.

Nair, P. K. 1991. "State-of-the-art of Agroforestry Systems," *Forest Ecology and Management* 45: 5–29.

Nations, J. D., and D. I. Komer. 1983. "Central America's Tropical Rainforests: Positive Steps for Survival," *AMBIO* 12 (5): 232–38.

Nepstad, D. C., C. Uhl, and E.A.S. Serrão. 1991. "Recuperation of a Degraded Amazonian Landscape: Forest Recovery and Agricultural Restoration," *AMBIO* 20 (6): 248–55.

Norman, M. J. T. 1979. *Annual Cropping Systems in the Tropics: An Introduction*. Gainesville: University Presses of Florida.

NRC (National Research Council). 1990. *The Improvement of Tropical and Subtropical Rangelands*. Washington, D.C.: National Academy Press, NRC.

———.1993a. *Managing Global Genetic Resources: Agricultural Crop Issues and Policies*. Washington, D.C.: National Academy of Sciences, NRC.

———.1993b. *Sustainable Agriculture and the Environment in the Humid Tropics*. Washington, D.C.: National Academy of Sciences, NRC.

Padoch, C. 1988. "Aguaje (Mauritia flexuosa L. f.) in the Economy of Iquitos, Peru," *Advances in Economic Botany* 6: 214–24.

Padoch, C., and W. de Jong, 1991. "The House Gardens of Santa Rosa: Diversity and Variability in an Amazonian Agricultural System," *Economic Botany* 45 (2): 166–75.

Padoch, C., J. Chota Inuma, W. de Jong, and J. Unruh. 1985. "Amazonian Agroforestry: A Market-Oriented System in Peru," *Agroforestry Systems* 3: 47–58.

Pagiola, S. 1995. "Environmental and Natural Resource Degradation in Intensive Agriculture in Bangladesh."

World Bank, Environment Department Paper 15, Washington, D.C.

Parrotta, J. A. 1993. "Secondary Forest Regeneration on Degraded Tropical Lands: The Role of Plantations as 'Foster Ecosystems.'" In H. Lieth and M. Lohmann, eds., *Restoration of Tropical Forest Ecosystems*. Amsterdam: Kluwer.

Parsons, J. J. 1969. "Ridged Fields in the Rio Guayas Valley, Ecuador," *American Antiquity* 34 (1): 76–80.

———.1986. "Now This Matter of Cultural Geography: Notes From Carl Sauer's Last Seminar at Berkeley." In M. Kenzer, ed., *Carl O. Sauer: A Tribute*. Corvalis: Oregon State University Press.

———.1989. "Forest to Pasture: Development or Destruction." In W. M. Denevan, ed., *Hispanic Lands and Peoples: Selected Writings of James J. Parsons*. Boulder, Colo.: Westview Press.

———.1991. "Giant American Bamboo in the Vernacular Architecture of Colombia and Ecuador," *Geographical Review* 81 (2): 131–52.

Parsons, J. J., and W. A. Bowen. 1966. "Ancient Ridged Fields of the San Jorge River Floodplain, Colombia," *Geographical Review* 56 (3): 317–43.

Peters, W. J., and L. F. Neuenschwander. 1988. *Slash and Burn Farming in the Third World Forest*. Moscow: University of Idaho Press.

Pimm, S. L., 1984. "The Complexity and Stability of Ecosystems," *Nature* 307 (5949): 321–26.

———.1991. *The Balance of Nature? Ecological Issues in the Conservation of Species and Communities*. Chicago: University of Chicago Press.

Pimm, S. L., and J. L. Gittleman. 1992. "Biological Diversity: Where Is It?" *Science* 255: 940.

Plucknett, D. L. 1979. *Managing Pastures and Cattle under Coconuts*. Boulder, Colo.: Westview Press.

Plucknett, D. L., and M. E. Horne. 1992. "Conservation of Genetic Resources," *Agriculture, Ecosystems, and Environment* 42: 75–92.

Porter, V. 1993. *Pigs: A Handbook to the Breeds of the World*. Ithaca, N.Y.: Cornell University Press.

Qualset, C. O., A. B. Damania, A. C. A. Zanatta, and S. B. Brush. In press. "Locally Based Crop Plant Conservation." In N. Maxted and others, eds., *Plant Conservation: The In Situ Approach*. London: Chapman and Hall.

Rege, J. E. O. 1994. "International Livestock Center Preserves Africa's Declining Wealth of Animal Biodiversity," *Diversity* 10 (3): 21–25.

Revkin, Andrew. 1990. *The Burning Season: The Murder of Chico Mendes and the Fight for the Amazon Rain Forest*. Boston: Houghton Mifflin.

Roger, P. A., K. L. Heong, and P. S. Teng. 1991. "Biodiversity and Sustainability of Wetland Rice Production: Role and Potential of Microorganisms and Invertebrates." In D. L. Hawksworth, ed., *The Biodiversity of Microorganisms and Invertebrates: Its Role in Sustainable Agriculture*. See Altieri 1991.

Ruddle, K. 1974. *The Yupka Cultivation System: A Study of Shifting Cultivation in Colombia and Venezuela*.

Berkeley: University of California Press.

Rudel, T. K., and B. Horowitz. 1993. *Tropical Deforestation: Small Farmers and Land Clearing in the Ecuadorian Amazon.* New York: Columbia University Press.

Ruthenberg, H. 1980. *Farming Systems in the Tropics.* Oxford: Clarendon Press.

Salazar, J. J. 1973. "Effects of Crossing Brahman and Charolais Bulls on Native Breeds in Colombia." In M. Koger, T. J. Cunha, and A. C. Warnick, eds., *Crossbreeding Beef Cattle.* Series 2. Gainesville: University of Florida Press.

Sauer, J. D. 1979. "Living Fences in Costa Rican Agriculture," *Turrialba* 29 (4): 255–61.

———.1988. *Plant Migration: The Dynamics of Geographic Patterning in Seed Plant Species.* Berkeley: University of California Press.

Schneider, R. 1994. *Government and the Economy on the Amazon Frontier.* World Bank Environment Paper no. 11. Washington, D.C.

Seré, C., and L. S. Jarvis. 1992. "Livestock Economy and Forest Destruction." In T. E. Downing, S. B. Hecht, H. A. Pearson, and C. Garcia-Downing, eds., *Development or Destruction: The Conversion of Tropical Forest to Pasture in Latin America.* See Hecht 1992b.

Serrão, E. A. S. 1989. "Pecuária na Amazônia: a evolução da sustentabilidade das pastagens substituindo florestas," *Pará Desenvolvimento* 25: 117–27.

Siemens, A. H. 1983. "Wetland Agriculture in Pre-Hispanic Mesoamerica," *Geographical Review* 73 (2): 166–81.

———.1995. "Land-Use Succession in the Gulf Lowlands of Mexico." In B. L. Turner II, A. Gómez, F. González, and F. Castri, eds., *Global Land Use Change: A Perspective from the Columbian Encounter.* Madrid: Consejo Superior de Investigaciones Científicas.

Siskind, Janet. 1973. *To Hunt in the Morning.* London: Oxford University Press.

Skole, D. L., W. H. Chomentowski, W. A. Salas, and A. D. Nobre. 1994. "Physical and Human Dimensions of Deforestation in Amazonia," *Bioscience* 44 (5): 314–22.

Sluyter, A. 1994. "Intensive Wetland Agriculture in Mesoamerica: Space, Time, and Form," *Annals of the Association of American Geographers* 84 (4): 557–84.

Smale, M., P. W. Heisey, D. Byerlee, and E. Souza. 1995. "The Private Cost of Genetic Diversity in Farmers' Fields." Paper presented at the Annual Meetings of the American Agricultural Economics Association, 7–9 August, Indianapolis.

Smith, N. J. H. 1982. *Rainforest Corridors.* Berkeley: University of California Press.

———.1990. "Strategies for Sustainable Agriculture in the Humid Tropics," *Ecological Economics* 2: 311–23.

———.1995. "Human-Induced Landscape Changes in Amazonia and Implications for Development." In B. L. Turner II, A. Gómez, Fernando González, F. Castri, eds., *Global Land Use Change: A Perspective from the Columbian Encounter.* See Siemens 1995.

Smith, N. J. H., J. T. Williams, D. L. Plucknett, and J. P. Talbot. 1992. *Tropical Forests and Their Crops.* Ithaca,

N.Y.: Cornell University Press.

Smith, N. J. H., E. A. S. Serrão, P. Alvim, and I. C. Falesi. 1995. *Amazonia: Resiliency and Dynamism of the Land and its People.* Tokyo: United Nations University Press.

Smith, N. J. H., T. J. Fik, P. Alvim, I. C. Falesi, and E. A. S. Serrão. 1995. "Agroforestry Developments and Potential in the Brazilian Amazon," *Land Degradation and Rehabilitation* 6: 251–63.

Sponsel, L. E. 1986. "Amazon Ecology and Adaptation," *Annual Review of Anthropology* 15: 67–97.

Stakman, E. C., R. Bradfield, and P. C. Mangelsdorf. 1967. *Campaigns Against Hunger.* Cambridge, Mass.: Belknap Press of Harvard University.

Sternberg, H. O'R. 1973. "Development and Conservation," *Erdkunde* 27 (4): 253–65.

Stewart, D. I. 1994. *After the Trees: Living on the Transamazon Highway.* Austin: University of Texas Press.

Toledo, V. M., B. Ortiz, and S. Medellín. 1994. "Biodiversity Islands in a Sea of Pasturelands: Indigenous Resource Management in the Humid Tropics of Mexico," *Etnoecológica* 2 (3): 37–49.

Torres-Lima, P., B. Canabal-Cristiani, and G. Burela-Rueda. 1994. "Urban Sustainable Agriculture: The Paradox of the Chinampa System in Mexico City," *Agriculture and Human Values* 11 (1): 37–46.

Thrupp, L. A., G. Bergeron, and W. F. Waters. 1995. *Bittersweet Harvests for Global Supermarkets: Challenges in Latin America's Agricultural Export Boom.* Washington, D.C.: World Resources Institute.

Turner, II, B. L. 1974. "Prehistoric Intensive Agriculture in the Maya Lowlands," *Science* 185: 118–24.

Uquillas, J., A. Ramírez, and C. Seré. 1992. "Are Modern Agroforestry Practices Economically Viable? A Case Study in the Ecuadorian Amazon." In G. Sullivan, S. Huke, and J. Fox, eds., *Financial and Economic Analysis of Agroforestry Systems.* Honolulu: East-West Center.

Valverde, O. 1971. "Shifting Cultivation in Brazil: Ideas on a New Land Policy," *Heidelberger Geographische Arbeiten* 34: 1–14.

Verdade, F. 1974. *Problemas de Fertilidade do Solo na Amazonia.* Cadernos de Ciências da Terra, No. 53. Universidade de São Paulo, Instituto de Geografia.

Vincent, J. R., and Y. Hadi. 1993. "Malaysia." In *Sustainable Agriculture and the Environment in the Humid Tropics.* Washington, D.C.: National Academy Press, National Research Council.

Waage, J. K. 1991. "Biodiversity as a Resource for Biological Control." In D. L. Hawksworth, ed., *The Biodiversity of Microorganisms and Invertebrates: Its Role in Sustainable Agriculture.* See Altieri 1991.

Watters, R. F. 1971. *Shifting Cultivation in Latin America.* Forestry Development Paper 17. FAO. Rome.

Weischet, W., and C. N. Caviedes. 1993. *The Persisting Ecological Constraints of Tropical Agriculture.* Harlow: Longman Scientific and Technical.

Westoby, Jack. 1989. *Introduction to World Forestry.*

Oxford: Basil Blackwell.

Wilbanks, T. J. 1994. "'Sustainable Development' in Geographic Perspective," *Annals of the Association of American Geographers* 84: 541–56.

Wilcox, B. A., and K. N. Duin. 1995. "Indigenous Cultural and Biological Diversity: Overlapping Values of Latin American Ecoregions," *Cultural Survival Quarterly* (Winter): 51–3.

Wilken, G. C. 1969. "Drained-field Agriculture: An Intensive Farming System in Tlaxcala, Mexico," *Geographical Review* 59: 215–41.

Wilkes, G. 1989. "Germplasm Preservation: Objectives and Needs." In L. Knutson and A. K. Stoner, eds., *Biotic Diversity and Germplasm Preservation, Global Imperatives.* See Gámez 1989.

Wood, D. 1993. *Agrobiodiversity in Global Conservation Policy.* Biopolicy International Series No. 11. African Centre for Technology Studies (ACTS). Nairobi.

World Bank. 1991. *Environmental Assessment Sourcebook, Volume II: Sectoral Guidelines.* Washington, D.C.

Zimmerer, K. S. 1991. "Managing Diversity in Potato and Maize Fields of the Peruvian Andes," *Journal of Ethnobiology* 11 (1): 23–49.

———.1995. "The Origins of Andean Irrigation," *Nature* 378: 481–83.

5. Effects of Agricultural Development on Biodiversity: Lessons from Iowa

*Gordon L. Bultena, Michael D. Duffy, Steven E. Jungst,
Ramesh S. Kanwar, Bruce W. Menzel, Manjit K. Misra,
Piyush Singh, Janette R. Thompson, Arnold van der Valk,
and Richard L. Willham*

Numerous ecological studies have shown that human population growth is forcing many plant and animal species into extinction. Communities of all living organisms, such as those found in prairies, marshes, woodlands, and lakes, interact in many ways with their surrounding environments. A recent report of the 1995 UN Conference on Biodiversity in Indonesia found that human population growth and economic development are depleting the planet's biological resources. Although environmental awareness is growing, damage to global biodiversity continues. More than 30,000 plant and animal species face possible extinction worldwide and some forty to a hundred species become extinct every day.

Trends in biodiversity, population, and development in Iowa are quite similar to those observed on a global scale. In 1780 about 1,200 American Indians lived in Iowa (Torrell 1971). Iowa's population rose from 10,500 in 1836 to 97,000 in 1846. Today Iowa's population is close to 2.8 million (Legislative Fiscal Bureau 1995). Similarly dramatic increases in human population in some 150 years have driven the destruction of many of the most productive natural ecosystems of the world.

This chapter presents the status of natural habitats and biodiversity in Iowa before and after European settlement. Both the positive and negative effects of past and current agricultural practices on biodiversity and related socioeconomic and policy issues are discussed. Policy implications of Iowa's experience with agricultural development and biodiversity management are also examined. Some of the positive effects on biodiversity that can be achieved with various management systems in current agricultural production systems are also highlighted in this chapter.

Natural Habitats in Presettlement Iowa

Iowa was once covered by vast prairie grasslands and open savannas. Thick woodlands bordered many of the state's rivers and streams. A large variety of wildlife lived in its prairies, woodlands, and wetlands. The total land area of Iowa—about 36 million acres—and prairies, including prairie wetlands, covered more than 30 million acres of the landscape in presettlement times (Hayden 1945; Shimek 1911).

The landscape was characterized by smooth and gently rolling plains with soils derived from glacial deposits. Most of the area was covered with deep deposits of finely divided glacial and wind-blown material. Modern soils were chiefly formed under prairie conditions over till, loess, paleosols, and bedrock, primarily limestone. Prairie soils characterized by deep topsoil were rich in humus, nitrogen, and minerals conducive for plant growth. These soils also tended to be poorly drained and included wetlands in areas of low relief. It is generally believed that prairies persisted because of fire, despite the long-term climatic change to cooler and more humid conditions. Prairie plants were deeply rooted and thus capable of withstanding periodic drought and fire, whereas trees were vulnerable to both.

The exact composition of the prairies of Iowa's past is not known because many plant and animal species may have disappeared before their presence was ever recorded. Nonetheless, the state's remaining prairie areas can give us a glimpse of what Iowa looked like about 150 years ago. The prairie was a complex of native grasses (such as big bluestem, Indiangrass, bluejoint reedgrass, and coarse prairie cordgrass), legumes, and flowering plants. Iowa's prairies provided habitat for such wild flowers as purple prairie clover, compass plant, and black-eyed Susan. Shimek (1931) documented 265 plant species as the bulk of Iowa's prairie flora, although the total number of plant species that originally grew in the state's prairies was probably closer to 400. Plant community structure and species distribution depended on topography and soil characteristics (Crist and Glenn-Lewin 1978). Many animals lived on the prairies, including dozens of mammals, birds, reptiles, and insects. Meadow voles, bobolinks, and box turtles were among the animals that made their homes in Iowa's prairies.

In eastern Iowa trees flourished on the uplands as well as along streams. These woodlands were home to a wide variety of trees, shrubs, and wild flowers. Iowa's upland forests were dominated by large oaks, hickories, and walnut trees, whereas cottonwood, maple, and green ash characterized lowland forests. Western Iowa had fewer trees. Even the timber along the streams was thin and meager along the western boundary of the state (Peterson and Englehorn 1946). Thus in its natural condition Iowa was in a transition zone between the arid, grassy plains to the west and the subhumid, deciduous forests to the east. On an annual basis the state was wettest and warmest in the southeast and driest and coldest in the northwest.

Abundant wetlands, riparian forests bordering Iowa's rivers and streams, and prairie potholes supported diverse plant and animal life. Prairie wetlands that dotted the landscape of much of north-central Iowa were among the most productive ecosystems in the world. Some unusual plants, such as the fly-eating sundew plant and duckweed, the world's smallest flowering plant, could be found only in wetlands.

Iowa wetlands were home to frogs, salamanders, muskrats, ducks, and turtles. As many as 250 species of animals, including black bear, wolves, bison, wapiti, and mountain lion, once made homes in Iowa's native vegetation (INAI 1984). Similarly, many bird, amphibian and reptile, fish, and invertebrate species were abundant before people settled in Iowa.

Effects of Presettlement Cultures and the Pioneer Era on Biodiversity

By 2000 B.C. various native cultures flourished in the part of the world later to be known as Iowa. Archeological evidence suggests that several societies flourished in the state, primarily associated with major rivers. These cultures were largely based on hunting and fishing, but they were also the first farmers in Iowa. Crops of maize, beans, squash, and sunflower were raised a millennium ago.

In historical times at least seventeen native tribes occupied Iowa. Torrell (1971) reported an estimate of 1,200 American Indians living in Iowa in 1780. As in the case of their ancestors indigenous cultures of the eighteenth century were based on hunting, gathering, and limited agriculture. Native American farmers began cultivating small tracts of land on the river flood plains. They used fire to clear their land as well as to enhance their ability to hunt buffalo, deer, and elk. Fire destroyed the woody plant growth and made hoeing and digging easier. It also enabled new shoots of grass to easily emerge from the soil after the winter. Native Americans first altered Iowa's natural environment with fire, which affected not only plant growth but also the composition of plant communities. They also began to change the area's biodiversity by adding plants that they cultivated for food. The most significant plant introductions that altered Iowa's biodiversity were maize (both flint and dent), beans, squash, sunflower, and tobacco.

In the late 1600s French explorers and fur traders were the first Europeans to penetrate Iowa. Skins of beaver, mink, and other fur bearers were taken by the French or obtained by trade with natives to supply European fashion markets. Although several European states claimed title to Iowa and its neighboring areas through the 1700s, the environmental repercussions of these claims were minimal until the nineteenth century. In 1800 Napoleon reclaimed lands west of the Mississippi from Spain and sold them to the United States in 1803 as the Louisiana Purchase. For most of the next thirty years Iowa and other western territories were regarded as Indian land by the federal government and remained largely free of settlement. Beginning in the 1820s, however, various treaties with the natives began ceding the western lands to the government.

Encouraged by the availability of inexpensive land ($1.25 an acre), settlers began flooding across the Mississippi River in the early 1830s from eastern states into what was then part of the Michigan Territory. Iowa subsequently became part of the Wisconsin Territory (1836 to 1838), the Iowa Territory (1838 to 1846), and finally Iowa became the twenty-ninth state in 1846. Although the first settlers were from the eastern United States, pioneers soon arrived from Europe, especially from Denmark, Germany, Holland, Norway, and Sweden. Each group brought its own approach to agriculture and tended to settle in different parts of the state.

The pace of settlement in Iowa was remarkable. U.S. Census statistics for 1836 recorded a total non-native population of 10,531; ten years later, more than 90,000, mostly engaged in farming. In 1860 the Census reported nearly 675,000 citizens (Dinsmore 1994). Initially, settlement was primarily confined to the borders of the Mississippi River. The first pioneers, accustomed to farming in forestlands of the eastern United States, tended to establish their claims in the woodlands of eastern Iowa. Prairie areas were habitually avoided for settlement because of the lack of useful timber, the threat of fire in summer and deep snow in winter, and difficulty in breaking the thick sod. However, the prairies and the larger interior rivers did permit relatively rapid travel, and settlers quickly spread throughout the state. By the time of the Civil War in 1861 nearly all of Iowa's present ninety-nine counties had at least a few settlers. The last county to be settled, in northwestern Iowa, had its first permanent residents in 1871 (Dinsmore 1994). Thus the pioneer era in Iowa spanned approximately four decades.

Agricultural Development and Habitat Loss

Habitat destruction has been by far the greatest contributor to Iowa's loss of biodiversity. Although agricultural development is considered the main cause, other human activities, such as railroad construction, also contributed to the decline of natural habitat. Many plants and animals disappeared along with the loss of habitat because they were an integral part of the natural ecosystems. One hundred plant species are considered endangered in Iowa, while 52 are threatened, 61 are presumed extirpated, and 25 are of undetermined status (INAI 1984). Among animals 37 species are endangered, 35 are threatened, 29 are locally extinct, and 12 are of undetermined status. The Indiana bat, bald eagle, peregrine falcon, Iowa Pleistocene snail, Higgins' eye pearly mussel, and fat pocketbook pearly mussel are Iowa species listed by the U.S. Fish and Wildlife Service as federally endangered (INAI 1984). Habitat destruction from farming was especially pronounced in forests, prairie land, and wetlands. Loss of habitat and biodiversity in each ecosystem is discussed separately in the following sections.

Effects on Forests and Their Biodiversity

Agriculture's main assault on the natural habitats of Iowa began with settlers during the early 1830s. Iowa's forests were the first to go. Trees provided wood for building homes, fences, and other structures. Wood was also in demand to provide heat for homes and later to fuel steamships. From 1830 to 1850 about 7.6 percent of Iowa's land was converted to farm land (table 5.1). Iowa's forests were quickly cleared to grow crops. The pioneers believed that soil under prairie was not fit for cultivation. Also, there were no means for plowing the thick prairie sod.

During the 1832–75 period Iowa's forested area decreased from more than 6.6 million acres to less than 2.6 million acres, and by 1974 forested area had shrunk to about 1.6 million acres (IAN 1992; Ostrom 1976). The most recent inventory, conducted by the U.S. Forest Service in 1990, shows an increase of 500,000 acres in total forest acreage compared to 1974 inventory (Brand and Walkowiak 1991).

Table 5.1 Major trends in Iowa's agricultural history

Period	Farmland as percentage of total land area	Average farm size (acres)	Major agricultural developments
1850s	7.6	185	Use of steel moldboard plow to break prairie sod.
1880s	69.1	134	Expansion in farmland.
1900s	96.5	151	Tile drainage; small-farm equipment (for example, seed drill binder and shellers).
1930s	94.0	158	Livestock production begins; rapid mechanization of farms, especially tractors; ammonia synthesized and applied as nitrogen fertilizer; soil conservation practices begin.
1940s	95.3	162	Advances in genetic research to produce hybrid maize.
1950s	95.3	175	Use of synthetic organic pesticides and increased use of nitrogen fertilizers; ecosystem disaster era.
1970s	95.5	265	Ecosystem disaster era until 1985.
1990s	93.0	322	Ecosystem awakening continues from 1985.

Source: USDA 1995; Iowa Farm Bureau Federation 1995; Murray 1946.

Much of the recent increase in forest cover is because of a decline in the cattle industry between 1974 and 1990. Land with tree cover is not included as forest land by the U.S. Forest Service if it is being grazed because cattle cause soil compaction, a reduction in the number of understory species, and the loss of natural vegetation. Although land with tree cover has been reclassified as forest, in most cases biodiversity has been severely reduced.

Today nearly all of Iowa's forest lands are privately owned (figure 5.1). Because the preponderance of forest land belongs to private landowners, it is reasonable to expect that most of the effects on forest land over the past 150 years have been a result of agricultural activities. Throughout the early history of Iowa and continuing to the 1970s, forests were logged to clear land for pasture or cultivation.

Although the dimension of forest loss is difficult to determine precisely because of differences in methods used in 1832 and 1990, figures show the magnitude—approximately two-thirds of forest cover is now gone. The remaining forests have also been altered by human activities. Although the number of tree species throughout the state has not declined, fragmentation of forest coverage has lead to a reduction in the natural "transferability" of genetic variation among trees. More and more frequently, forests exist as small islands within a sea of cultivated land. This island effect reduces the transfer of genetic traits among trees and causes loss of diversity because the remaining small populations are in isolated patches.

The island effect also reduces the preferred habitat of wildlife species that seek interior-type habitat. Large predators (such as wolves, cougars, and black bears that were once native to Iowa) need vast, continuous tracts of forest cover for hunting. They could not survive in fragmented and disturbed forest ecosystems. However, the small islands or patches of natural ecosystems are suitable for a variety of plants (trees, shrubs, wildflowers) and wildlife species that prefer edge-type habitat. A large variety of birds and small animals, such as squirrels, raccoons, rabbits, and occasionally white-tailed deer, rely on small patches of woodland (Johnson, Beck, and Brandle 1994).

Biodiversity is also reduced when cattle graze in wooded areas. Cattle grazing greatly reduces the biodiversity of understory plants in the forest as well as inhibiting natural regeneration of the forest. If grazing continues for a long enough period, the combination of loss of natural

Figure 5.1 Ownership of timberland in Iowa, 1990

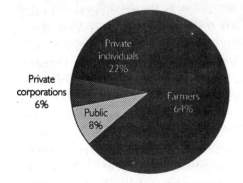

Source: Brand and Walkowiak 1991.

regeneration and soil compaction ultimately leads to a complete loss of forest cover. Even if cattle are only grazed for a few years, biodiversity of the forest is affected for many years. The most significant is a reduction in understory diversity and a shift from species that are "desirable" for such things as timber production, wildlife habitat, and recreation to species that are generally "undesirable." Species in this category include Honey Locust (*Gleditsia triacanthos*), Prickly Ash (*Zanthoxylum Americanum*), and Multiflora Rose (*Rosa multiflora*).

Effects on Prairies and Their Biodiversity

The tough sod of prairies was the main obstacle to their agricultural development. Plows of the early 1800s were useless against the thick network of plant roots, but introduction of the steel moldboard plow in the 1850s finally made it possible to plow the grasslands. The advent of this improved technology also signaled the prairie's end. Iowa's prairie was essentially gone by the end of the nineteenth century. Thirty million acres of prairie were quickly converted to farm land at a pace of about 2 million acres a year (see table 5.1). Recent inventories indicate that only about 30,000 acres of prairie remain. Of this area about 5,000 acres are in state-owned preserves. Hayden Prairie, a 240-acre tract located in Howard County, is among the largest of the state-owned preserves. Other small unprotected prairie remnants persist along railroad rights-of-way, in areas cut off from cultivated ground by roads or railroads, in old cemeteries and prairie hayfields, on steep slopes, or as fringes around other natural areas (Thompson 1992). These remnants are too small to affect the biodiversity in surrounding agricultural fields.

Drastic reduction of total prairie area and breakup of the original contiguous prairie have resulted in lower plant species diversity on remaining prairies, less genetic diversity of remaining plant species, and fewer animal species that inhabit the prairie (especially forms that had coevolved with specific relationships to plants, such as butterflies, that are critical pollinators). Iowa's prairie ecosystems not only provided a suitable habitat for plant and animal diversity but also helped to build and maintain the productivity of the soils as well as control noxious weeds.

A recent experimental study has demonstrated that plant diversity in grassland ecosystems improves productivity and promotes more efficient nutrient use and better nutrient retention (Tilman, Wedin, and Knops 1996). Thus prairie communities should be used as a model to design more productive agricultural systems that maintain or improve ecosystem characteristics; for example, use of perennial polyculture or prairie fallow periods to protect or enhance soil properties (Drake 1978). Prairie communities are already being used in roadside management programs to control weeds effectively, without the economic and ecological costs associated with mowing or spraying herbicides. Prairie corridors stretching across agricultural landscapes may also contribute to gene flow for both plant and animal species.

The rich genetic resource represented by the remaining hundreds of prairie plants has been largely untapped. The prairie community represents thousands of years of natural selection, hence a renewable source that is well adapted to local climatic and edaphic conditions and very productive in terms of total annual biomass. These features of the prairie community merit additional attention and add to the value of prairie ecosystems as a part of the Iowa landscape.

Effects on Wetlands and Their Biodiversity

During the early 1900s subsurface drains were installed in prairie marshes and wetlands, which were especially abundant in north-central Iowa. A large proportion of the wetlands had been drained in this manner by 1915 (Peterson and Englehorn 1946). Although lakes, streams, and reservoirs are all classified as wetlands, marshes and overflow wetlands are the most diverse and the most productive wildlife ecosystems. About 7.6 million acres of prairie-marsh habitat once covered north-central and northwestern Iowa. In about 100 years Iowa's natural marshes were reduced to about 26,000 acres (IAN 1992).

The drainage of wetlands and their subsequent degradation because of sediment and nutrients in agricultural runoff (the major source of water for many of the remaining wetlands) has resulted in a number of direct and indirect changes in Iowa's fauna and flora. The direct effect has been local extinction of numerous plant species, such as whitetop and wild rice, as well as several animal species, including the trumpeter swan, the marbled godwit, the long-billed curlew, and the common loon. Many other plants and animals adapted to wetlands have suffered significant reduction in range because of habitat degradation or destruction. About eighty-five wetland plant species are now rare and restricted to only a few sites (Galatowitsch and van der Valk 1994). Many animals have suffered the same fate (Dinsmore 1994).

Indirect effects of agriculture include a significant degradation of the remaining wetlands and a subsequent loss of species from them. One of the most profound changes has been the spread of cattail, which now dominates these wetlands. Higher nutrient levels in the remaining wetlands probably account for the cattail's proliferation. Agricultural activities have also resulted in the introduction of alien plants that have become a nuisance in wetlands. Reed canary grass, planted to stabilize drainage canal banks, now dominates the wet meadow zones in many Iowa wetlands, displacing a host of native species. This wetland habitat degradation has also had adverse effects on many animal populations.

The benefits of wetlands in agricultural landscapes have recently been widely recognized. Not only do they provide a habitat for diverse plant and animal communities, but they also function as natural filters, removing nutrients and sediments from agricultural runoff and preventing floods. Many wetlands in Iowa have consequently been restored. For example, the Clean Water Alliance in the Iowa Great Lakes region has restored wetlands around the lakes to reduce nutrient inputs. This is providing a unique opportunity to reestablish wetland species and to increase biodiversity in a way that is congruent with agricultural interests.

Effects of Mechanization and Farming Practices on Biodiversity

Changes in farm practices, particularly the use of large machinery and the introduction of tractor power during the past fifty years, have destroyed most of the natural areas that existed in Iowa before World War II. As large farm equipment became available, Iowa farmers were able to cultivate larger areas with row crops. The landscape slowly changed from a series of small fields surrounded by brushy fence rows and grassland pastures to vast areas of nearly uninterrupted cropland. Farm size initially averaged about 185 acres but dropped to about 134 acres during 1870s, as farmers realized that they did not have the technology and resources to cultivate all the land. Today the average farm size in Iowa is about 322 acres (see table 5.1) and is likely to increase.

Rapid farm mechanization resulted in a drastic reduction of hours of labor required for agricultural and livestock production. From 1915 to 1919, for example, about thirty-four hours of labor were required per acre for maize production. Between 1982 and 1986 this figure was reduced to about three hours (table 5.2).

The rapid mechanization of farms and the resulting reduced labor inputs triggered a major population shift from rural to urban areas. The proportion of Iowa's population living in rural areas declined from about 70 percent to 40 percent between 1910 and 1990.

Farm produce from Iowa was in great demand during World War II, and farmers were

Table 5.2 Hours of labor for agricultural and livestock production

Year	Maize (per acre)	Soybean (per acre)	Maize (per 100 bushels)	Soybean (per 100 bushels)	Hogs (per 100 lb.)	Cattle (per 100 lb.)
1915–19	34.2	19.9	132	143	3.6	4.5
1925–29	30.3	15.9	115	126	3.3	4.3
1935–39	28.1	11.8	108	64	3.2	4.2
1945–49	19.2	8.0	53	41	3.0	4.0
1955–59	9.9	5.2	20	23	2.4	3.2
1965–69	5.8	4.8	7	19	1.4	2.1
1975–79	3.6	3.7	4	12	0.5	1.3
1982–86	3.1	3.2	3	10	0.3	0.9

Source: USDA 1983, 1994, and 1995.

Table 5.3 Percentage of farmland acres by crop in Iowa

Year	Maize	Maize yields[a]	Soybean	Hay	Oats	Other
1910	28	41.5	0	14	15	43
1920	28	46.0	0	11	18	43
1930	29	34.0	0	10	19	42
1940	25	52.5	2	13	15	45
1950	27	48.5	6	11	19	37
1960	36	63.5	8	10	12	34
1970	30	86.0	17	7	5	41
1980	40	110.0	25	7	3	25
1990	37	126.0	24	6	2	31
1994	39	152.0	27	5	2	27

a. In bushels per acre.
Source: USDA 1983, 1994, and 1995.

urged to cultivate as much land as possible. The main crops grown included maize, soybean, oats, alfalfa, sweet clover, and red clover. Similarly, the opening of world markets in the 1970s propelled Iowa to the status of "the bread basket of the world," which further increased the value of farmland. The conversion of wetlands and woodlands to farmland became economically feasible.

Iowa agriculture has been rapidly transformed from an enterprise characterized by diversity into one based on specialization and monoculture production. For example, livestock were once common on Iowa farms, but a majority of farms today have no cattle, horses, or pigs. Considerable crop diversity and complex crop rotations once prevailed, but today most farmers plant only two or three crops and practice simple two-crop rotations involving maize and soybeans (table 5.3). About 90 percent of the cropland is devoted to just two crops—maize and soybean.

A constant flow of innovative agricultural practices and technologies, coupled with powerful economic forces (such as international banking, credit, and marketing), federal farm policies, and dominant societal values, have driven the dramatic changes in farming patterns. Modern farming patterns are neither particularly attuned to preservation of natural landscapes nor to the promotion of biodiversity.

Effects of Livestock Industry on Biodiversity

Settlers brought stock of diverse genetic origin to Iowa. By the late 1800s, however, breeds of stock were being imported because they were perceived as being ideal for commercial agricul-

ture. A breed is a group of animals that has resulted from selection for a desirable type and subsequent intense inbreeding among the best to fix the type.

Use-specification of stock was concurrent with breed formation. Thus one finds dairy and beef breeds in cattle, light and draft breeds in horses, mutton and wool breeds in sheep, egg and broiler breeds in poultry, and lard and bacon breeds in swine. Swine breeds used in Iowa were developed primarily in the United States, but European breeds were imported for the other livestock species. Commercial herds and flocks developed by using males of a breed repeatedly, called *grading up*. So intense was the use of these breeds by grading up that the well-adapted indigenous stock was lost. Iowa agriculture developed with five dairy, three beef, five horse, six swine, five sheep, and six poultry breeds.

With the advent of hybridization of maize in the 1930s stock breeders also tried to obtain crossbreeding (heterosis) in commercial production. Inbred lines of maize are crossed, but except for poultry, inbreeding before crossing was too costly. Researchers then demonstrated that the crossing of breeds produced economically important heterosis. Commercial swine, sheep, and beef cattle are crossbred. Holsteins dominate milk production at the expense of other dairy breeds. Poultry is vertically integrated, using inbred-line crosses for either egg or broiler production. Swine production is beginning to emulate poultry, including specialized breeding companies. Beef producers have many breeds to select from, especially since the late 1960s when importation was possible from continental Europe. The genetic diversity of poultry, dairy, sheep, and swine in Iowa has thus declined dramatically. Horses have maintained their breed diversity, but genetic variation within breeds has suffered because of smaller populations.

Two schools of thought have emerged on the need to maintain a diverse genetic base within livestock species. According to the first school of thought, diversity in the genetic base is essential if resource bases are expected to shift quickly. But the second school of thought holds that the genetic base is sufficient to move the species toward new adaptations fast enough. It is expensive to maintain a broad genetic base in the animal species, but with new technologies it may be economically feasible to achieve this goal.

Effects of Water Use and Drainage Developments on Biodiversity

Iowa's natural drainage network includes two major river systems. Streams in the northern and eastern two-thirds of the state flow to the Mississippi River, whereas the Missouri River drains in western and south-central Iowa. Most of the streams are warm water, but spring-fed, cold water streams flow in the northeast. Early accounts describe the north-central and eastern streams as being of permanent and clear water, while those of the west tended to be more intermittent and carried greater sediment loads.

Although irrigation needs were minimal, waterways posed problems for early settlers. Meandering streams would periodically flood farms and towns. Heavy rains caused curved sections of the rivers to scour out new channels. These natural changes made farming unpredictable and were a danger to farms and towns. Necessity of flood control and efforts to create navigational routes led to channelization and deepening of the Mississippi and Missouri Rivers.

Construction of navigation locks and dams wrought major changes to the Mississippi by creating a series of stair-step "pools." The Mississippi was also dredged to facilitate navigation. The meandering Missouri was channelized by building training structures, such as dikes and revetments; this channelization resulted in its narrowing and deepening. The nature of these mighty rivers was thus forever changed. The diverse habitats of these rivers was exchanged for straight channels to allow the unimpeded passage of barge traffic.

Dams along the rivers did create habitat for lake wildlife but also acted as barriers to migrating fish and formed reservoirs that collect silt. Dredging and stabilizing the banks of rivers also changed the environment for aquatic life. Channelization resulted in shorter courses and much less river habitat. At least 1,000 miles—and perhaps as much as 3,000 miles—of Iowa's streams and small rivers have been eliminated by straightening (Bulkley 1975). Destruction of adja-

cent wetlands also played a part in altering river habitat by speeding the removal of water from the land and quickening the current of rivers. The floods of 1993 in the midwestern United States probably best underscore the elusiveness of technical solutions once considered adequate for managing the state's water resources.

Drainage of wetlands for reclamation and conversion to crop land was especially pronounced in the early 1900s. In 1902 the Experiment Station at the State College in Ames declared that more than 4 million acres of land required drainage to improve agricultural production. Moreover, wetland drainage had exacerbated the problem of flooding.

The State Drainage, Waterways, and Conservation Commission was created in 1909 to further improve drainage of agricultural land, among other goals. The legislation provided for the establishment of drainage districts under the supervision of county governments. Such districts were formed by petition of neighboring farmers. County engineers assisted in drainage planning, and the state provided partial subsidies for construction work. The system permitted construction of buried communal drains so that even fields far removed from receiving streams could be drained by tilling.

The construction of mill dams also created adverse effects on wildlife. Virtually every prosperous pioneer farming community had a water-driven mill to grind local grain products or to cut lumber. In most cases this involved construction of a lowhead dam across the local river to divert water to the mill wheel. More than a thousand mill dams had been built by 1880. They had the unintentional side effect of blocking the migratory movements of fish and thus interfered with fish reproduction and other critical life activities. In 1874 a state commission was established to encourage construction of "fishways" over these dams.

Effects of Agricultural Management Systems

Historically, agricultural management systems have had negative effects on the environment and biodiversity. Growing environmental awareness has, however, led to improved management systems.

Negative effects on the environment and biodiversity. Agriculture has also seriously affected the biodiversity of the remaining natural ecosystems in the state. For a long time environmental concerns were essentially limited to soil erosion from plowed fields, which reduced soil fertility; siltation of lakes and streams; and loss of habitat for aquatic life.

The intensive use of agricultural chemicals created another serious environmental threat for biodiversity as well as for human health. The application of modern pesticides, introduced in the mid-1940s, soon became common practice. The industrial synthesis of ammonia in 1920s resulted in a cheap supply of nitrogen fertilizer; farmers responded by applying increasingly liberal amounts of the synthetic fertilizer, and crop yields increased dramatically (Schaller and Bailey 1983). In 1945 less than 0.2 lb. of nitrogen fertilizer was applied per acre to Iowa's croplands, but application rates rose to 144 lb. per acre by 1985. In 1995, 11.5 million acres of maize received nitrogen fertilizer. Further, 20.7 million acres of maize and soybeans received herbicide treatment.

The quality of surface and groundwater suffered because of the off-site impact of field-applied agricultural chemicals. Beginning in the 1950s, research slowly defined the nature of water quality problems caused by agricultural chemicals. Runoff from agricultural land was shown to be a major cause of surface water contamination from pesticides and other agricultural chemicals (Nicholson 1969). Similarly, many studies conducted in Iowa have shown that subsurface drainwater leaving agricultural watersheds carries agricultural chemicals into surface and groundwater sources (Baker and Laflen 1983; Kanwar, Colvin, and Karlen 1995).

Serious environmental concerns arise because of the adverse impact of agricultural chemicals and pesticides on the biodiversity of aquatic ecosystems. Toxic levels of some chemicals disrupt the flora and fauna of aquatic ecosystems. Excessive amounts of others in surface water bodies acclerate eutrophication. Water quality problems not only trigger biodiversity loss in aquatic ecosystems but also pose serious health problems for people, livestock, and wild animals (Schaller and Bailey 1983).

Effects of conservation efforts and improved management systems. Growing environmental awareness among farmers and implementation of government conservation programs have resulted in some reduction in the environmental degradation associated with agricultural practices and the restoration of some natural habitats to a healthier state so that they are once again attractive to wildlife.

Serious conservation efforts began in the 1930s, with the introduction of such soil conservation practices such as contouring, terracing, and tree planting in sloughs and gullies (Schwieder 1993). Legislation was introduced to study soil erosion in 1933, create the Soil Conservation Service in 1935, and create soil conservation districts.

By the 1980s farmers had become increasingly aware of the need for conservation and adopted several ameliorative practices, such as conservation tillage, crop rotation, strip cropping, and reduced application of agrochemicals. More comprehensive government conservation programs were also implemented during the 1980s, including the Conservation Reserve Program (CRP), Conservation Compliance, Sodbuster, and Swampbuster. In 1990 the Food, Agriculture, Conservation, and Trade Act added the Wetlands Reserve Program (WRP), with a target of improving conservation on 1 million acres.

On a national scale soil erosion was reduced on about 22 percent of the 37 million hectares under CRP. Six percent of CRP land is under trees, while another 6 percent has been set aside specifically for wildlife (Osborn 1993). Some 5,200 miles of buffer strips have been created along waterways as a result of CRP. WRP provides another option for enhancing biodiversity within agricultural landscapes. According to the U.S. Fish and Wildlife Service, because of various conservation practices of CRP and efforts under WRP, more than 900,000 acres of wetland systems have been affected (Lant, Kraft, and Gillman 1995). Wetland protection in agricultural areas has improved significantly in the last decade, although more work needs to be done (Robinson 1993).

Improved management systems. In the past fifteen to twenty years improved management systems have also been developed in Iowa to check soil erosion and reduce the loss of chemicals to water. In the process they are restoring habitat for wild plants and animals. For example, no-till and minimum-till farming leaves between 30 and 90 percent of crop residue on the surface, which reduces runoff volume, erosion, and chemical losses. Other advantages include reduced time and energy for field preparation. Conservation tillage systems are also more conducive to biological activity in the topsoil, increasing the populations of microbes, earthworms, and other living organisms in the soil (Kennedy and Papendick 1995).

Strip cropping, in which different crops are planted in alternate strips across the slope, also reduces soil erosion and pesticides in runoff. Some crops in strips may require fewer or no chemical inputs. Similarly, the use of terraces, detention ponds, constructed wetlands, buffer strips, vegetative filter strips, and grassed waterways in agricultural fields are enhancing the environment for wildlife and plant biodiversity.

Management systems initially designed for enhancing soil, water, and crop quality have thus enhanced biodiversity within agroecosystems (table 5.4). For example, strip cropping and wind breaks are reported to provide a suitable habitat for wildlife adapted to "edge" environments, including the northern oriole, American robin, the woodpecker, and introduced pheasant. These species thrive along the interface between habitats (Johnson, Beck, and Brandle 1994).

Forest land in Iowa is frequently managed for one or more of the following goods and services: timber, wildlife habitat, or recreation. Of the three, management for wildlife habitat would be most positive for biodiversity. As a management objective landowners would maintain a high level of plant diversity to attract a variety of wildlife. Recreation, if managed properly, could have little or no impact on biodiversity, but timber production would be expected to reduce biodiversity. In the case of timber production landowners usually favor a select group of high-value trees over other vegetation.

Efforts currently under way to create greater biodiversity through forestry activities center on

Table 5.4 Current agricultural management systems and their potential impact on biodiversity

	Impact on biodiversity	
Agricultural management system	*Field scale*	*Watershed scale*
Tillage and residue management		
Conventional tillage	D	D
Chisel plow	C	C
Ridge-tillage	B	B
No-tillage	B	B
Mulching	B	B
Soil conservation practices		
Contouring with conservation tillage	A	A
Strip cropping	A	A
Terracing	B	B
Wind breaks	A	A
Vegetative waterways	A	A
Crop management		
Crop rotations	B	A
Transgenic (weed-resistant) varieties	A	A
Tolerant varieties	A	A
Nutrient and chemical management		
Split or multiple application	B	A
Banding	B	A
Incorporating	B	A
Animal waste management	B	B
Pest management		
Biological control	B	B
Resistant cultivars	C	B
Early harvest and delayed planting	C	C
Insecticides	D	D
Crop rotations	B	A
Water management		
Irrigation (sprinkler, drip, flood)	C/D	C/D
Subsurface drainage	D	D
Water table management	C	C
Sediment control basins	C	B
Grade stabilization	B	B
Riparian zone management	A	A
Wetland management and restoration	A	A
Salinity management	A	A
Forestry management		
Timber production	D	D
Recreation	B/C	B/C
Wildlife management	A	A

A. High positive impact (direct habitat gain)
B. Moderate positive impact (enhancing the quality of existing natural habitat)
C. Little or no positive impact
D. Negative impact (direct loss or degrading quality of existing natural habitat)
Source: Authors' compilation.

agroforestry and woody biomass production. Two of the most significant projects to date involve establishment of constructed multi-species riparian buffer strips along waterways (Schultz and others 1995) and development of rapid-growing tree plantations for the production of woody biomass. The purpose of the buffer strips is to shore up stream banks, decrease siltation from field runoff, and reduce the amount of chemicals reaching streams. Wildlife is taking advantage of the increased plant biodiversity associated with riparian buffer strips. The number of bird species in buffer strips increases eightfold, compared to nearby areas without such vegetation.

The purpose of woody biomass research has been to select species that will generate significant amounts of woody biomass, either for fuel or to produce paper and its byproducts. Taken by themselves, the plantations are typically monocultures. However, when introduced into agricultural landscapes, they probably provide additional biodiversity. Studies to evaluate the impact of biomass crops on biodiversity in existing landscapes is in process (Ferrell and others 1995). Ultimately, the success of these efforts will be dependent on the willingness of private agricultural enterprises to return land from cultivation to less intensive use.

Genetic diversity. Although modern agricultural practices have reduced the biodiversity of prairies, forests, and wetlands, they have enhanced the genetic diversity used for improvement of two main crops: maize and soybean. Greater genetic diversity within maize is evident from the Iowa soybean and maize yield trials data. The maize yield trials were started in 1920, and that year 128 entries were received (Iowa Corn and Small Grain Grower's Association 1921). In 1995, by contrast, 715 entries were submitted, indicating a larger genetic base available to the Iowa farmer for planting.

From the genetic diversity standpoint the number of cultivars planted on the farm is only a fraction of the protovarieties held in reserve in public and private breeding programs. In the case of maize, for example, 454 cultivars were available for planting in the United States in 1981, compared to the impressive array of experimental hybrids in advanced trials: 6,042 in the private sector and 1,600 in public programs (table 5.5).

Table 5.5 Cultivars in U.S. maize and soybean genetic base, 1981

Development stage	Maize	Soybean
Cultivars planted	454	25
Advanced trials	7,642	6,382
Preliminary trials	60,625	46,271
Inbred lines (tested)	2,799	—
Inbred lines (top-cross)	22,525	—
Inbred lines in nurseries (partial)	769,535	518,350

Source: Duvick 1984.

The number of hybrids in preliminary trials in 1981 in the private sector program was 54,010 and in the public sector program, 6,615, for a total of 60,625. In early stages of development these experimental hybrids are not offered for sale. They are a genetic reserve, and any of them can be put into circulation should a special need arise, such as resistance to a disease or a pest. In addition 2,799 tested inbred lines, 22,525 inbred lines at the top-cross stage, and 769,535 partially inbred lines were reported to be on hand. The lush maize fields of Iowa may appear to be genetically uniform, but they are not a true indication of the total genetic diversity of the crop in Iowa. A similar pattern prevails for soybean (see table 5.5).

Modern agricultural practices have consistently increased food production and more than met the food needs of Iowans (figures 5.2 and 5.3). The food security of people cannot be ignored in the biodiversity debate; however, food supply, agriculture, and biodiversity are inextricably linked.

Iowa is headquarters to the Germplasm Enhancement Maize (GEM) project. Exotic materials are bred with local materials to select lines that carry the exotic trait. Landraces from twelve countries (Argentina, Bolivia, Brazil, Chile, Colombia, Guatemala, Mexico, Paraguay, Peru, Uruguay, United States, and Venezuela) are being adapted to Iowa and the central "corn" belt, which could provide valuable genetic diversity in the future. Some 12,000 accessions (each is potentially different) were evaluated earlier in an attempt to rescue endangered and irreplaceable maize germplasm that otherwise could have been lost.

The north-central regional plant-introduction station in Ames, Iowa, is one of four plant-introduction stations in the country devoted exclusively to the preservation of genetic resources. Founded in 1948, the Ames station currently contains 39,800 accessions, representing 320 genera, including more than 14,000 accessions of maize germplasm. Its mission is to conserve the genetic diversity of crops and wild relatives under *ex situ* conditions and to make it available for public use. The germplasm is carefully maintained, and accessions are propagated when the supply or the viability of a lot falls below a predetermined level. A portion of the

Figure 5.2 Maize yield (in bushel per acre) and cultivar types in the United States, 1865–1993

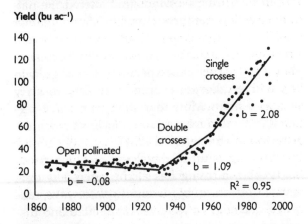

Yield (bu ac⁻¹)

Source: Hallauer 1996.

Figure 5.3 Maize yield (in bushel per acre) and cultivar types in Iowa, 1930–93

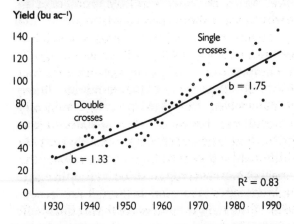

Yield (bu ac⁻¹)

Source: Hallauer 1996.

seed from any accession is available to plant breeders worldwide.

Sociocultural and Policy Effects on Biodiversity

The dominant social paradigm of American culture and policy limitations also have serious effects on biodiversity.

Sociocultural paradigms. The orientations of Iowa farmers toward the natural environment are consistent with a larger set of beliefs and values (the dominant social paradigm) that has long characterized American culture. Included are perceptions that natural resources are limitless; humans are dominant over nature; nature can, and should, be exploited to serve human needs; modern science and technology will solve all environmental ills; and economic growth is synonymous with progress.

Sociological studies in Iowa and elsewhere confirm this paradigm. It guides, perhaps unconsciously, daily decisions about farming practices and permissible environmental tradeoffs. When conflicts arise between economic goals and protection of environmental amenities and biodiversity, economic goals commonly prevail.

Evidence of disenchantment with the paradigm, however, is accumulating. An alternative is now being advocated by some, a paradigm that stresses ecological values and gives greater weight to enhancing biodiversity in agricultural decisionmaking. The emerging paradigm draws only narrow support within the general farm population but nevertheless is strongly endorsed by farmers who are seeking to make their agricultural practices and local communities more sustainable (Bird, Bultena, and Gardner 1995).

The diffusion of a competing paradigm portends possible changes in agricultural and environmental trends in the state. If alternative beliefs and values are endorsed more broadly and translated into action, both the structure of Iowa agriculture and characteristics of extant farming practices are likely to change. One consequence would be a transformed landscape, one that is more biologically diverse and sustainable.

Policy limitations. Agricultural conservation programs span more than sixty years. These efforts have stressed education, technical assistance, financial subsidies (or cost-sharing), and voluntary actions—the same basis for the creation of federal conservation agencies during the 1930s. But these voluntary educational and technical assistance programs may not have been particularly cost-effective (Ervin 1993). Attempts have been made to alter agricultural policy significantly (U.S. Congress decreed that control of industrial water pollution should include nonpoint source control; agriculture was perceived as the major contributor), but they were curtailed largely because of insufficient public funding. The major shift in agricultural policy came with the 1985 farm bill, which contains the most ambitious agricultural conservation and environmental agenda thus far. Mandatory compliance in exchange for commodity program payments replaced the previous voluntary approaches.

The main conservation and environmental challenges currently facing agricultural policy include significant budget pressures at all levels of government to cut expenditure for conservation programs; rapidly changing world markets in conjunction with less federal price and income support; and increasing local and state environmental regulations in response to growing public demands for environmental protection.

Large government subsidies are unlikely to continue because of federal and state budget problems. Farmers and ranchers will thus have to adjust to prices and costs aligned more with world market forces and less with commodity support programs. In general that means lower returns for crop production and fewer incentives to implement conservation programs. Increasing public pressure regarding conservation may also stimulate a rise in local and state environmental regulation, which might further increase production costs (Ervin 1993).

According to a recent survey in cornbelt counties, economic considerations constitute the primary reason farmers hesitate to enroll their eligible farm wetlands in CRP or WRP: the lands are too productive as croplands to convert to wetlands; restoring wetlands on these lands would interfere with farm activities on other croplands; and restoring wetlands would reduce the flexibility to change land uses as economic conditions warrant (Lant, Kraft, and Gillman 1995). About a third of the farmers were also concerned with time and cost factors in establishing and maintaining wetlands. Similarly, about half the farmers surveyed would use preserved wetlands for crop production without Swampbuster restrictions. This survey showed a clear need for additional economic incentives and technical support to enhance conservation efforts.

New Directions: Striving for Balance

Iowa's natural landscape has been modified more extensively than any other state in the United States. A prairie ecosystem of nearly 30 million acres is essentially gone. Nearly two-thirds of the state's forests has been cleared. More than 95 percent of Iowa's natural wetlands have

been drained. Channelization of rivers has eliminated bordering wetlands and altered the natural flow of water throughout the state. Together with habitat loss, a significant number of plant and animal species have disappeared. For example, of 250 higher plant species that once grew in the native tallgrass prairie, only fifty to sixty species remain. More than thirty species of vertebrates have disappeared from Iowa since the time of settlement (INAI 1984).

While agricultural development has destroyed habitat, farming has also triggered several indirect effects on biodiversity. Waterways, railways, and highways have fragmented and disturbed natural habitats that are no longer suitable for many native animal species. The genetic base of Iowa's livestock population has also shrunk considerably because of breeding and selection for a few preferred breeds.

The intensive use of chemicals in crop production has also caused adverse effects on biodiversity in remaining natural habitats. Drainage water leaving heavily treated agricultural fields may contaminate streams, lakes, and wetlands. Toxic levels of agricultural chemicals may also be detrimental to aquatic plants and wildlife species as well as to human health.

Although crop and livestock productivity are still in the forefront of Iowa's economy, sustainability issues regarding agricultural production and recognition of the need to conserve biodiversity are beginning to emerge. Only recently have Iowans collectively come to appreciate the magnitude and importance of environmental losses that have been incurred by agricultural progress. The past two decades have been marked by increasing environmental and conservation programs introduced by federal and state agencies and more public awareness about environmental issues as related to agricultural development.

Several socioeconomic issues are associated with the state's agricultural development and changes in biodiversity. Farming, the wellspring of Iowa's economy, has also resulted in the loss of much of its biodiversity. The dominant social paradigm (unlimited natural resources, dominance of humans over nature, progress measured by economic growth, and technology as a panacea) has affected farming decisions and permissible environmental tradeoffs. When conflicts arise, economic considerations usually prevail over saving natural habitats and wildlife.

Nonetheless, a new paradigm is emerging as concern about adverse environmental consequences of some conventional farming practices mounts. Interest is growing in alternative farming practices that conserve resources and protect biodiversity. Many Iowa farmers are working to reduce their nutrient and chemical applications. There is also increasing public support and funding for corrective actions that protect the natural environment. A harmonious balance of the need for human food, respect for nature, and conservation of natural resources can and must be agriculture's mission in coming years.

Indeed, a social-economic-political system is needed in which economic development and biological diversity gain from each other. Based on collective knowledge and experiences, it should address future needs for a vital economy, meeting society's food requirements, good quality surface and groundwater, and healthy ecosystems with diverse biological populations.

References

Baker, J. L., and J. M. Laflen. 1983. "Water Quality Consequences of Conservation Tillage," *Journal of Soil Water Conservation* 38 (3): 186–93.

Bird, E. A., G. L. Bultena, and J. C. Gardner, eds., 1995. *Planting the Future: Developing an Agriculture that Sustains Land and Community.* Ames: Iowa State University Press.

Brand, G. J., and J. T. Walkowiak. 1991. *Forest Statistics for Iowa, 1990.* U.S. Department of Agriculture (USDA), Forest Service Resource Bulletin NC-136, North Central Forest Experiment Station. St. Paul, Minn.: USDA.

Bulkley, R. V. 1975. "A Study of the Effects of Stream Channelization and Bank Stabilization on Warm Water Sport Fish in Iowa. Subproject No. 1. Inventory of Major Stream Alterations in Iowa." Completion Rep. U.S. Fish and Wildlife Service, Contract No. 14-16-0008-745.

Crist, A., and D. C. Glenn-Lewin. 1978. "The Structure of Community and Environmental Gradients in a Northern Iowa Prairie. " In D. C. Glenn-Lewin and R. Q. Landers, eds., *Fifth Midwest Prairie Conference Proceedings.* Ames: Iowa State University Press.

Davidson, J. B. 1946. "The Role of Machinery in Iowa Farming." In Members of the Staff of Iowa State College and the Iowa Agricultural Experiment Station, eds., *A Century of Farming in Iowa 1846–1946.* Ames: Iowa State College Press.

Dinsmore, J. J. 1994. *Country So Full of Game: The Story of Wildlife in Iowa.* Iowa City: University of Iowa Press.

Drake, L. D. 1978. "Prairie Models for Agricultural Systems." In D. C. Glen-Lewin and R. Q. Landers, eds., *Fifth Midwest Prairie Conference Proceedings.* Ames: Iowa State University Press.

Duvick, D. 1984. "Genetic Diversity in Major Farm Crops on the Farm and in Reserve," *Economic Botany* 38 (2): 161–78.

Ervin, D. E. 1993. "Conservation Policy Futures: An Overview," *Journal of Soil and Water Conservation* 48 (4): 300–03.

Ferrell, J. E., L. L. Wright, G. A. Tuskan, S. B. Mclaughlin, and A. R. Ehrenshaft. 1995. "Biofuels Feedstock Development Program: 1995 Activities and Future Directions," *Biologue* 13 (2): 33–39.

Galatowitsch, S. M., and A. G. van der Valk. 1994. *Restoring Prairie Wetlands: An Ecological Approach.* Ames: Iowa State University Press.

Hallauer, A. 1996. "Maize Yields and Cultivar Types in the United States (1865–1993) and in Iowa (1930–93)." Department of Agronomy, Iowa State University.

Hayden, A. 1945. "The Selection of Prairie Areas in Iowa Which Should be Preserved," *Proceedings of the Iowa Academy of Sciences* 52: 127–48.

IAN (Iowa Association of Naturalists). 1992. *Habitat Loss in Iowa.* Guthrie Center, Iowa: Conservation Education Center, IAN.

INAI (Iowa Natural Areas Inventory). 1984. *An Inventory of Significant Natural Areas in Iowa: Two-Year Progress Report of the Iowa Natural Areas Inventory.* Des Moines: Iowa Conservation Commission, INAI.

Iowa Corn and Small Grain Growers' Association. 1921. *Report of the 1920 Corn Yield Contest.* Ames: Iowa Corn and Small Grain Growers' Association.

Iowa Farm Bureau Federation (Communications Division). 1995. *Facts on Iowa's Agriculture.* Des Moines: Iowa Farm Bureau Federation.

Iowa State University. 1995. *The 1995 Corn Yield Test Report, PM 660–95.* Ames: Iowa State University.

Johnson, R. J., M. M. Beck, and J. R. Brandle. 1994. "Windbreaks for People," *Journal of Soil and Water Conservation* 49 (6): 546–47.

Kanwar, R. S., T. S. Colvin, and D. Karlen. 1995. "Tillage and Crop Rotation Effects on Drainage Water Quality." In *Proceedings of the Conference on Clean Water—Clean Environment, 21st Century.* Vol. 3:163-66. St. Joseph, Michigan: American Society of Agricultural Engineers.

Kennedy, A. C., and R. I. Papendick. 1995. "Microbial Characteristics of Soil Quality," *Journal of Soil and Water Conservation* 50 (3): 243–48.

Lant, C. L., S. E. Kraft, and K. R. Gillman. 1995. "The 1990 Farm Bill and Water Quality in Corn Belt Watersheds: Conserving Remaining Wetlands and Restoring Farmed Wetlands," *Journal of Soil and Water Conservation* 50 (2): 201–05.

Legislative Fiscal Bureau. 1995. *1994 Iowa Fact Book.* Des Moines, Iowa: Government Press.

Murray, W. G. 1946. "Struggle for Land Ownership." In Members of the Staff of Iowa State College and the Iowa Agricultural Experiment Station, eds., *A Century of Farming in Iowa 1846–1946.* Ames: Iowa State College Press.

Nicholson, H. P. 1969. "Occurrence and Significance of Pesticide Residues in Water," *Journal of the Washington Academy of Science* 59: 77–85.

Osborn, T. 1993. "The Conservation Reserve Program: Status, Future, and Policy Options," *Journal of Soil and Water Conservation* 48 (4): 272–79.

Ostrom, A. J. 1976. *Forest Statistics for Iowa, 1974.* USDA Forest Service Resource Bulletin NC-33, North Central Forest Experiment Station. St. Paul, Minn.: USDA.

Peterson, J. B., and A. J. Englehorn. 1946. "The Soil That Grows Crops." In Members of the Staff of Iowa State College and the Iowa Agricultural Experiment Station, eds., *A Century of Farming in Iowa 1846–1946.* Ames: Iowa State College Press.

Robinson, A. Y. 1993. "Wetlands Protection: What Success?" *Journal of Soil and Water Conservation* 48 (4): 268–70.

Schaller, F., and G. W. Bailey, eds. 1983. *Agricultural Management and Water Quality.* Ames: Iowa State University Press.

Schultz, R. C., J. P. Colletti, T. M. Isenhart, W. W. Simpkins, C. W. Mize, and M. L. Thompson. 1995. "Design and Placement of a Multi-Species Riparian Buffer Strip System," *Agroforestry Systems* 29: 201–26.

Schwieder, D. 1993. *75 Years of Service: Cooperative Extension in Iowa.* Ames: Iowa State University Press.

Shimek, B. 1911. "The Prairies," *Bulletin of the Laboratory of Natural History* 6: 169–240.

———.1931. "Relation between Migrant and Native Flora of the Prairie Region," University of Iowa, *Studies in Natural History* 14 (2): 10–16.

Thompson, J. R. 1992. *Prairies, Forests, and Wetlands: The Restoration of Natural Landscape Communities in Iowa.* Iowa City: University of Iowa Press.

Tilman D., D. Wedin, and J. Knops. 1996. "Productivity and Sustainability Influenced by Biodiversity in Grassland Ecosystems," *Nature* 379: 718–20.

Torrell, J. U. 1971. *American Indian Almanac.* New York and Cleveland: World Publishing Company.

USDA (U.S. Department of Agriculture). 1983. *Iowa Agricultural Statistics.* Washington, D.C.: National Agricultural Statistics Service, USDA.

———1990. *Seeds for Our Future: The U.S. National Plant Germplasm System.* Washington, D.C.: USDA.

———1994. *Iowa Agricultural Statistics.* Washington, D.C.: National Agricultural Statistics Service, USDA.

———1995. *Iowa Agricultural Statistics.* Washington, D.C.: National Agricultural Statistics Service, USDA.

6. Livestock Production Systems and the Management of Domestic Animal Biodiversity

Harvey Blackburn, Cornelis de Haan, and Henning Steinfeld

pproximately four thousand breeds of domesticated animals have been developed around the world—a number about equal to the number of mammalian species (Hammond and Leitch 1996). The biodiversity inherent in breeds is an important resource to help meet food security needs of growing human populations and to promote economic development. If livestock are to be productive, they must be able to adapt to an ever-changing ecological landscape; the maintenance of breed diversity is critical to this genetic elasticity. Over the past decade it has become increasingly apparent that livestock breeds in the developing world are better able to withstand environmental challenges such as disease, internal and external parasites, and erratic or poor-quality feed and water supplies than breeds introduced from temperate countries.

This chapter presents findings from a multidonor study designed to explore interactions between livestock and the environment. The goals of the study are to assess those interactions; to suggest technologies, policies, and research that will help mitigate negative environmental consequences of livestock production; and to encourage practices that improve environmental and economic conditions for livestock owners. The study presents its findings in the context of the pressure-state-response model (OECD 1994). In this model humans exert pressure on the natural resource base (the state) when they exploit resources such as forage for livestock. Societal decisions and actions are the response to such

pressures. As values placed on natural resources by society change, they may alter the pressure on the state variable. Alterations would then be manifested through various human activities.

This model can be adapted to the livestock sector (figure 6.1). The information, material flow, and feedback processes of the adapted model are the same as those articulated by the Organisation for Economic Co-operation and Development (OECD 1994). The system can be in a steady state, or the natural resource base can be enhanced or degraded. The status of the system depends on how society responds to its needs to promote economic growth, feed an increasing population, and conserve its natural resource base. The model is a viable framework for developing and monitoring livestock programs from both economic growth and environmental conservation perspectives.

Pressures on Animal Genetic Resources

Animal genetic resources are under the same types of pressures from human population as other natural resources. Shifts in farming systems, market value, and habitat, for example, can affect animal genetic resources by decreasing the number or herd size of breeds (table 6.1). When breeds disappear, or when herd size of a distinct breed diminishes, genetic diversity is lost.

Agricultural intensification is under way in both industrial and developing countries, and breed choice, as well as selection within breeds, is part of this widespread intensification.

Figure 6.1 Global or local pressure-state-response framework for livestock systems

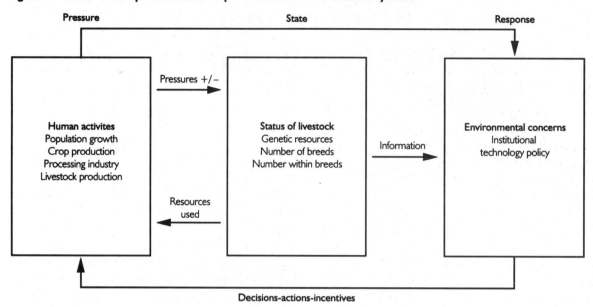

Source: Authors' rendering.

Genetic change is an essential part of intensification. Intensification has also been achieved by developing improved feed, more efficient feed-distribution systems, better management, and quality health care, all of which are necessary to support highly productive genotypes. This type of feedback or interaction has been the driving force of the intensive, highly productive livestock systems, especially in the OECD. Genetic resources are thus often lost as agriculture is intensified. For example, switching from draft to mechanical power causes a massive decrease in genetic variation as those types of animals used for plowing or pulling wagons and carts vanish from the landscape.

Industrialization also affects breeding structure. Market demands, for example, have changed the value of Holstein and Jersey dairy cattle; Holstein are more popular now because they produce larger quantities of milk. Another example is the total replacement of poultry stocks when highly intensive production systems are established. In the United States and Europe increased production means fewer animals are needed, and the gene pool shrinks. Genetic variation also declines, and inbreeding can become a problem (box 6.1).

The successes achieved through selecting animals for high production in the industrial world has discouraged producers and scientists in

Table 6.1 Driving forces that threaten the diversity of livestock breeds

Reason	Description
Development policy	Lack of incentives to develop and use breeds, giving preference to those few developed for use in high-input, high-output relatively benign environments. Commercial interests in donor communities promote the use of a few temperate climate breeds and create overexpectation for modern breeds in developing countries.
Specialization	Undue emphasis placed on a specific product or trait, leading to the rapid dissemination of one breed of animal to exclusion and loss of others.
Crossbreeding	Indiscriminate crossbreeding that can quickly lead to the loss of original breeds.
Storage	Failure of cryopreservation equipment and inadequate supply of liquid nitrogen to store samples of semen, ova, or embryos, or inadequate maintenance of animal populations for breeds not currently in use.
Technology	Introduction of new machinery to replace animal draft and transport, resulting in permanent change of farming system.
Biotechnology	Artificial insemination and embryo transfer leading to rapid replacement of indigenous breeds.
Violence	Wars and other forms of sociopolitical instability.
Disaster	Natural disasters such as floods, drought, or famine.

Source: Hammond and Leitch 1996.

**Box 6.1 Livestock population size—
a critical balancing point**

When livestock population size shrinks, genetic diversity is affected in two ways. First, certain genes or gene combinations are lost from the population. Second, when there are few representatives of a breed, the probability that parents of a new individual are related to each other increases. The mating of two such individuals not only increases the inbreeding of offspring, which can depress animal performance, but it also decreases genetic variability (Cunningham 1995).

The impact of small population size on genetic diversity within a population is also affected by the following:

- *Generation turnover.* Long generation intervals, as in horses, can delay the negative effects of small population size and inbreeding.
- *Current and prospective changes in population size.* If effective population numbers have been declining and are likely to continue downward, then calculations based on current size will underestimate the risk.
- *Changes in herd structure.* In some small populations the total number of herds may be quite small. The smaller the number, the greater the risk to the breed arising from the termination of any one herd.
- *Extent of crossbreeding.* While crossbreeding can remedy the effects of inbreeding, it can also result in a reduction of genetic diversity.

developing countries from attempting similar efforts with their indigenous genetic resources. The prevailing wisdom permeating many development activities has been that it is quicker and easier to import breeds developed for use in high-input farming systems than to work with indigenous stock. Although imported breeds are proven winners in their areas of origin, their productivity decreases dramatically when they are introduced to harsher environments typical of developing countries. The development strategy has been to try and alter the environment to accommodate these imported breeds rather than work on preadapted breeds. Excessive reliance on importing exotic genetic stocks has in many instances resulted in crossbreeding with indigenous breeds. Such crossbreeding serves initially to increase genetic variation. If crossbreeding continues indiscriminately, however, the genetic resources of the indigenous stock can be swamped. In West

Africa, for example, demand for heavier cattle has led to substantial crossbreeding of larger *Bos indicus* exotic cattle on the smaller, indigenous population of humpless *Bos taurus*. Such crossbreeding can eventually replace the domestic gene pool, thereby reducing genetic diversity.

Natural hazards and social insecurity can also undercut animal genetic resources. In Somalia, for example, drought and political instability have reduced cattle population by 70 percent and small ruminant population by 60 percent. The decrease in animal numbers undermines the food security and economic well-being of the livestock owners as well as the vitality of the national economy. Further, crashes in livestock populations can create evolutionary bottlenecks that render populations more vulnerable to environmental changes.

Production Systems

Livestock uses, genetic variance, and the degree of genetic diversity vary across production systems. As these different production systems evolve, pressures will be exerted on the existing breeds. The following is a brief assessment of how the genetic resources within different production systems are affected.

Grassland systems. Pastoral systems account for approximately two-thirds of the world's agricultural area and are used mostly for cattle and sheep production. Because stocking rates are low, they account for some 12 percent of the approximately 900 million cattle in developing countries and 15 percent of the 1.1 billion sheep and goats (Seré 1994). In Latin America pastoral systems have important implications for biodiversity. The Andes, for example, harbor four representatives of the camelid family (box 6.2). Cattle predominate in Latin America's humid and subhumid tropical grasslands. Genetic resources of cattle in Latin America can be traced to the original criollo types, which are *Bos taurus* cattle with 500 years of adaptation to tropical conditions, *Bos indicus* breeds derived from Indian imports during the past century, and European and North American breeds, also imported in recent times.

Arid and semiarid grasslands in Sub-Saharan Africa are grazed extensively by cattle and small

Box 6.2 Genetic resources of the Andean *Camelidae*

The *Camelidae* evolved in the New World, and four species survive in Latin America: the llama (a beast of burden), alpaca (raised primarily for wool production), the wild vicuña, and the guanaco (Philipsson and Wilson 1995). The first two species formed the mainstay of livestock in Andean agricultural systems in the pre–Colombian period, but they have been largely replaced by cattle and sheep. Vicuña have long been periodically rounded up to shear their fine wool, while the guanaco has been hunted for its meat. Today approximately 6 million alpaca and llama are raised mainly in Peru and Bolivia, while smaller numbers of the nondomesticated species survive in certain areas.

Most alpaca and llama belong to small farmers in the more difficult Andean areas above 3,000 meters. Data on fertility, mortality, and growth indicate low productivity. Nevertheless, these populations have held their place in competition with other species because of their adaptations to harsh climatic conditions and high altitudes.

ruminants and are an important source of genetic diversity. West Asia and North Africa are important reservoirs of sheep germplasm. The intensification and development of African systems has begun more recently, so livestock populations in that region are under more rapid genetic pressure than those elsewhere. Because of the diversity of systems and the shortage of objective information on the livestock resource, little is known about the status of African ruminant livestock populations.

Mixed farming systems. In developing countries more than 60 percent of cattle, 55 percent of sheep and goats, and about 70 percent of pigmeat production comes from mixed farming systems. The greatest challenge is likely to be in Asia, which accounts for 42 percent of developing country cattle, 46 percent of sheep and goats, almost 90 percent of pigmeat production, and practically all of the world's water buffaloes (Seré 1994). Major pressures and challenges include:

- Rapid genetic erosion of pig breeds in China, where more than 100 distinct breeds are found, many with unique and potentially valuable characteristics
- Widespread transformation of dairy cattle populations in countries such as India, where

crossbreeding of local breeds with introduced strains is proceeding on a massive scale

- Conservation of noncattle bovid species in tropical Asia—such as banteng, gaur, mithun, and yak—and the region's unique buffalo resources
- Expanded use of small ruminants, rabbits, the guinea pig, and other species in mixed farming systems.

In some countries, particularly India, government and nongovernmental agencies have well-developed programs to conserve local genetic resources. Unfortunately, such an extensive infrastructure is not operational in most developing countries, thus underscoring the need for more research, documentation, and educational activities related to indigenous breeds and local livestock species.

The genetic future of livestock populations in mixed farming systems is linked closely to crop integration. As human pressures increase in these systems, livestock's role for draft, feed-base use (most of which is crop waste), and the relatively high value of dung for fuel and manure will become even more critical in maintaining genetic diversity.

Landless systems. Pigmeat production in industrial countries has shifted almost entirely to industrial-scale units, often far removed from their feed sources. Production in Asia is moving in the same direction. In 1994 about 30 percent of production came from such systems (Seré 1994). Similar trends are under way in poultry. An inevitable consequence of this trend is a move away from local genetic sources to internationally competitive stock and husbandry systems. The growth of these systems therefore underscores the need for conservation of livestock populations that persist in traditional systems.

Wildlife interactions. Much discussion has focused on livestock-wildlife interactions. As with any evolutionary process involving human modifications of the environment, wildlife habitats are often affected by development. As more land is brought into agricultural production, wildlife habitat is typically lost. This point has been articulated by Reid, Wilson, and Kruska

(1996), who showed how bird, large mammal, and tree species decreased when human populations exert intense pressure on the environment, especially in urban settings. Bird species increased on small-holdings that employ animal traction, however. The crucial point is that land-use systems vary enormously in their impact on biodiversity, and generalizations often obscure the issue. Further, because the natural resource base is so diverse and changing constantly, it is impossible to maximize the habitat for all wildlife at the same time. If the objective of natural resource management is to maximize biodiversity by providing a diverse array of habitats within a landscape, prescribed sheep grazing is a promising tool for creating or maintaining such diversity because of the sheep's ability to consume a broad array of plant types (Mosley 1994).

In the western United States it is becoming increasingly evident that livestock can help enhance the environment for wildlife because of differences in dietary selection. In that region about 600,000 hectares have been invaded by leafy spurge, a noxious weed that crowds out plant species important in the diet of antelope, deer, and elk. Grazing leafy spurge with small ruminants, especially goats, helps suppress this weed, however, thereby boosting plant and animal biodiversity. This method is becoming increasingly popular as the most environmentally benign method for controlling leafy spurge (Walker and others 1994).

In the past wildlife and livestock were regarded as competitors for the same feed resources and were also considered incompatible because of the possibility of disease transmission. Evidence is accumulating, however, that livestock and wildlife are often synergistic. The diets of livestock and most wildlife species rarely overlap significantly, and a better understanding of which wild species are reservoirs of pathogens, combined with better disease control techniques, have reduced the danger of disease transmission in either direction.

Synergisms rather than antagonisms between livestock and wildlife have finally come to the surface in many debates on the improvement of pastoral and other livestock production systems (Western 1989). In developing countries work in Kenya especially has demonstrated some of

these complementarities. Livestock productivity can be enhanced by making provisions for wildlife. In comments to the authors Western said that about 80 percent of the big game animals in Kenya are currently outside national parks (Western 1996). Rapid population growth will allow only a modest increase in the area or number of national parks. Improved habitat conditions for wildlife outside the park system are therefore the only viable option. Over the past decade wildlife populations outside protected areas have been growing, while the number of big game animals in the protected parks has decreased. Wildlife can be managed for income alongside livestock, thereby enhancing biodiversity and income levels of pastoralists and ranchers. Fortunately livestock-wildlife combinations do not require significant reductions in livestock stocking rates. Western commented that in southern Kenya cattle stocking rates only have to be trimmed by 20 percent to allow most wildlife species to prosper.

In Texas many ranchers consider the blend of livestock and wildlife to be a very important component of the overall ranch enterprise because it contributes significantly to ranch income. Similar experiences pertain in Africa. The combination of livestock raising and wildlife management among the Masai, for example, generally resulted in higher incomes than if either were carried out alone. The key ingredient in this success is the sharing of game park revenues with the Masai, which in turn induced them to protect wildlife resources.

In mixed farming systems livestock can assist in preserving biodiversity. Livestock provide a reason for maintaining a mosaic of land-use patterns and contribute manure, which not only provides soil nutrients but also enhances soil organic matter. The beneficial effects of hedgerows and shelterbelts are widely known for controlling wind erosion, and their importance in promoting biodiversity is becoming increasingly clear. Livestock integration into the cropping system can further promote development of hedgerows and shelterbelts.

Numerous studies have shown a positive correlation between plant biomass production and species diversity. Biomass generation contributes to soil organic matter. In temperate areas soil organic matter ranges between 1 and 4 percent in well-managed cropland, between 4 and 8 percent in productive pastures, and between 6 and 15 percent in forests (Pimentel and others 1992). Livestock contribute to biomass production through controlled grazing and manure application. In grassland plots in Japan, for example, the species diversity of the macrofauna more than doubled when manure was added to the land (Pimentel and others 1992). Increased biomass production not only fosters a vibrant biodiversity, but it also helps to conserve water, slow runoff, and decrease soil erosion.

Status of Breeds

Concern about the erosion of livestock genetic diversity has prompted the United Nations Food and Agriculture Organization (FAO) to establish a global program on animal genetic resources (Hammond and Leitch 1996). This program's first initiative was to produce a World Watch List of breeds at risk. Of breeds with adequate data for assessment 19 percent are classified as endangered (table 6.2). In developed countries 21 percent are at risk (table 6.3).

Market forces are diminishing much of the diversity in the OECD countries. In Europe Holstein cattle account for 60 percent of dairy cattle and in North America, 90 percent. The inbreeding of Holsteins in the United States is expected to increase by 0.725 percent a year from 1990 to 2015. This corresponds to an effective population size of sixty-six animals (Hanson 1995).

Table 6.2 Threatened breeds of domestic animals by species, worldwide, 1996

Species	On file	With population data	At risk	Projected at risk
Ass	77	24	9	9
Avians	863	733	372	195
Buffalo	72	55	2	2
Camelid and dromedary	69	59	3	3
Cattle	787	582	135	80
Goat	351	267	44	37
Horse	384	277	120	96
Pig	353	265	69	52
Sheep	920	656	119	85
Yak	6	6	0	0
Total	3,882	2,924	873	559

Note: At risk is based on breeds with population data having less than 1,000 breeding females or less than 20 males and for which there is no conservation program in place.
Source: Hammond and Leitch 1996.

Two-thirds of the world's livestock are located in the developing world, but reliable information on breeds in the tropics and subtropics is far from complete. The data from both industrial and developing countries show that erosion of biodiversity at the breed level is not simply a concern for the distant future but a current issue.

Critical Indicators of Genetic Diversity

Critical indicators identified for determining the status of genetic diversity in animal populations include population size, breeding structure, and interpopulation gene flow. Risk assessment for a breed should take into account:
- Increasing or decreasing population size
- Decreasing number of herds
- Extent of crossbreeding.

Thresholds recommended for these factors include:
- Population size (number of females) falls more than 10 percent a year.
- Effective population size drops below fifty.
- Number of breeding herds decreases below ten.
- Proportion of matings to animals from outside the population exceeds 10 percent (Simon and Buchenauer 1993).

Breeding structure, the second crucial indicator, refers to the composition of the breed's population and includes the following factors:
- Replacement rates for males and females
- Ratio of breeding males to females
- Age structure of the population
- Extent of natural versus artificial insemination
- Pattern of acquisition of breeding material, such as from hatcheries or breeding companies.

For well-documented populations annual statistical reports normally include most of these factors.

Probably the most important factor affecting the genetic constitution of populations has been the movement of genetic material among populations (Cunningham 1995). This most often takes the form of crossbreeding through introducing males from outside. For each population it is important to monitor the inward gene flow. As for other aspects of genetic change, the requirements for monitoring are different for well-documented

Table 6.3 Breeds of domestic animals at risk, by region

Region	On file	With population data	At risk	Projected at risk
Africa	396	239	27	27
Asia and Pacific	996	710	105	97
Europe	1,688	1,501	638	358
Latin America	220	143	29	27
Near East	378	214	15	9
North America	204	117	59	41
World	3,882	2,924	873	559

Note: At risk is based on breeds with population data having less than 1,000 breeding females or less than 20 males and for which there is no conservation program in place.
Source: Hammond and Leitch 1996.

breeds and for undocumented, localized, indigenous stock. For indigenous stock regular (five yearly) analyses should be done on the pattern of genetic movement into the population. This analysis should include an estimation of:

- Extent of crossbreeding (generally the proportion of females mated to males from outside the population).
- Source of external genetic material.
- Nature of the crossbreeding. In some cases this may be terminal crossing to produce slaughter animals, with no permanent genetic effect on the population. In other cases it may be a pattern of continuous crossing in which the population's genetic resources are gradually replaced. It can also take the form of partial or complete replacement of existing breeding structures by a planned provision of hybrids.
- Extent to which breeding animals are produced at home or provided by outside breeding companies or organizations.
- Use of DNA techniques to track the nature and extent of gene infusion.

In documented breeds annual statistics covering the same range of factors are generally produced. Because gene movement between populations is well documented in these cases, the use of DNA techniques may be less informative and therefore less necessary.

Societal Response

Society's response to the use of animal genetic resources has ebbed and flowed over the past three decades. In developing countries breed substitution through crossbreeding was the most common mechanism used to increase the genetic potential of livestock for a specific characteristic such as milk production during the 1960s and 1970s. During the mid- to late 1980s awareness increased that indigenous breeds are highly adapted to rigorous environments. With this realization came a series of initiatives to conserve animal genetic resources.

Actors

Effective use and conservation of animal genetic resources requires a concerted effort by a number of actors (table 6.4). These include individual breeders, breed associations, national governments, and international agencies.

Livestock owners and breeders bear ultimate responsibility for managing the genetic future of livestock populations. Their actions are determined in large part by economic returns. Conservation programs must therefore sensitize livestock owners to their important role as guardians of livestock genetic resources and help find ways to increase revenue from threatened breeds.

Breed associations are responsible for maintaining pedigree information, developing breed standards, and collecting and analyzing data on animal performance. In many cases public funds have assisted the development and functioning of these breed societies.

National governmental authorities are also involved in managing and safeguarding animal genetic resources through various programs and regulations. Governments provide many services, including supervision of breed societies, supervision of imports, and services such as animal

Table 6.4 Relative importance of actions by various participants in animal genetic resource conservation

Actions	Participants			
	Breeder or farmer	Breed associations	National governments	International agencies
In situ conservation	Strongly relevant	Strongly relevant	Moderately relevant	Slightly relevant
Ex situ conservation	Slightly relevant	Moderately relevant	Strongly relevant	Slightly relevant
DNA characterization	Not Applicable	Slightly relevant	Strongly relevant	Slightly relevant
Data base collection and management	Slightly relevant	Moderately relevant	Moderately relevant	Strongly relevant

Source: de Haan, Steinfeld, and Blackburn 1996.

recording and artificial insemination. Many zoos are government-operated and therefore could play an important role in conservation of near relatives and wild populations of livestock species.

International agencies provide the critical glue for a successful gene conservation program. These institutions provide a forum for the development of international accords and conventions. Such institutions also play a crucial role in planning for both the compilation and management of international genetic resource databases. International agencies will be increasingly instrumental in the transfer of genetic resources, such as in cryopreservation form, dissemination of DNA techniques in breeding and conservation work, and standardization of procedures.

Costs and Benefits

The preferred path to conserving a breed is for it to function in an economically viable farming system. In some situations modest subsidies to support the conservation of crucial genetic resources may be warranted, as in the case of Kerry, a dual-purpose cattle breed from Ireland (box 6.3). In other cases it may be possible to alter other components of the farming system so that performance of the conserved breed is enhanced, thereby helping it to be economically competitive.

Regardless of the benefit, costs will clearly play a role in determining the amount of animal genetic resources that can be preserved via *in*

situ or *ex situ* methods (box 6.4). Financial resources are currently insufficient to assess and preserve all breeds adequately. DNA techniques, however, can be used to assess the genetic differences between breeds and thereby determine which breeds are truly unique and scarce. Although such an approach entails a high initial cost, it is relatively cost-effective over the long term. Further, applying DNA techniques focuses the greatest effort on those breeds that are in critical need of preservation.

Costs associated with development of data bases, DNA analysis, and international protocols and accords fall into the category of public goods. But the maintenance costs of data bases could be shared with livestock owners, breed associations, national authorities, and international agencies. The costs are modest when considered per head. For example, long-term costs for semen and embryos depend on scale but can be in the order of $1 per unit per year. Genotyping the DNA of a breed within a country for a cross-breed comparison can be performed for approximately $1,000–$3,000 ($5–$10 a head), and once this work is done, it does not have to be repeated.

To recover these costs, fairly modest incremental benefits are required. For example, at a discount ratio of 7.5 percent, an incremental benefit of 80 times the annual cost could repay a twenty-five-year investment in the conservation of a breed. Thus a return of $800,000 would be required to recover the costs of a breed conservation program covering 10,000 animals over twenty-five years. Assuming that such benefits would affect 10 million animals, the incremental yields per animal required to repay the investment would be less than 10 cents.

Monitoring Genetic Diversity

It is possible to measure changes in genetic diversity directly with commonly used monitoring techniques. Several indicators can be monitored:

Genetic parameters. The amount of genetic variation for a trait in a population is normally measured as its heritability. This is the ratio of the additive genetic variance to the total phenotypic

---

Box 6.3 Conservation of Kerry cattle

The Kerry is a remnant of a once numerous population of small black cattle native to southwestern Ireland. A breed society was formed in 1887, but the number of registered females declined to about 200 in the 1970s, with an effective population size of about 50. Since then a conservation scheme has provided a small subsidy per calf registered, ensured long-term storage of semen, and provided breeders with relationship information between animals that enables them to minimize inbreeding. The number of breeders has doubled, and numbers of animals have increased by more than half. Recent DNA analysis has shown that the breed is significantly different from all other European breeds with which it has been compared.
Source: Cunningham 1995.

Box 6.4 Tools for genetic conservation of livestock

Several tools are available for the conservation of livestock genetic resources. Among them are:

- In situ *conservation*. The maintenance of livestock with viable population sizes can be accomplished by enhancing the economic value of the animals in the farming system.
- Ex situ *conservation*. Maintain animals by freezing semen and embryos. This technology is not adequately developed for all species, however. Although labor and animal facility costs are saved, the approach requires the continual use of frozen nitrogen and a secure facility.
- *DNA technology*. This can provide important information concerning the evolutionary history of a breed or species.
- *Breeds and landraces*. Thorough documentation currently in existence will provide a basis for evaluating breed differences.
- *International accords*. Such accords provide a framework for global animal genetic resources.

variance. A narrowing of the genetic variance is the major concern, although experimental and field data have shown that this is surprisingly well maintained even in populations under intense selection. In well-documented populations these statistics are routinely calculated, while in many local breeds, suitable data are seldom available.

Measurement of genetic trend. Genetic response to selection in a population is a function of the selection goals pursued, the heritability of these goals, the genetic variance for the traits concerned, and the selection intensity applied. In many modern populations these factors are all quantified as part of the process of calculating breeding values for individuals. The routine tracking of genetic trends in the population is feasible and should be part of annual population reporting.

Degree of inbreeding. As populations become smaller, average inbreeding increases. This can be accentuated by deliberate patterns of mating related individuals, or by isolation of the population into subpopulations. Because increased inbreeding is associated with a decline in a range of fitness factors, it can be an important determinant of a population's prospects for survival. It is therefore a critical indicator. In most circum-

stances calculating effective population size will permit a good estimate of the rate of inbreeding. However, this should be supplemented by periodic analyses of pedigree data to measure directly the accumulation of inbreeding in the population. This will take account of mating patterns, genetic grouping within the population, and nonrandom variability in family size.

Measuring genetic diversity at the DNA level. DNA techniques developed within the past five years now make feasible the routine monitoring of genetic variability within a population at the molecular level (Cunningham 1995). Such techniques include:

- Polymerase chain reaction, which permits the extraction and rapid multiplication of selected segments of DNA from very small samples of tissue, including blood, hair, and milk.
- Discovery of microsatellites, highly variable repeat segments of nonfunctional DNA, has uncovered an enormous reservoir of genetic variability useful in tracking genetic change within and between populations.
- Sequence analysis makes possible the rapid evaluation of genetic differences between individuals in the structure of functional genes at a reasonable cost.

The rapid and ongoing development of DNA techniques has opened up a wide variety of options for monitoring genetic change. The genetic consequence of inbreeding is an increase in homozygosity within individuals. With the use of DNA techniques this phenomenon can now be measured directly. The degree and nature of variability within a population can tell a great deal about its evolutionary history and about its relationship to other populations. Such information is invaluable for planning conservation programs.

Monitoring interpopulation differences. Genetic differences among populations should be carefully documented. This is seldom the case, and comparisons often include many environmental factors in addition to genetic ones. Interpopulation genetic comparisons can be made in two ways. One is carefully controlled experimentation in which breeds, and sometimes their crosses, are compared for a range of production traits. Another is the use of DNA techniques to document the extent of their common or divergent genetic heritage.

Matching Genotypes to the Environment

Past attempts at improving livestock productivity in developing countries have focused largely on importation of exotic breeds because crossbreeding was thought to be a faster means of achieving increased production than within-breed selection. Imported breeds were chosen based on a partial analysis that indicated that they could produce higher quantities of milk, meat, or wool. But the analysis lacked a full appreciation for genetic-environmental interactions and lifetime productivity.

The imported breeds were then crossed with existing genetic stocks, thereby extinguishing indigenous breeds. Significant genetic variability was thus lost before its potential benefits could be assessed. Indigenous breeds often contain traits that could be exploited more fully for improving local incomes or that could be transferred to other breeds (box 6.5). This practice of selecting for individual production characteristics (growth rates or meat or milk production) instead of lifetime productivity and biological efficiency has carried over to selective breeding of indigenous populations. The result is a partial analysis of how

indigenous breed types perform. Because the entire process of animal production has not been evaluated, these actions have also contributed to the displacement and loss of biodiversity. Further, the exotic breeds have not been able to maintain high levels of productivity in many cases. The result is not only a loss in biodiversity but also a loss in economic returns.

Compounding the problems of partial analysis has been a disregard for genetic traits for fitness associated with the adaptation complex. Animals in a specific environment have developed resistance or adaptation to a full range of environmental challenges such as ticks, internal parasites, and temperature extremes (Hammond and Leitch 1996). For the most part these characteristics have not been fully accounted for in planning and executing breeding and selection schemes in industrial or developing countries.

The manner in which genotypes respond to different types of environments can be envisioned in a three-dimensional schematic (figure 6.2). By viewing breeds in the context of composite productivity, it becomes much more apparent how indigenous breeds or those breeds that have been selected for a different set of characteristics can achieve higher levels of productivity.

An alternative approach to breeding animals for perceived economic returns and conserving

---

Box 6.5 Improving competitiveness of indigenous livestock breeds

An important tactic for conserving indigenous genetic resources is to make those breeds more beneficial. A program that focuses on the traits that increase the economic value of the breed is such a mechanism. The N'Dama cattle of southern Senegal have traditionally been an important component of farming systems in the forested Casamance. Trypanosomiasis is prevalent in that region, and other breeds cannot survive there. Although the N'Dama are able to withstand the trypanosome challenge, their productivity is low: two-year calving intervals, low-growth rates, and milk production averaging about 700 kilograms per cow. A research program has been initiated to improve the performance of the N'Dama. The protocol used feed products that were readily available, such as groundnut hay and cotton-seed meal. By improving the N'Dama's nutrition, performance was doubled.
Source: Philipsson and Wilson 1995.

Figure 6.2 Relative performance of selected and indigenous livestock genotypes across environments

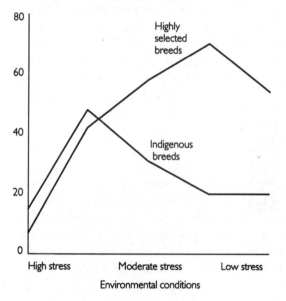

Source: Adapted from de Haan, Steinfled, and Blackburn 1996.

genetic resources is matching genotypes to environments. Instead of importing a genotype and attempting to modify the environment through increased input levels, indigenous breeds should be used. Imported breeds may be justified when appropriate evaluation trials have been conducted to verify their performance advantage over indigenous stock. The basis for comparing performance would be lifetime productivity (number of offspring per female), economic returns for the herd or flock (versus individual performance), and biological efficiency (output and input). Such a strategy implies that general recommendations are not possible because accounting has to be made for the specific environment in which the breeds are expected to perform.

Studies to characterize this reranking of genetic types in differing environments are not easy to design or conduct, but simulation models have been developed to screen breed types in different environments. This approach has been used to assess the introduction of the Boer goat in the United States.

The Texas and Oklahoma goat industries are interested in importing and using the Boer goat, which originated in South Africa. High-growth rates and meaty characteristics of the Boer make it an attractive candidate for substituting for the indigenous Spanish meat goat. The Spanish meat goat has been traditionally produced in this region with minimal inputs and very little genetic selection. In essence this is a case of reverse gene flows (from developing country to industrial country) and potential breed replacement. Although Boer goats fetch extremely high prices, no information is available on how they will perform in the extensive rangelands of Texas or the monoculture pastures in Oklahoma. A simulation model was used, however, to compare the performance of the Boer goat with the indigenous Spanish meat goat under varying levels of nutrition (Blackburn 1995). Results from this study demonstrated that:

- Although the Boer goat produced more sale weight per doe and had higher growth rates, no difference was noted between the two breeds for biological efficiency.
- When nutritional stress was imposed on both breeds, the Spanish goats had higher sale weights per doe and biological efficiencies, indicating that this breed has a greater ability to withstand typical environmental challenges (figure 6.3).

Conclusions drawn from this example indicate that although the Boer goat may confer an advantage in growth rate, it does not achieve this increase more efficiently than the Spanish goats, which are better adapted to the local conditions. For the Boer to be used successfully in Texas or Oklahoma, more inputs, particularly high-quality feed, would be required than are usual for the Spanish goats. Such additional production costs will lessen the Boer's potential profitability.

The shift in how breeds are evaluated, such as combining analysis of lifetime productivity

Figure 6.3 Comparison of Boer and Spanish goat performance under conditions prevailing in Oklahoma

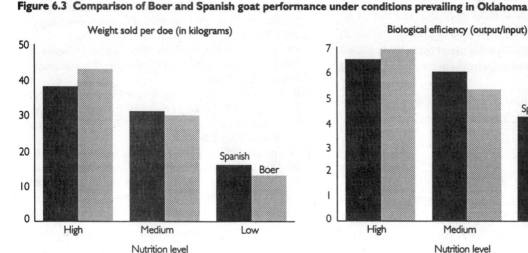

Source: Blackburn 1995.

and using simulation models to screen the magnitude of genetic environmental interactions, provides a mechanism to assess and conserve genetic resources. It also provides a basis to conduct and promote more sound animal breeding programs than currently prevail in the developing world.

Research and Policy Priorities

Using the preceding as a basis for determining conservation and better animal breeding practices, the following research and policy initiatives are warranted:

Policies

- Support implementation of the Biodiversity Convention, which includes development of national and regional infrastructures
- Assess roles of indigenous and nonindigenous breeds in meeting future domestic and export needs for food and other animal products
- Facilitate regional cooperation among countries to achieve economies of scale
- Support the international exchange and use of animal genetic resources.

Research Initiatives

- Shift the research focus from individual traits to lifetime and herd productivity using deterministic simulation models and live-animal experimentation where feasible
- Determine the critical number of breeds to conserve via DNA analysis of genetic variation
- Determine appropriate selection goals based upon the environmental capacity for animal production
- Learn more about genetic bases of adaptation, such as tick resistance and use of body reserves.

References

Blackburn, H. D. 1995. "Comparison of Performance of Boer and Spanish Goats in Two U.S. Locations,"

Journal of Animal Science 73: 302–09.

Cunningham, E. P. 1995. "Livestock and the Environment: Finding a Balance. Global Impact Domain, Animal Genetic Resources." Background paper for the Multidonor Livestock-Environment Study. Food and Agriculture Organization (FAO), Rome.

de Haan, C., H. Steinfeld, and H. Blackburn. 1996. *Livestock and the Environment: Finding the Balance.* Washington, D.C. and Rome: World Bank and FAO.

Hammond, K., and H. W. Leitch. Forthcoming. "The FAO Global Program for Management of Farm Animal Genetic Resources," *Journal of Animal Science.*

Hanson, L. B. 1995. "Breeding Schemes." In *Proceedings of the National Dairy Genetics Workshop.* Orlando: American Dairy Science Association.

Mosley, J. C. 1994. "Prescribed Sheep Grazing to Enhance Wildlife Habitat on North American Rangelands," *Sheep Research Journal* 10: 79–91.

OECD (Organisation for Economic Co-operation and Development). 1994. *Environmental Indicators.* Paris.

Pimentel, D., U. Stachow, D. A. Takacs, H. W. Brubaker, A. R. Dumas, J. J. Meaney, J. O'Neil, D. E. Onsi, and D. B. Corzilius. 1992. "Conserving Biological Diversity in Agricultural/Forestry Systems," *BioScience* 42: 354–62.

Philipsson, J., and R. T. Wilson. 1995. "Interactions between Livestock Production Systems and the Environment: Global Perspectives and Prospects." Background paper for the Multidonor Livestock-Environment Study. FAO, Rome.

Reid, R. S., C. J. Wilson, and R. L. Kruska. 1996. "The Influence of Human Use on Rangeland Biodiversity in Ghibe Valley, Ethiopia, as Affected by Natural Resource Use Changes and Livestock Disease Control." *Proceedings of the Fifth International Rangeland Congress.* Salt Lake City, Utah, and Denver, Colo.: Society for Range Management.

Seré, C. 1994. "Characterization and Quantification of Livestock Production Systems." Background paper for the Multidonor Livestock-Environment Study, FAO, Rome.

Simon, D., and D. Buchenauer. 1993. *Genetic Diversity of European Livestock Breeds.* Wageningen, Netherlands: Wageningen Press.

Walker, J. W., S. L. Kronberg, S. L. Al-Rowaily, and N. E. West. 1994. "Comparison of Sheep and Goat Preferences for Leafy Spurge," *Journal of Range Management* 47: 429–34.

Western, D. 1989. "Conservation without Parks: Wildlife in the Rural Landscape." In D. Western and M. Pearl, eds., *Conservation for the Twenty-First Century.* New York: Oxford University Press.

———. 1996. Personal communication.

7. Biodiversity and the World Bank's Agricultural Portfolio

Sakti Jana and Sanjiva Cooke

An intersectoral effort is currently under way at the World Bank to mainstream biodiversity conservation in environmentally sustainable development activities. Agriculture is a key component in these efforts to integrate biodiversity conservation in rural development, while enhancing agricultural productivity. This chapter assesses some of the World Bank's key analytical and development assistance instruments—country assistance strategies and agricultural and forestry sector reviews—and national environmental action plans as they apply to these concerns. Documents reviewed were those available for a sample of thirty-two countries, which included all developing megadiversity countries, countries with centers of agrobiodiversity not included in the first category and a random selection of other countries to make up at least five countries from each of the World Bank regions.

The agricultural development portfolio of projects initialed since fiscal 1988 and 1995 is examined in its entirety, focusing on its potential impact on biodiversity, especially agrobiodiversity.

Commitment and Funding for Biodiversity

The World Bank's development assistance relevant to biodiversity is channeled through three main forms: the International Bank for Reconstruction and Development (IBRD), International Development Association (IDA) credits, and Global Environment Facility (GEF) grants. The first two instruments are generated from the World Bank's resources, with IDA being the source of low-cost financing to countries unable to afford market rates. GEF grants have been administered on behalf of the international development community since 1991. From 1988 to mid-1995, $731 million was committed to eighty-four projects or project components in fifty-one countries with explicit objectives of conserving biodiversity, including $512 million in World Bank loans or IDA credits and $219 million in grants from the World Bank–administered GEF or the Brazilian Rain Forest Trust Fund (World Bank 1995a). These investments leveraged an additional $522 million in parallel financing from other donors and borrowing governments for a combined total commitment of $1.25 billion to biodiversity conservation.

Explicitly biodiversity-related project components in IBRD and IDA projects include:
- Establishment of new protected areas
- Management of existing protected areas
- Direct and indirect efforts to conserve biodiversity outside protected areas
- *Ex situ* conservation
- Studies, research, and monitoring
- Strategies, planning, policies, and institutions related to biodiversity.

Strengthening the management of existing protected areas and strategy (policy and plan development) account for more than 60 percent of the World Bank's biodiversity financing. A proposed World Bank assistance strategy for implementing the Biodiversity Convention intends for the World Bank to use its policy dialogue, country economic and sector work, and country assistance strategies to help mainstream biodiversity.

How does the World Bank work? In support of its lending operations, the World Bank jointly undertakes country economic and sector work with client governments (figure 7.1). This analytical work contributes to policy dialogue with governments, covering strategic issues of national economic and sectoral development. A country assistance strategy, prepared with the client government, sets out the agreed strategy for development assistance and indicates the level and composition of assistance to be provided. The World Bank's operational and sectoral policies guide the process throughout policy dialogue, economic and sector work, and the program or project lending cycle.

Figure 7.1 Regional distribution of IBRD/IDA agriculture sector portfolio, 1988–95

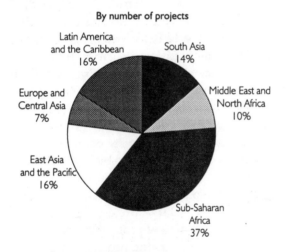

By number of projects

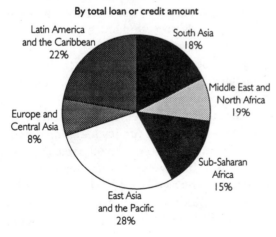

By total loan or credit amount

Policies That Support Biodiversity

The World Bank's basic support for biodiversity conservation includes protection of natural habitats. Wherever possible the World Bank tries to avoid damaging biodiversity by locating projects on lands already converted, not on lands cleared in anticipation of project funding.

The World Bank's sectoral and operational documents related to environment and forestry sectors illustrate this policy:

- *Operational Policies on Forestry.* This document requires a client country to undertake sustainable management and conservation-oriented forestry (World Bank 1993).

- *Operational Policies on Natural Habitats.* In this recently published manual, the World Bank gives unequivocal support for the protection, maintenance, and rehabilitation of natural habitats and their functions. Natural habitat protection is also emphasized in World Bank procedures. Task managers are required to identify natural habitat issues that are likely to arise in a project under preparation. Projects are classified as A (requiring full assessment) or B (partial assessment), depending on the degree of potential ecological effects. The compensatory costs of conservation of any natural habitats are included in the project's financing (World Bank 1995c).

- *Operational Directive on Environmental Assessment.* This document outlines the World Bank's policies and procedures for environmental assessment. It lists the issues to be addressed to ensure environmental soundness and sustainability in a project under preparation for World Bank financing. It includes several important aspects of biodiversity, such as conservation of endangered species, critical habitats, protected areas, wetlands and wildlands, and preservation of tropical forests and coastal and marine resources (World Bank 1991b).

Country Assistance Strategies

A World Bank–developed country assistance strategy provides the overall context for World Bank operations in that country. It is not a comprehensive treatment of development problems within a country; rather, it is a concise document focusing on the four or five most critical issues. The country assistance strategy describes the country's recent economic and social performance, development objectives, and lays out an agenda for action and support.

In a sample of country assistance strategies for sixteen countries, many included some environmental concern, none mentioned agrobiodiversity specifically, and only a few included management of the land or natural resources (table 7.1).

Brazil, Ethiopia, Madagascar, and Mexico were among the countries in which such issues gained attention in the country assistance strategy. In the case of Brazil accelerated deforestation attracted serious concern. Brazilian rain forests contain the largest repository of biodiversity in the world, and past development policies have contributed to deforestation and the loss of this rich heritage, much of it unique. Noting that policy and institutional changes to enhance environmental protection have been introduced in recent years, the World Bank's assistance objective is to help ensure that priority biomes are protected. Assistance is envisaged for strengthening federal and state environmental protection agencies; reforming laws, regulations, and policies affecting taxes and user fees, land ownership, forestry development, and indigenous reserves; and strengthening monitoring and enforcement capabilities (box 7.1). In addition to economic and sector work and grant

management of a pilot program to conserve the Brazilian rain forest through GEF, World Bank lending will encompass land management and a biomass pilot project.

Environmental degradation threatens biodiversity in several other "megadiversity" countries, such as Madagascar and Mexico. Deforestation for agriculture is accelerating in species-rich Madagascar, and its country assistance strategy expressed alarm. Protection of Madagascar's fragile environment represents a major challenge to its government, the World Bank, and other international agencies, donor countries, and NGOs.

In Mexico the disruption of ecosystems and resulting loss of biodiversity is a major problem. The country assistance strategy for Mexico assigns high priority to sustainable natural resources management and biodiversity conservation. The World Bank's strategy strives to increase public-private partnership for environmental management and conservation, enhance private incentives for appropriate environment protection, raise public awareness and participation in policy formulation and enforcement, strengthen the institutional framework, and enhance the capacity of state and municipal agencies (box 7.2). Proposed sector work includes a country environment memorandum that will also cover biodiversity and soil conservation. Two environmental projects and a forestry project are also part of the World Bank's lending program for Mexico.

Table 7.1 Incidence of biodiversity, environmental, and natural resource issues in selected World Bank country assistance strategies

Country	Natural resource management	Environment	Land management	Deforestation	Biodiversity	Agrobiodiversity
Argentina		•	•		•	
Bangladesh		•				
Brazil		•		•	•	
Chile		•				
Cambodia	•	•				
Colombia	•	•				
Ethiopia		•		•	•	
India		•		•		
Lebanon		•				
Madagascar	•	•		•	•	
Mexico	•	•		•	•	
Papua New Guinea		•		•		
Peru		•				
Russia		•				
Sri Lanka			•			
Zaire						

Source: Authors' sampling.

Box 7.1 Biodiversity in a country assistance strategy: Brazil

The World Bank's May 1995 country assistance strategy for Brazil endorses recent policy and institutional changes that have been introduced to enhance environmental protection. Among the changes:
- Fiscal incentives for investing in the Amazon region are now subject to environmental conditionality.
- Road building and colonization projects have been abandoned or scaled back.
- Environmental impact studies are mandated for all public works and private investments.
- Agricultural tax exemptions have been curtailed.
- Price and credit subsidies for ranching in the Amazon have been reduced or eliminated.

The sectoral reform agenda for natural resource management includes the following items:
- Set tax rates for native forests equivalent to or less than tax rates on agricultural land.
- Establish separate rules and regulations for native and plantation forests.
- Define a process for assigning *terra develuta* to alternate private uses within five years, including a settlement policy that takes into account the full environmental impact of forest conversion.
- Design policy and regulation such that conservation, agricultural development, and delivery of special services can be contracted out to the private sector, local communities, and nongovernmental organizations (NGOs).
- Decentralize to the states much of the responsibility for the implementation and enforcement of environmental protection.
- Provide incentives for collection of environmental user fees by allowing environmental agencies to retain a portion of the fees they collect.

Streamline and clarify procedures for identification and demarcation of indigenous reserves. Strengthen and coordinate protection of these reserves to reduce encroachment and illegal exploitation of indigenous reserves.

The World Bank has supported Ethiopia, another country rich in agrobiodiversity, in the preparation of a biodiversity strategy. But several countries with rich genetic heritages have not received similar treatment. The country assistance strategy for India, for example, a country with a wealth of genetic resources for a wide range of crops, does not mention agrobiodiversity conservation nor its importance for agricultural development.

Although other environmental issues related to biodiversity conservation, such as watershed management, soil salinity, and other forms of land degradation, were included generally in the sampled country assistance strategies, few of them mention biodiversity. Particularly striking is the absence of biodiversity concerns in the country assistance strategies for Colombia, India, Peru, and Zaire—all megadiversity countries. For most country assistance strategies few references are made to such cross-cutting issues as forestry, agrobiodiversity, or the vital links between agricultural development and biodiversity conservation.

National Environmental Action Plans

A national environmental action plan (NEAP) describes a country's major environmental problems, seeks to identify causes, and outlines a national plan to address problems. A NEAP encompasses both policy and technical aspects and is expected to be developed and implemented by the government with broad participation. As such, the document is envisaged as an integral part of overall planning to alleviate environmental problems.

The World Bank considers the preparation and implementation of a NEAP as a step toward integrating global environmental objectives into national strategies and action plans for sustainable development. Though not strictly a Bank instrument, the Bank encourages and assists borrowing countries in the preparation and implementation of NEAPs, if requested. The NEAP is expected to strengthen the Bank's dialogue with the borrowing country and improve the quality of Bank operations in the borrowing country by making them more environmentally sustainable.

A brief look at NEAPs for Bangladesh, China, India, Jordan, Madagascar, Sri Lanka, and Tunisia shows how differently environmental issues may be treated. In the case of Sri Lanka, for example, the NEAP outlines the country's environmental action plan for 1992–96 on several fronts: land resources, water resources, mineral resources, coastal resources, forestry, biodiversity and wildlife, urban pollution, industrial pollution, energy, environmental education, culture, and institutional capacity.

Sri Lanka has more endemic species per unit area than any other country in Asia. It is one of eleven areas in the tropics identified by the Committee on Research Priorities in Tropical Biology for special attention because of its high levels of biodiversity and endemism and high rates of forest conversion to other uses (Government of Sri Lanka 1991). To alleviate ecological problems associated with shifting cultivation (about half of agricultural production area), several immediate and long-term measures have been proposed:

- Confine shifting cultivation to certain areas and immediately encourage adoption of practices that help conserve biodiversity
- Forest rehabilitation with community participation over the long term
- Identification of degraded forest lands with high agricultural potential and their conversion to agricultural use over the long term.

The NEAPs for China and India are the most comprehensive. The China NEAP highlights biodiversity losses resulting from the degradation and shrinking of natural habitats and the illegal cutting of forests. If the present trend continues, China will soon lose almost all of its natural woodlands outside of nature reserves.

China is not only a megadiversity country, it is also a major center of diversity for many agricultural species and their wild relatives, yet the NEAP makes no direct reference to agrobiodiversity. Only a passing reference is made to the protection of farmlands, where some of the "critical species" may exist. More than a thousand designated "eco-farms" in China practice ecologically sustainable agriculture. A lack of funds is jeopardizing this innovative program.

Environmental strategy in the NEAP for India recognizes the tradeoffs between poverty reduction and protection of the environment and emphasizes complementary actions. Considerable attention has been paid to the management of natural resources (such as the conservation and sustainable use of biodiversity) including forests, soil, and water conservation and industrial pollution control because they are most likely to have an effect on the poor. Of the seven NEAPs reviewed, only the one for India recognizes the usefulness of complementary *ex situ* and *in situ* conservation of food crops and other commercially important species.

In the NEAP for Bangladesh wildlife preservation and the protection and sustainable management of the Sundarban mangrove forests receive high priority. Agricultural pollution of land and water, because of high-input intensive

---

Box 7.2 Biodiversity in a country assistance strategy: Mexico

The World Bank's May 1994 country assistance strategy for Mexico argues that aquifer depletion, soil erosion, devastation of ecosystems, and exceptional biodiversity are pressing environmental issues. On both environmental and economic grounds there is no time to loose. Failure to act will result in further degradation, thereby undercutting economic and social development. The World Bank's strategy for sustainable development and biodiversity conservation includes strengthening natural resource management, slowing soil erosion, and improving protection and management of forests, parks, and biological reserves.

The Mexican government is committed to improving its efforts to ensure sustainable use of resources and reduction of pollution. Its strategy encompasses two mutually reinforcing sets of initiatives: a multisectoral approach in subregions with high-priority environmental problems and a national approach in particular sectors, including sustainable natural resource management and biodiversity conservation.

The World Bank is actively supporting the development and implementation of Mexico's environmental strategy through analytical work, institutional development, and lending.

The World Bank plans to continue efforts to strengthen environmental institutions, extending ongoing initiatives at the central level to state and municipal agencies. While supporting geographically focused environmental lending, sector-specific efforts will include ensuring the sustainable use of national forests and other natural resources and harnessing private sector initiative through incentives for appropriate environmental protection. The World Bank intends to work with Mexico to identify priorities in the areas of soil conservation, water resources management (including aquifer protection), and biodiversity conservation. Public participation in environmental policy formulation and enforcement will be supported, as well as preparation and implementation of an environmental action plan.

agriculture, is also a serious national concern, but the effects of intensive agriculture and population on biodiversity are not considered.

Nestled in the fertile crescent of southwest Asia, Jordan is an important area for the genetic diversity of several cereal crops and food legumes, including their wild relatives. The NEAP for Jordan makes no mention of their status, nor whether a conservation strategy has been devised for this agrobiodiversity of global significance. Rather, threats to the Wadi Rum desert ecosystem and archaeological sites from tourism and other human activities are the NEAP's main concern.

The NEAP for Tunisia provides a synthesis of environmental and related social problems in the country, covering a wide range of factors, such as industrial and marine pollution, land and water resource degradation, rapid urbanization, and expansion of residential areas to agricultural land. The environmental effects of redirecting economic activities are also covered, but no assessment is provided of the impact of the above factors on the country's biological resources.

In general NEAPs are preoccupied with the physical environment rather than biological resources. Less attention is paid to the conservation of biodiversity. Agrobiodiversity is virtually ignored. NEAPs often overlook the critical role of agrobiodiversity for sustainable agricultural development. Only the NEAP for India incorporates a systematic concern for the conservation of agrobiodiversity. Agriculture is frequently depicted as a factor in environmental degradation, but this treatment is rarely balanced with a discussion of how agriculture can enhance biodiversity and the environment.

Sectoral Perspectives on Biodiversity

The World Bank also publishes agricultural sector reviews and forestry sector reviews that provide sectoral perspectives on biodiversity in various countries.

Agricultural Sector Reviews

The principal objective of a World Bank agricultural sector review is to highlight the role of agriculture in an economy and the constraints to

agricultural growth, to recommend remedial actions, and to propose a strategy for future World Bank assistance to the sector. Typically, it contains reviews and recommendations that vary greatly by country depending on economic, political, and infrastructural conditions as well as institutional capabilities. The most common points covered are production systems, agricultural support services, marketing, transport, credit, irrigation, land degradation (such as soil salinity because of irrigation), land reform, agricultural subsidies, administration, and in a few cases involvement by NGOs and the private sector.

The main thrust of the World Bank's agricultural sector reviews is to increase production and reduce rural poverty, yet the sustainability of agricultural production is rarely addressed and biodiversity issues are rarely mentioned. In most countries government ministries are the largest and most important institutions concerned with agricultural development. Among competing sectors, the forestry sectors in developing countries have weak institutional capacity, thus exacerbating universal problems associated with inadequate research and extension.

In a survey of agricultural sector reviews for twenty-four countries, agriculture dominates the national economies and provides a significant proportion of export earnings. Most of the export commodities are introduced cash crops. The reviews' recommendations often include diversification of agriculture to avoid relying heavily on cash crops of exotic origin, but measures to broaden the genetic diversity of crop species and the potential of many interesting indigenous crops are typically overlooked.

In many countries increases in agricultural production have been achieved at the expense of the natural resource base. In such countries greater emphasis is warranted on the management of biophysical resources to sustain agricultural growth. This approach would include the integration of biodiversity conservation in agricultural development, an issue that might be tackled profitably in future agricultural sector reviews.

Some highlights from the sector reviews of selected countries indicate the broad range but uneven concern regarding biodiversity issues.

Agrobiodiversity gets little attention. In countries of Eastern Europe and the Commonwealth of Independent States many difficult policy, technical, and institutional problems have emerged during the transition from a command economy to a market-oriented one. Their agricultural sector reviews thus reflect a preoccupation with these issues. Progress in land reform (farm restructuring) and privatization of production, trade, and distribution systems have been important in countries such as Armenia, Estonia, Kazakhstan, Latvia, and the Russian Republic.

In Armenia, for example, cropping patterns have changed substantially since 1991, with food crop production sharply increased at the expense of forage, perennial, and industrial crops. The sector review for Armenia describes several environmental problems affecting agricultural productivity, including soil erosion, soil salinity, water pollution from agrochemicals, and deforestation. The need to protect wheat genetic resources is highlighted (box 7.3). Limiting factors for boosting agricultural production include unsatisfactory access to open-pollinated seeds and lack of superior genetic material for crop and livestock improvement.

Box 7.3 Protecting agrobiodiversity in Armenia

The World Bank's February 1996 agricultural sector review for Armenia notes that the country has a diversified and unique assemblage of plant genetic material, including ancient varieties of several crops and their wild relatives. However, Armenia does not have a gene bank, and foreign financial and technical assistance is needed to preserve this germplasm under both *ex situ* and *in situ* conditions.

Armenia has a long history of setting aside specific habitats for conservation—a small part of Khosrov has been designated as a preserve since A.D. 333—but much remains to be done. The review recommends that immediate steps be taken to prevent the destruction of progenitors of wheat in the biological preserve and park complex near the city of Yerevan.

The recommended steps have implications for wheat growers and consumers not only in Armenia but around the world. If adequately protected, areas in Armenia could serve as examples of how

---

The review makes several recommendations to protect and better use the country's environmental and biological assets:

• Allow the market to set prices for fertilizers, herbicides, and pesticides to encourage their more efficient use and reduce runoff and consequent pollution of aquatic environments
• Regulate the storage and use of agrochemicals
• Establish a soil conservation directorate to help reduce erosion
• Provide tax credits to farmers who manage their land well
• Facilitate access to land for entrepreneurial farmers with a vested interest in long-term stewardship
• Reduce grazing pressure on pastures formerly open to communal use by providing exclusive, long-term leases.

For Estonia the combined agricultural and forestry sector review observes that past methods of forest management and use have been beneficial for maintaining high levels of biodiversity both in production and protected forests. About one-quarter of forest area is classified as protected, but only 1 percent is totally excluded from harvesting, a fact that may endanger the chances of maintaining current levels of biodiversity. This combined review for Estonia is one of the few sectoral documents that address the biodiversity issue, albeit briefly. It does not, however, suggest any steps other than the use of protected areas that might foster the preservation of forest biodiversity, nor does it mention crop diversity or broadening genetic diversity within crops.

For Latvia the agricultural sector review recommends a crop production strategy that includes minimum tillage, crop rotation, and effective soil conservation measures. Changes in crop production patterns to increase feed and forage production and improvement of feeding and livestock management practices to enhance feeding efficiency and increase livestock production are also discussed. The recommendation for crop rotation would increase the agrobiodiversity of areas currently monocropped. Forests are important natural resources in Latvia and are derived largely from afforestation of agricultural land. The agricultural sector review points out the potential for increased forest production with proper management. However, the biodiversity of forest trees—and the importance of genetic resources for forestry—are not discussed.

For Kazakhstan the agriculture and forestry sector review comments on the negative environmental effects of outdated cultivation practices but does not elaborate. The country's crop research is conducted by public institutions, primarily based on imported germplasm. From Africa a few observations from the agricultural sector reviews for Egypt, Ethiopia, Madagascar, and Zaire show similarly varied concerns.

In the case of Egypt, except for a brief reference to the use of locally established strains of dual-purpose birds such as poultry, the agricultural sector review does not consider agrobiodiversity and its potential in agricultural development in this highly populated country. For Ethiopia the sector review ignores the country's wealth of crop genetic resources, especially with respect to Arabica coffee, teff, and ensete (a relative of the banana). The agricultural sector review emphasizes the importance of research in agroforestry and cropping systems involving legumes and forage legumes in crop rotation.

In Madagascar geographic isolation and varied terrain, climate, and soils have fostered the evolution of many unique plants and animals. Diverse altitudinal zones, ranging from temperate to tropical, have also promoted a diverse agriculture. The agricultural sector review recognizes that natural resource degradation reduces biodiversity and constrains agricultural growth (box 7.4).

Zaire, with the largest tropical rainforest in Africa (about 10 percent of the global tropical forest area), has substantial biodiversity to conserve. Loss of genetic resources would constrain efforts to boost the country's productivity of such cash crops as oil palm, rubber, and cotton. The sector review notes that the country has great potential for forestry and fishery development and recommends development of a forestry management and protection plan to promote the rational use of forest resources.

The sector reviews for Sri Lanka and Papua New Guinea skim over biodiversity and agrobiodiversity. The agricultural sector review for Sri Lanka pinpoints tree crops, especially tea, rubber, and coconut, for particular attention in agricultural development, but replanting rates are

---

Box 7.4 Biodiversity concerns and constraints to agricultural growth in Madagascar

The World Bank's February 1994 agricultural strategy note for Madagascar recognizes that the country has impressive agricultural potential and significant constraints to achieving that potential. Among the constraints are inadequate land tenure legislation and limited use of technology. Both these constraints are seen as a negative impact on the natural resource base and hence the island's unique biodiversity.

Because of the lack of land tenure security, conflicts over the use of natural resources (land, forest, water, fish) arise out of the ambiguous definition of resource user's rights. The current system clearly needs revamping.

The expansion of farmland with continued reliance on traditional techniques alone has accelerated natural resource degradation:

- Hillside cultivation has provoked massive deforestation and serious soil erosion.
- Bush fires set by farmers and by those involved in land-use disputes between pastoralists and cultivators are exceeding the regenerative capacity of the plant cover.

In the past thirty years 80 percent of the west coast deciduous natural forests and 50 percent of humid tropical forests in the eastern region have disappeared. Most of this loss is a result of clearing new lands for cultivation. A marked reduction of government services in the field has contributed to the destructive process: nominally protected forests are not supervised adequately, rangelands are not managed properly, land-tenure rights are not clarified in a timely fashion.

Heightened governmental awareness of these issues and a massive donor response have resulted in an environmental program that includes the establishment and protection of fifty parks and reserves; introduction of sustainable production systems in environmentally sensitive areas; accelerated titling of agricultural land; and improved management of gazetted forests. The program, however, is facing a bottleneck caused by the need to build implementation capacity on the ground. The program is initially concentrating on the protection of biodiversity, more attention over the long term will need to be given to soil erosion, deforestation caused by shifting cultivation, and bush fires. Accordingly, the World Bank's strategy for agriculture in Madagascar highlights the proper management of natural resources.

currently inadequate. Crop diversification is encouraged, for which two avenues exist: promising new lines of high-value crops and traditional supplementary crops. Biodiversity, however, is not mentioned.

As in several other biodiversity-rich developing countries, the problems of agriculture in Papua New Guinea are soil erosion, soil salinity, waterlogging, and unchanged cropping patterns. Land tenure is a particularly difficult problem in Papua New Guinea because most of the land is community owned. With rapid population growth and the increased adoption of cash crops, the sustainability of the traditional land-tenure system is being challenged. Without elaboration the sector review asserts that the introduction of new crops, rather than improving local crops, is the most promising avenue for agricultural development. It expresses concern for increasing pressure on land, particularly in areas of high-population density, as well as for the sustainability of traditional production systems. Agrobiodiversity in this ecologically diverse country gets no notice.

Shifting to Latin America—specifically, to Argentina, Brazil, and Ecuador—uneven attention to biodiversity is again the case. The sector review for Argentina claims that the country has some of the most counter-productive agricultural sector policies among the world's major agricultural exporters. Application of biotechnologies is seen as a key for improving crops and livestock, but broadening their genetic base is largely overlooked.

For Brazil the agricultural sector review ignores biodiversity and agrobiodiversity, but these topics are covered in a separate sector report (World Bank 1994). This report recognizes the abundance of biodiversity, ecosystems, and diversity of agriculture. Indicative problems cited are agrochemical hazards, soil erosion, and land degradation. Issues in forest biodiversity conservation include management of conservation units and differential taxing of land in native forest and cleared areas. The issue of indigenous rights is also broached. Also it credits agricultural research in Brazil with the development of high-yielding varieties and assembling a large collection of genetic resources.

Noticeably, the agricultural sector review for Ecuador acknowledges the remarkably rich bio-

diversity in the country and identifies deforestation as one of the most significant threats to its genetic heritage. Crop agriculture and the livestock industry are described as the driving forces behind deforestation. The review recommends changes in property rights, implementation of various measures to slow the conversion of logged forests to agriculture, and strengthening the national research system for agriculture and forestry. Significantly, local communities are heavily involved in reforestation and agroforestry projects in Ecuador. Involvement of local stakeholders is essential for the long-term conservation and management of biodiversity.

Forestry Sector Reviews

The World Bank's forestry policy emphasizes collaboration among conventional forest services, agricultural extension agencies, and NGOs (World Bank 1991). Biodiversity conservation is clearly a concern in forestry sector reviews. Deforestation and loss of habitat because of agricultural expansion, soil degradation, and declining fertility appear to be the most serious environmental problem. Mexico exemplifies the importance of public awareness and participation in the management and conservation of biodiversity. In general, however, biological resources are undervalued in most countries. Observations from the forestry sector reviews of Argentina, India, and Mexico are indicative of this.

The forestry sector review for Argentina cites with dismay institutional capacity of the forestry sector. Although laws have been promulgated to safeguard the environment and to establish national parks, enforcement is lax, as it is in many other developing countries.

For India the forestry sector review contends that biodiversity conservation could be improved through a spectrum of interventions to meet different needs. A three-pronged strategy is proposed:

1. Extending and improving the protected area network
2. Increasing benefits to local populations in and around protected areas through joint management and other ecodevelopment activities
3. Including biodiversity objectives in management of multiple-use forest lands.

Population pressure and poverty are major problems facing forest conservation in Mexico, home to numerous endemic plant and animal species. The greatest threat comes from land-use conversion of natural habitat, especially forests, to agriculture and ranching. Most of the officially protected areas are too small to be ecologically viable. While the habitat types with the highest endemism and diversity (for example, oak and cloud forests, dry scrubland, and tropical moist forests) are underprotected, low-diversity ecosystems (conifer forests) are overrepresented in the country's system of protected areas. On the other hand preservation of biodiversity is considered to be an ecological, economic, and cultural issue in Mexico; such grassroots concern bodes well for future conservation efforts.

Agriculture Sector Portfolio

Between July 1988 and June 1995 the World Bank initiated 402 agricultural development projects in ninety-seven countries. These projects supported a wide range of activities, from genetic engineering of livestock to improved marketing of crops (table 7.2).

Forty projects explicitly involved conservation and management of biodiversity. Ten projects were concerned with agrobiodiversity (box 7.5).

However, biodiversity conservation was not usually well integrated with other project activities. Except for two projects, one in Ghana (the 1989 Forestry Project) and one in Brazil (the 1992 Mato Grosso Natural Resource Management Project), conscious efforts toward sustainable management of both natural and agricultural habitats were absent or indiscernible. Little interest was evident in "alternative agriculture" concerned with ecological restoration and environmental conservation.

About thirty-six (73 percent) of the agriculture sector projects required a partial environmental assessment (category B), and 37 percent called for no assessment. Only 4 percent of agricultural projects merited a full environmental assessment (18 percent was pending assignment, and 7 percent was categorized as environmental from the outset). While some environmental assessment and analysis sections of project documents are limited to listing envisaged environmental benefits, many consider the environmental impact of project activities and suggest remedial or mitigating actions for incorporation into project design.

Very few environmental assessments discuss biodiversity issues directly, and even fewer approach it from the "mainstreaming" point of view. When biodiversity is mentioned, it is usually in the context of possible effects of agricultural

Table 7.2 Overview of the World Bank's agriculture sector portfolio
IBRD/IDA agriculture sector loans and credits, 1988–95
(millions of U.S. dollars)

Subsector	1988	1989	1990	1991	1992	1993	1994	1995
Sector loan	2,118.5	1,701.7	1,380.5	2,151.6	1,744.1	1,117.5	1,818.4	994.4
	(22)	(21)	(20)	(19)	(26)	(22)	(21)	(18)
Agroindustry	376.3	635.2	228.0	3.0	0.0	493.1	0.0	92.0
	(3)	(5)	(3)	(1)	(0)	(2)	(0)	(2)
Fisheries	0.0	0.0	44.6	22.0	95.0	0.0	0.0	9.0
	(0)	(0)	(1)	(2)	(2)	(0)	(0)	(1)
Forestry	167.5	89.8	536.0	19.9	291.1	91.5	565.4	113.0
	(6)	(3)	(8)	(1)	(7)	(2)	(8)	(2)
Irrigation and drainage	956.2	580.4	713.8	980.4	1,019.7	920.0	1,025.9	781.9
	(14)	(5)	(8)	(10)	(8)	(11)	(8)	(9)
Livestock	378.6	53.6	0.0	40.8	0.0	22.5	0.0	0.0
	(2)	(2)	(0)	(2)	(0)	(1)	(0)	(0)
Perennial crops	90.5	25.1	365.8	16.5	114.6	92.0	70.0	0.0
	(4)	(1)	(5)	(1)	(2)	(1)	(1)	(0)
Research and extension	37.5	247.5	270.4	196.1	296.6	53.1	87.9	347.6
	(2)	(10)	(10)	(7)	(6)	(3)	(5)	(7)
Other	383.3	168.3	117.0	277.0	342.9	477.0	339.7	311.4
	(4)	(5)	(1)	(4)	(4)	(3)	(5)	(3)
Total amount	4,508.4	3,501.6	3,656.1	3,707.3	3,904.0	3,266.7	3,907.3	2,649.3
Total number	(57)	(52)	(56)	(47)	(55)	(45)	(48)	(42)

Note: Figures in parentheses are number of loans.
Source: World Bank data.

Box 7.5 Agrobiodiversity issues addressed in the World Bank's agriculture portfolio

The China National Afforestation Project (1990) is establishing approximately one million hectares of forest with 75 percent native species. Genetic uniformity is being avoided by planting blocks of single species that do not exceed 100 hectares; further, the blocks are divided by strips of natural or planted broad-leafed trees. A mosaic of different species including natural vegetation thus characterizes this afforestation project, unlike many others that tend to involve planting of a single species over vast areas. The Zaire Agriculture Research Project (1992) includes germplasm conservation among twelve priority research programs identified in a master plan for research in the country. The Congo Wildlands Protection Project (1993) supports capacity building at the national herbarium. The Gabon Forestry and Environment Project (1993) finances refrigeration facilities for seed storage at the country's national arboretum.

Source: World Bank data.

Table 7.3 Some agricultural development targets of World Bank projects and their potential impact on biodiversity

Target	Impact	Target	Impact
Agricultural diversification	+/–	Agricultural expansion	–
Agricultural intensification	–	Agroindustry	+/–
Agroforestry	+	Agropastoral system	+/–
Animal breeding	+/–	Annual to perennial crops shift	+/–
Archaeological sites protection	+	Biodynamic farming	+
Biotechnology	+/–	Broadening crop gene pool	+
Community pasture development	+	Crop diversification (polyculture)	+
Crop rotation	+	Ecological agriculture	+
Ecosystem preservation	+	Ecotourism	+
Endangered species protection	+	*Ex situ* preservation of genetic resources	+
Germplasm preservation	+	Green and organic manure use	+
Habitat restoration	+	Habitat protection	+
High-yielding varieties	+/–	High-input farming (purchased agrochemicals)	–
Integrated pest management	+	Improved strains of livestock	+/–
Irrigation	–	*In situ* conservation of diversity	+
Low-input sustainable agriculture	+	Irrigation dams	+/–
Managed forests	+	Multiple variety or strain development	+
Mixed farming	+	Mixed cropping	+
Natural reserves (parks, botanical gardens, arboretums)	+	Multiline development	+
		Natural resources management	+
Natural habitats protection and restoration	+	New crop introduction	+/–
Nitrogen fixation	+	New livestock introduction	+/–
Pest-resistant varieties	+/–	Organic farming	+
Plantation systems	+/–	Plant breeding	+/–
Rare-species recovery	+	Protected-area management	+
Seed health and quality	+	Rural transportation	+/–
Soil conservation	+	Traditional agro-ecosystem protection	+/–
Wild crop relatives conservation	+	Varietal diversification	+
Wildlife protection	+	Wetland management	+

Note: Impacts are catergorized as potentially + positive, – negative, or either +/– positive or negative.
Source: Prepared by the authors.

activity on protected areas or the formation of such areas to mitigate project activities. However, in a few cases biodiversity is a major project concern. For example, the environmental assessment section of the 1988 Brazil Agriculture Credit Project (World Bank 1988) notes that removal of subsidized credit provides greater parity between private and social costs of investment in ecologically fragile areas, thereby contributing to more sound husbandry of the country's natural resources.

To determine the potential impact of the World Bank's agriculture sector portfolio on biodiversity, 361 projects with sufficient information were broadly grouped by: (1) obvious relation with biodiversity, (2) potential relation with biodiversity, and (3) no apparent relation with biodiversity. Each project's objectives and method of procedure suggested its potential effect on biodiversity, including agrobiodiversity. Using a number of key agricultural and development activities, which have known or anticipated effects on biodiversity, it was further possible to characterize projects by potentially negative, positive, or mixed effects (table 7.3). For example, some activities such as agroforestry, integrated pest management, natural resources management, rare and endangered

species protection, ecological restoration, crop rotation, and genetic resources preservation are known to have positive effects. On the other hand promotion of pesticide use, plantation of introduced cash crops, and canal construction through nature reserves have potentially negative effects on biodiversity. Still other activities have potential to convey mixed or ambivalent effects.

The typology and categorization of projects in table 7.3 simplifies the interrelationships between agricultural activities and their effects on biodiversity, but it points out the complexity of the issue because of the many variables involved. For instance, field-scale and off-site effects of some practices differ considerably (box 7.6).

Biodiversity-friendly projects are apparently on the increase (figure 7.2). This encouraging trend has occurred despite the fact that biodiversity conservation was not the motivation of these agricultural projects. A window of opportunity clearly exists, therefore to mainstream biodiversity conservation in most, if not all, of the World Bank's agricultural development projects.

Issues and Future Direction

Biodiversity is a concern in a relatively small portion of the World Bank's policy and strategy documents. The central role of biodiversity in sustainable development warrants stronger emphasis. A recent policy paper pinpoints several areas for adjustment and improvement to procedures and analytical approach (box 7.7). Environmental concern in agricultural and forestry projects has emphasized physical aspects, such as soil and water, while much less attention has been paid to the biotic environment and consequently to biodiversity conservation. Agriculture's contribution to environmental problems, such as habitat destruction and soil degradation, are relatively well documented, but discussions on the constraints to agriculture have generally not included biodiversity issues. In country assistance strategies, for example, a country's biological richness is rarely taken into account, particularly as it applies to improving agriculture. Crop diversification is recommended in some cases, but measures to broaden genetic diversity of crop species are almost always overlooked.

Agrobiodiversity is thus seldom a matter of concern. In many examples a country's environmental problems, ranging from industrial and marine pollution to land and water resource degradation, will be scrutinized but the country's biological resources ignored. Effective planning and complementary strategies for agricultural development and conservation of the genetic diversity of crops and livestock, their wild relatives, and evolutionary progenitors are needed. The conservation and potential use of

---

Box 7.6 Possible biodiversity tradeoffs within agroecosystems

Several agricultural practices assist in protecting soil and water quality while maintaining or increasing productivity. These practices have the potential to significantly decrease farmers' encroachment on fragile areas and natural habitats. They indirectly enhance biodiversity by mitigating many of the adverse environmental effects of modern agriculture, especially pollution of aquatic environments with agrochemicals and excessive soil erosion.

No-tillage reduces soil erosion and pesticide losses with surface runoff (Baker and Johnson 1979). Crop residues left on the ground help build up organic matter, thereby restoring the natural fertility of the soil. Increased organic matter and soil moisture in no-tillage fields foster greater biological activity in the soil, such as activity by earthworms (Woomer and Swift 1994).

On the other hand pest and weed control may be a problem in no-till fields. In conventional tillage systems plowing helps control weeds, and farmers who adopt no-tillage systems may have to increase their use of herbicides. Also, by leaving more crop residue in the fields, diseases and pests can build up faster

under conventional tillage, so some pesticides may have to be used more frequently, at least during the transitional phase (Hinkle 1983).

Evidence is growing that increased activity by earthworms and soil insects in no-tillage systems creates an intricate network of macropores (usually destroyed in conventional tillage systems) that facilitate the movement of water, dissolved solutes, and suspended sediment to shallow groundwater or deeper soil layers where biological degradation is much lower (Baker 1987; Kanwar, Baker, and Laflen 1985; Wagenet 1987).

Contamination of shallow groundwater systems with persistent agricultural chemicals could eventually lead to degraded quality of surface aquatic systems (as surface and groundwater systems are hydrologically linked) and associated flora and fauna. No-tillage practice therefore may positively affect biodiversity on a field scale, but its short-run off-site impacts could be negative or positive, depending on the hydrology of the area and on farmers' ability to master all the aspects of no-tillage.

Source: Singh 1996.

Figure 7.2 Trends in the potential impact of World Bank agriculture sector projects on biodiversity, 1988–95

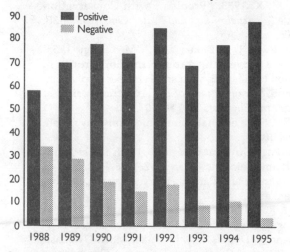

Source: Authors' compilation.

agrobiodiversity for long-term economic benefits for the country and world should be investigated and incorporated into World Bank analytical documents. One option is to place greater emphasis on natural resource management problems in agriculture. This should include biodiversity (including agrobiodiversity) management and the integration of biodiversity with agricultural development.

The major portion of the World Bank's investment in biodiversity conservation has aimed at the establishment and management of protected areas. Numerous issues relevant to biodiversity in agriculture are not broached. Fortunately, however, as analysis of the agriculture sector portfolio reveals, the trend toward biodiversity-friendly practices in agricultural development projects is increasing, despite the fact that biodiversity conservation was not a primary concern of these agricultural projects.

A comprehensive agricultural development policy should maximize the economic benefits to society while preserving its biological wealth. To achieve this dual goal, the World Bank can assist national governments in several key areas:

- Develop environmentally sustainable national agricultural developmental strategies
- Provide both economic and ecological rationales for biodiversity conservation
- Promote an ecosystem-approach to development and pursue conservation methods that

---

Box 7.7 Mainstreaming biodiversity in development

In a recent policy-oriented paper the following actions are cited as a way to strengthen the role of biodiversity in the World Bank's work:

- Integrate biodiversity conservation and sustainable use with its overall policy dialogue and country assistance strategies
- Adjust traditional economic and sector work to include biodiversity issues and priorities.
- Ensure that biodiversity objectives are appropriately reflected in the design of individual investment projects across sectors of the economy
- Enhance environmental assessment practices.
- Support the development of human resources and institutions that are required to facilitate the mainstreaming of biodiversity
- Adopt internal operational policies and development practices that support the mainstreaming of biodiversity in the World Bank's development programs
- Learn from others' experiences, strengthen existing collaborations, and establish new partnerships, drawing on others' skills and resources, the development of good practices, and the increasing public awareness of biodiversity's value.

Source: World Bank 1995a.

---

will maximize agricultural and natural biodiversity and also allow its sustainable use
- Formulate economic and noneconomic incentives for biodiversity conservation.
- Encourage legal and regulatory reforms
- Strengthen institutional capacity and organizations.

In the short term the World Bank could identify and further encourage the adoption of biodiversity-friendly agricultural policies, practices, and approaches. A sound-practices manual or guide for task managers at the World Bank and other organizations involved in agricultural development would be a step in that direction. A sound-practices guide would include a checklist of practices that significantly diminish negative downstream effects of farming and livestock operations and suggest measures that can be taken to reduce encroachment into natural habitats and fragile areas. A checklist would not constrain agricultural growth; rather, it would point to opportunities for incorporating greater biodiversity in agricultural landscapes while reducing collateral damage to the environment. However, biodiversity conservation needs to be recognized as a long-term investment. The ecological, genetic, and social interactions that create and maintain biodiversity are the result of evolutionary processes not confined to a fiscal year or five-year project envelopes. Investment strategies need to be adjusted accordingly.

Poverty alleviation cannot be achieved in the absence of the sustainable use of natural resources, but an environmental strategy must recognize that tradeoffs exist between immediate poverty reduction and protection of the environment. Also environmental concerns cannot be divorced from social considerations because the causes of encroachment and resource over-exploitation are usually social and economic. Governments should be encouraged to include greater public participation to share with society the responsibility of protecting its biological resources.

Many intergovernment organizations and national and international NGOs are actively engaged in worldwide biodiversity conservation, particularly in biodiversity-rich developing countries. While developing a comprehensive strategy for biodiversity conservation, the role and contributions of these local and international participants in agricultural development and biodiversity conservation should be reviewed, and lessons from experience should be used.

References

Baker, J. L. 1987. "Hydrologic Effects of Conservation Tillage and Their Importance Relative to Water Quality." In T. J. Logan, J. Davidson, J. L. Baker, M. R. Overcash eds., *Effects of Conservation Tillage on Groundwater Quality: Nitrates and Pesticides*. Chelsea, Mich.: Lewis Publishers.

Baker, J. L., and H. P. Johnson. 1979. "The Effects of Tillage Systems on Pesticide in Runoff from Small Watersheds," *Transactions of the American Society of Agricultural Engineers* 22: 554–59.

Hinkle, M. K. 1983. "Problems with Conservation Tillage," *Journal of Soil and Water Conservation* 38: 201–06.

Kanwar, R. S., J. L. Baker, and J. M. Laflen. 1985. "Nitrate Movement through the Soil Profile in Relation to Tillage System and Fertilizer Application Method," *Transactions of the American Society of Agricultural Engineers* 28: 1,802–07.

Singh, P. 1996. Personal communication. Iowa State University.

Sri Lanka, Government of. 1991. "National Environmental Action Plan 1992–1996." Ministry of Environment and Parliamentary Affairs. Colombo, Sri Lanka.

Wagenet, R. J. 1987. "Processes Influencing Pesticide Loss with Water under Conservation Tillage." In T. J. Logan, J. Davidson, J. L. Baker, M. R. Overcash eds., *Effects of Conservation Tillage on Groundwater Quality: Nitrates and Pesticides*. Chelsea, Mich.: Lewis Publishers.

Woomer, P. L., and M. J. Swift, eds. 1994. *The Biological Management of Tropical Soil Fertility*. Chichester, U.K.: John Wiley.

World Bank. 1988. "Staff Appraisal Report, Agricultural Credit Project: Brazil." Report no. 7199, Washington, D.C.

———.1991a. *The Forest Sector: A World Bank Policy Paper*. Washington, D.C.

———.1991b. "Operational Directive 4.01, Environmental Assessment." *Operational Manual*. Washington, D.C.

———.1993. "Operational Policy 4.36, Forestry." *Operational Manual*. Washington, D.C.

———.1994. "Brazil: The Management of Agriculture, Rural Development and Natural Resources." World Bank Sector Report. Washington, D.C.

———.1995a. "Mainstreaming Biodiversity in Development: A World Bank Assistance Strategy for Implementing the Convention on Biological Diversity." Environment Department. Washington, D.C.

———.1995b. *Mainstreaming the Environment. The World Bank Group and the Environment since the Rio Earth Summit*. Washington, D.C.

———.1995c. "Operational Policy 4.04, National Habitats." *Operational Manual*. Washington, D.C.

8. Toward a Strategy for Mainstreaming Biodiversity in Agricultural Development

Jitendra P. Srivastava, Nigel J. H. Smith, and Douglas A. Forno

A strategy is needed to help policymakers reconcile the task of preserving biodiversity while at the same time increasing agricultural productivity. Preceding chapters have explored some of the important relationships between agriculture and biodiversity and have argued that biodiversity conservation and agricultural development can be complementary activities. Each chapter has offered suggestions to ameliorate damage to biodiversity resulting from agricultural practices and policies. Here we explore some tentative steps toward an overall strategy for better mainstreaming biodiversity in agricultural development.

Biodiversity and Agriculture: Partnership for Sustainable Development

The expansion of the agricultural frontier, population growth, and an emphasis on maximizing agricultural output using potent agrochemicals are exerting pressure on habitats for wild plants and animals. In many cases the conversion of wildlife habitats to farmland and adoption of "modern" farming practices that rely heavily on purchased fertilizers, pesticides, and herbicides trigger a loss of biodiversity and the extinction of species. How to conserve biodiversity while addressing the need to increase agricultural production in developing countries—where most of the earth's biodiversity is located—is a major challenge facing humanity.

An effective strategy to conserve biodiversity and further agricultural development requires greater comprehension on the part of both sides. On the one hand those interested in preserving wildlife, and the habitats they depend on, would benefit from an appreciation of people's roles in shaping a wide array of cultural habitats on the earth, many of which contain considerable biodiversity both in space and over time. And those concerned with agricultural development might improve their success rate by a better appreciation of the value of conserving biodiversity and the importance of devising land-use practices that enhance rather than destroy biological riches and the ecosystems that support them.

Agenda for Action

Various policies and practices can be devised to promote biodiversity conservation in managed landscapes and to enhance the greater use of bioiversity in agriculture (table 8.1). Some of the major points for policy consideration are summarized here.

Toward a Balanced Conservation Strategy

Too often conservation is posed as an either-or proposition. Some argue that resources should be concentrated in maintaining animal and plant genetic resources in places where they occur naturally (*in situ*), while others suggest that genetic variation is more useful and often safer if it is maintained in seed or field gene banks (*ex situ*). Both strategies are needed to sustain the productivity of agricultural systems.

Table 8.1 Policies and practices that promote biodiversity conservation

Objective	Proposed action	Responsible organizations
COMMITMENT TO ENHANCING BIODIVERSITY IN AGRICULTURE		
Increase government commitment to mainstreaming biodiversity in agriculture and rural development.	Conduct substantive dialogue with client countries on the need to conserve and manage biodiversity resources.	MDBs, bilateral aid agencies, and NGOs.
Increase farmer commitment to incorporate greater diversity in farming systems.	Support efforts to establish property rights so that farmers are more willing to invest in long-term strategies to incorporate more biodiversity such as intercropping with perennials; identify other incentives that encourage farmers to promote agrobiodiversity in their cropping systems.	National governments.
Generate greater understanding of how to implement policies and sound practices to enhance biodiversity in agricultural development.	Prepare training manuals and packets for human resource development.	MDBs, bilateral aid agencies, IARCs, NGOs, and agricultural extension agencies.
Diversify farming operations with viable alternative crops.	Support more research in lesser known or more localized crops.	NARs.
Collect sufficient data on potential impact of agricultural development projects on biodiversity and agrobiodiversity.	Develop methodologies and performance indicators for assessing agrobiodiversity in areas targeted for agricultural development.	MDBs, bilateral aid agencies, NARs, NGOs, and farmers.
NEW AGRICULTURAL RESEARCH AND EXTENSION PARADIGM		
Increase participation of farmers in design and implementation of agricultural development projects to enhance agrobiodiversity.	Conduct substantive dialogue with developing country institutions on the need to incorporate, not just consult, local farmers in agricultural research and development projects.	Farmers, MDBs, IARCs, and NGOs.
Increase deployment of genetically diverse (heterozygous) populations of crop varieties and animal breeds on managed landscapes.	Provide greater support for developing polygenic resistance, multilines, high-yielding, open-pollinated varieties instead of hybrids.	IARCs and NARs.
Improve productivity of farming and livestock raising in marginal environments.	Increase research on undervalued crops and livestock that are better adapted to difficult environments than the "mega" crops and livestock.	Farmers, IARCs, and NARs.
Create greater awareness of appropriate practices for enhancing biodiversity in agricultural development.	Develop and disseminate "sound practices" tailored to task managers in developing country institutions and international development agencies.	MDBs, bilateral aid agencies, NGOs, NARs, and agricultural extension agencies.
Create rich landscape mosaics with a variety of habitats for wildlife as well as crop and livestock production.	Develop an understanding of factors that motivate farmers to retain or destroy buffer strips and woodlots or to plant a wider variety of crops; suggest policies to promote landscape mosaics.	Research: universities and NARs. Implementation: agricultural extension agencies.
Develop understanding of how to implement policies and sound practices to enhance biodiversity in agricultural development.	Prepare training manuals and packets for human resource development.	MDBs, bilateral aid agencies, IARCs, NGOs, and agricultural extension agencies.
APPROACHES TO CONSERVATION OF AGROBIODIVERSITY		
Achieve appropriate balance between *in situ* and *ex situ* approaches by crop.	Develop methodology for estimating the value of *in situ* conservation of genetic resources as a basis for allocating limited funds.	IARCs (especially IPGRI), universities, and FAO.
Create incentives for *in situ* conservation of crop and livestock genetic resources.	Identify and implement a new system of intellectual property rights applicable to traditional varieties and breeds to benefit local people.	FAO.
Create incentives to maintain materials in *ex situ* collections through recognition of their tangible economic value.	Explore the possibility of recognizing intellectual property rights for some genetic materials in collections with royalties to be paid to gene banks and groups that provided the germplasm.	FAO.

Note: FAO (Food and Agriculture Organization); IARCs (international agricultural research centers); IPGRI (International Plant Genetic Resources Institute); MDB (multilateral development banks); NARs (national agricultural research programs); NGOs (nongovernmental organizations).

While measures to improve the usefulness of *ex situ* collections of plant and animal genetic resources are warranted, considerable attention is now being focused on ways to promote *in situ* conservation of plant and animal genetic resources. A wide assortment of approaches to *in situ* conservation is being tried, and a review of their effectiveness would generate helpful information for policy formulation.

The following approaches to *in situ* conservation of crops and livestock appear to warrant particular support:

- Emphasize a new dimension to existing wilderness parks and biological reserves, safeguarding plants and animals for the future improvement of agriculture. Some existing parks and reserves contain wild populations or near relatives of crops and livestock; highlighting such attributes would strengthen the case for their better protection and management. A major problem is that many areas under consideration for protection have not been adequately inventoried from the botanical standpoint.

- Create world heritage sites for genes for agricultural development. Most parks and reserves have been set up to protect spectacular animals or rare and endangered plants and habitats. While such efforts deserve continued support, the agrobiodiversity aspect of environmental conservation has been largely overlooked. Many areas are "hot spots" for agrobiodiversity and warrant better conservation and management in their own right.

- Protect sacred sites and agrobiodiversity. Some sites that are revered and protected for religious purposes contain groves of wild populations of crops or their near relatives. Their contribution to agrobiodiversity has been largely ignored. The World Bank has a policy of helping to protect cultural patrimony. Some sacred places could be envisaged as a form of cultural patrimony with an added twist: agrobiodiversity conservation.

- Integrate agrobiodiversity in ecotourism where appropriate. A virtually untapped market exists for showing tourists who visit nature reserves and major archaeological sites "traditional" villages and farmlands in the surrounding area.

- Help find markets for lesser known crops and local varieties under the motto "use it or lose it." If a highly localized crop that is on the decline suddenly ignites interest in a distant market, growers will be motivated to look around for highly productive varieties. This search for planting material might save varieties that might otherwise be abandoned. If the crop becomes highly successful and commercialized, the number of varieties that are eventually grown is likely to decline. But if the crop is valuable, some efforts may be taken to save at least some of the variation that used to exist in the crop.

- Help find ways for livestock owners to generate more revenues from threatened breeds. If such breeds can "pay" for themselves, they are less likely to be replaced by the more widespread breeds, or their identity is lost in continuous crossbreeding. Ecotourism is one way to generate income from rare breeds. Another way would be to eliminate fiscal incentives for livestock owners to import exotic breeds or to use artificial insemination based on a few "super" sires. Incentives might be provided to promote more widespread adoption of indigenous stock that is in many cases better adapted to harsh environments than exotic breeds.

Greater Involvement of the Private Sector

Too often biodiversity conservation is seen as a public sector responsibility. Experience has shown that reliance on parks and reserves alone to conserve biodiversity does not work because local populations often do not receive any benefits from such protected areas. Indeed they may even suffer damages from wildlife damaging crops or livestock or be denied access to resources they once depended on for part of their subsistence or income.

To counteract reliance on formal protected areas, community empowerment and management of natural resources have become a rallying cry among donors and organizations that promote conservation and rural development. The decentralization of control over natural resources can bring many benefits, but community management alone may not work in all cases.

Both protected areas and community or local initiatives to manage and conserve biodiversity warrant continued support, but they are not enough. A third, parallel approach is called for, particularly in the case of agrobiodiversity: greater involvement of the private sector. Market forces can and should be harnessed to conserve and better use biodiversity. Some specific steps that can be taken to facilitate this process include:

- *Promoting policies that encourage market diversification.* Create enterprise funds or generate other mechanisms to increase investments in developing new crops and "forgotten" crops so that their potential can be tapped for national and international markets.
- *Engaging private landowners in the conservation and management of biodiversity.* More studies need to be undertaken to understand factors that influence landowners in their decisions to maintain or destroy forests or other reservoirs of biodiversity. Provide tax incentives or other measures to encourage landowners to keep relatively undisturbed areas out of production for crops or livestock.

Tapping Indigenous Knowledge

This is a theme that cross-cuts so many aspects of the dynamic interplay between biodiversity and sustaining agricultural production. In the past local or farmer knowledge about production systems has been largely overlooked, especially in developing countries. Increasingly, though, farmers are seen as partners in efforts to conserve and manage biodiversity, whether for nature reserves or to improve crop and livestock yields.

As a matter of policy all agricultural research programs and development projects should include components that seek to incorporate farmers in the design and implementation of research and development efforts. The benefits of such collaboration far outweigh the costs of taking the time and trouble to improve the channels of communication between the research establishment and the intended beneficiaries: farmers and livestock managers. Some specific contributions of indigenous knowledge to sustainable agriculture include:

- Crop varieties adapted to harsh growing conditions

- Cropping patterns that minimize the buildup of diseases
- Breeds of livestock that tolerate poor feed or resist diseases and pests that afflict imported breeds
- Intimate knowledge of botanical resources in forests and other habitats that could provide leads for plant domestication or other uses.

Respect for the importance of local or "traditional" knowledge for agricultural development should include renewed efforts to demarcate and protect the territories of indigenous groups. This does not imply that indigenous people should be cut off from the outside world and discouraged from changing their cultural systems. They should be allowed to do so at their own pace, however, and with their lands intact. In this manner information on biodiversity resources can be shared between indigenous groups and the national society. Too often "development" arrives at the door of indigenous lands and destroys the rich and unique knowledge systems that have coevolved with the environment.

Greater Support for Systematics

The task of *in situ* conservation and agrobiodiversity surveys before agricultural development will be made much easier if competent specialists are available to identify and sort materials. Currently, not nearly enough taxonomists are available to analyze plant and animal materials collected, particularly in the tropics. This shortage stems in part from the pull of "glamour" fields such as microbiology and biotechnology. Development organizations and donors could help fill this need by:

- Providing support to expand room for botanical and zoological collections in museums, universities, and other research-oriented institutions in developing countries
- Providing scholarships for students from developing countires to undertake taxonomic training in both developing and industrial countries.

Rapid Agrobiodiversity Assessment Teams

Surveys of agrobiodiversity are needed before a development project is implemented. Currently, many development organizations, including the

World Bank, have procedures for screening projects for their environmental effects before such projects are approved. For the most part screening focuses on off-site impacts of agricultural development and includes an assessment of whether the project is likely to lead to the loss of forest or other "natural" habitats.

An assessment of biodiversity before a project is approved and implemented would encompass two main topics: biodiversity in relatively undisturbed habitats and agrobiodiversity. For both situations biodiversity indicators would need to be established and their significance for decision-making assessed. Rapid assessment methodologies have been tried and tested more fully with the first category. Much work remains to be done in designing methodologies for adequately assessing agrobiodiversity.

An understanding of the historical processes that have shaped the current mix of land-use systems in the area targeted for agricultural development is warranted. A survey of biodiversity and agrobiodiversity would include identification of the driving forces that are propelling:

1. The shifting boundaries of different land-use systems, particularly if they are encroaching on relatively undisturbed habitats
2. The adoption or abandonment of technologies and practices within land-use systems that are enhancing or destroying biodiversity.

Biodiversity in Relatively Undisturbed Habitats

A map using geographic information system techniques would be needed, delineating habitats with minimal disturbance where much of native biodiversity is concentrated. Such mapping would also be useful in categorizing landscape units on a sliding scale of biodiversity richness or uniqueness, thereby providing a tool to help establish priorities for conservation.

For the different "natural" habitats an inventory of the plant and animal species would be called for, and any species with restricted distributions noted (this is already part of the environmental assessment process) and any wild populations of domesticated plants and animals that could be of special interest to breeders would be identified. Efforts should be made to establish if spontaneous introgression is occur-

ring between weedy populations and crops; such exchange of genes often improves the hardiness of crops. The implications of the agricultural development project in terms of the expected shift in land-use patterns would need to be analyzed, with special attention paid to the likelihood that the project might exert greater pressure on remaining relatively intact habitats.

Possible off-site effects of the proposed agricultural development project on biodiversity, such as diversion of water courses for irrigation or use of agrochemicals, can adversely affect fisheries and other wildlife.

Agrobiodiversity

A survey is warranted to document:
- *The diversity of crops cultivated by local farmers.* Would they reduce their number of cultivated species if the project is implemented?
- *Varietal diversity of each crop.* Are the varieties unique to the area? If so, have they been collected for *ex situ* collections? Would they be displaced by technologies associated with implementing the agricultural development project? Strategies need to be identified that would promote the use of traditional varieties without compromising the income-generating capacity of farmers.
- *The number of livestock species raised.* Would local farmers simplify their livestock production systems if the project is implemented? If so, is the tradeoff worthwhile in the long run?
- *The number of breeds per livestock species.* Are the breeds unique to the area? Would any of them disappear because of the agricultural development project?
- *Assessment of land-use practice on soil biodiversity as an indicator of soil "health."* In general the greater the quantity of organic matter in the soil, the greater the biodiversity of soil microorganisms. Would the proposed project accelerate the loss of soil organic matter and associated biodiversity?

Performance Indicators

In chapter 4 some performance indicators with respect to agriculture's impact on biodiversity are identified. Performance indicators can serve as warning bells when agricultural practices threaten to impair the integrity of both "natural" and cultural habitats. Chapter 4 also highlights possible mitigating actions to address danger signs that are identified in the performance indicators matrix. Dangers signs include:

- Natural habitat loss
- Habitat fragmentation
- Species loss even when natural habitat is still intact
- Decline in biodiversity of crop species on farms
- Decline in biodiversity within species.

The following is a sample of remedial measures that can be adopted to address biodiversity loss associated with agricultural development:

- Minimize habitat fragmentation by providing wildlife corridors along bridges of natural habitat.
- Shift to integrated pest management strategies, such as crop rotation and reliance on biocontrol agents to check crop and livestock pests.
- Eliminate fiscal or regulatory measures that promote homogeneity in crop and livestock production.
- Support research on traditional varieties that can achieve high yield.
- Support research on modern varieties that are genetically resistant to pests and diseases.

More work will be needed to operationalize an indicator matrix, particularly with regard to methodologies for measuring indicators.

Adjusting Policy Environment

A wide range of policy areas are involved, such as credit, trade, intellectual property rights, and land tenure. Specific policy levers that would help conserve and better use agrobiodiversity include:

- *Promoting quality pricing.* If farmers receive premium prices for unusual but attractive varieties of crops, they will be encouraged to grow them. A price grading system that rewards farmers not only for producing "clean" produce but also for offering a diverse array of fruit and leaf types will help generate heterogeneity on agricultural landscapes. In some markets specialty growers are

making more money than farmers who concentrate on common, mainstream varieties.

Incentives can easily be created to encourage growers to target produce for a variety of niche markets. Such incentives do not imply a burden on taxpayers. Sometimes lesser known varieties have superior taste or other qualities but are not promoted by marketing organizations. Quality pricing is especially important for fruits, vegetables, coffee, and cacao because a discriminating pricing structure would send signals to farmers that some of the lesser known varieties also have market value, and it is worth their trouble to take care with processing and handling of produce.

- *Opening credit to nonrecommended varieties and livestock.* For the most part farmers can only obtain credit for government-approved varieties, or "super" breeds. If a variety is not on the recommended checklist, farmers usually cannot obtain credit. Likewise, a farmer interested in acquiring a few cows for dairy production may only be able to obtain a Holstein cow when some local breeds may be better adapted to the environment. Such widespread discrimination accelerates the process of abandoning traditional varieties and breeds and contributes to genetic erosion.
- *Continuing to encourage reduction of farming subsidies.* This process is well under way in many countries, in part because of international trade agreements, and should be encouraged because agricultural subsidies often trigger biodiversity loss. Such losses occur because farmers may use more purchased inputs, such as environmentally damaging pesticides and fertilizers or irrigation water, than they would if they had to pay market prices. A highly subsidized crop may also tempt farmers to clear land that would otherwise be left in a relatively undisturbed state.

Toward a New Agricultural Research and Development Model

This new agricultural research paradigm is already evolving along many fronts and at different rates in various parts of the world. The shift can be summerized as follows: the old research model emphasized maximizing output at almost any cost. Research tended to be commodity-focused, rather than on production systems as a whole. The interrelatedness of the parts of farming systems was neither appreciated nor understood, with sometimes adverse effects on the landscape and peoples' livelihoods. The new vision for agricultural research adopts a more holistic approach that is more sensitive to environmental concerns, while still addressing the need to boost yields and incomes of rural producers and caretakers of the land.

The new or evolving agricultural research paradigm includes but is not restricted to:

- *Integrated pest management.* Integrated pest management strategies include the release of biocontrol agents; deployment of genetically resistant cultivars and breeds; more judicious use of pesticides and herbicides; altering cropping patterns to help thwart buildup of pests and diseases; greater emphasis on crop rotation where economically feasible to retard soil degradation and reduce pest pressure.

- *A participatory approach with farmers.* Two types of on-farm research are typically found: demonstration plots on farmers' land and experimental work that involves farmers and other stakeholders in the design of models from the ground up. Demonstration plots on farmers' land is much more common and is often more akin to experiment station work in which pieces of farmers' property are used for the trials with little or no input from the farmers. Much more of the second type of on-farm research is needed, which involves farmers, pastoralists, and other "clients" of agricultural research and development from the inception of the study design. In this manner research would be more demand-driven.

- *Better use of indigenous knowledge.* How and why local people use natural resources can provide important information for more appropriate agricultural research and development efforts.

- *Greater support for research, development, and dissemination of lesser known crops and animals.* Neglected traditional varieties and breeds, many of which are particularly well suited to difficult environments, would also be included in such a broadened research effort.

Some agrobiodiversity is underused, and such neglect is environmentally and socially costly. Sustained support for research on the major food and industrial crops as well as livestock is essential. Any significant cutbacks on such mainstream crops and livestock could bring disastrous consequences. But relatively minor investments in some neglected crops and livestock breeds could generate significant dividends.

- *Support for research on new crops and livestock.* Scope exists for new crops and livestock to fill specialty market and environmental niches. In some cases natural vegetation communities could be managed for the production of new domesticated animals. A better commitment to research on crop and livestock candidates would thus underscore the value of conserving biodiversity and natural habitats.

- *Greater sensitivity to the value of a mosaic of land uses.* Even land uses that are desirable from the biodiversity viewpoint can be promoted too far. Biodiversity in managed landscapes is often best served by promoting a mixture of land uses that provides varied habitats for wildlife adapted to altered areas.

- *Greater diversity of habitats within land-use systems.* Biodiversity within a land-use system, such as intensive cereal cropping, can be achieved by allowing for a variety of habitats, such as riparian buffer strips, shelterbelts, windbreaks, strip cropping, and wetlands. Diversity of habitats on the landscape creates more niches for wildlife, some of which are beneficial in controlling crop pests. More diverse habitats, including managed ones, also promote the more efficient use of nutrients and creates microclimates that can help buffer crops from inclement weather.

- *Greater reliance on recycling organic matter.* Such measures as incorporating livestock or green manure—no-till or minimum-till farming—help sustain the diversity of soil microorganisms that are so important in nutrient recycling.

- *Shifting research focus from individual traits to lifetime and herd productivity characteristics.* Deterministic simulation models and live animal experimentation can be used in some cases to achieve this goal.

- *Determining the critical number of breeds for conservation purposes.* DNA analysis of genetic variation can be used to highlight the genetic spacing between breeds and to identify those breeds that are significantly different or unique from others.
- *Learning more about genetic components of adaptation in livestock.* A better understanding of such traits as tick resistance and use of body reserves would aid breeding efforts and would likely underscore the importance of safeguarding so-called "minor" breeds.

Institutional Development

The notion of a new research paradigm has implications for institutional development and exploring new ways of doing business. Innovative institutional arrangements would include more effective partnerships between:
- Agricultural research centers and NGOs
- Agricultural research centers and growers' associations
- Agricultural research centers and private companies involved in the manufacture and selling of agricultural technologies
- Universities and agricultural extension agencies
- Development lending institutions and all of the above entities.

To some degree all of these connections are being explored and tested. Results are mixed. Initial suspicion between some national agricultural research centers and NGOs has gradually subsided, while in other cases misgivings about interinstitutional collaboration have been borne by experience. Links between agricultural extension agencies and generators of technology are with few exceptions weak. To facilitate future collaborative ventures in the management of agrobiodiversity, organizations' roles and responsibilities will have to be established more clearly at the outset.

Intersectoral Links to Agrobiodiversity

The conservation and management of biodiversity of relevance to agricultural development impinges on several sectors and associated activities, including energy development and ecotourism. Institutional mechanisms are needed to ensure that activities in a diverse array of sectors do not adversely affect efforts to conserve and better use biodiversity for agriculture. Conversely, efforts in other sectors, such as parks and reserves, could be enhanced by systematically incorporating agrobiodiversity dimensions, such as wild populations of crops and near relatives of livestock.

Future Imperatives

Two main points can be distilled from the plethora of policy recommendations, covering a diverse array of activities in biodiversity conservation and agricultural development: establishing performance evaluation criteria and crafting incentives to safeguard and manage agrobiodiversity more effectively. If the policy establishment can get these two items right, virtually all of the recommendations are likely to follow suit.

Performance Evaluation Criteria

Chapter 4 provides a tentative outline on ways to proceed with such performance criteria. But much work remains to be done to broaden this first step in designing a checklist that can be operationally useful for task managers at development agencies and lending institutions.

Incentives to Safeguard and Manage Agrobiodiversity

Factors that encourage farmers to innovate with a diverse array of crops and varieties for marketing purposes need to be better understood. Policies that create a favorable business environment for entrepreneurs to explore opportunities to process fruit, nuts, and other agricultural products for new markets need to be identified (and successes analyzed). Such information would help both the urban and rural poor in many developing countries.

Distributors of World Bank Publications

Prices and credit terms vary from country to country. Consult your local distributor before placing an order.

ALBANIA
Adrion Ltd.
Perlat Rexhepi Str.
Pall. 9, Shk. 1, Ap. 4
Tirana
Tel: (42) 274 19; 221 72
Fax: (42) 274 19

ARGENTINA
Oficina del Libro Internacional
Av. Cordoba 1877
1120 Buenos Aires
Tel: (1) 815-8156
Fax: (1) 815-8354

AUSTRALIA, FIJI, PAPUA NEW GUINEA, SOLOMON ISLANDS, VANUATU, AND WESTERN SAMOA
D.A. Information Services
648 Whitehorse Road
Mitcham 3132
Victoria
Tel: (61) 3 9210 7777
Fax: (61) 3 9210 7788
URL: http://www.dadirect.com.au

AUSTRIA
Gerold and Co.
Graben 31
A-1011 Wien
Tel: (1) 533-50-14-0
Fax: (1) 512-47-31-29

BANGLADESH
Micro Industries Development
Assistance Society (MIDAS)
House 5, Road 16
Dhanmondi R/Area
Dhaka 1209
Tel: (2) 326427
Fax: (2) 811188

BELGIUM
Jean De Lannoy
Av. du Roi 202
1060 Brussels
Tel: (2) 538-5169
Fax: (2) 538-0841

BRAZIL
Publicacões Tecnicas Internacionais Ltda.
Rua Peixoto Gomide, 209
01409 Sao Paulo, SP.
Tel: (11) 259-6644
Fax: (11) 258-6990

CANADA
Renouf Publishing Co. Ltd.
1294 Algoma Road
Ottawa, Ontario K1B 3W8
Tel: 613-741-4333
Fax: 613-741-5439

CHINA
China Financial & Economic
Publishing House
8, Da Fo Si Dong Jie
Beijing
Tel: (1) 333-8257
Fax: (1) 401-7365

COLOMBIA
Infoenlace Ltda.
Apartado Aereo 34270
Bogota D.E.
Tel: (1) 285-2798
Fax: (1) 285-2798

COTE D'IVOIRE
Centre d'Edition et de Diffusion
Africaines (CEDA)
04 B.P. 541
Abidjan 04 Plateau
Tel: 225-24-6510
Fax: 225-25-0567

CYPRUS
Center of Applied Research
Cyprus College
6, Diogenes Street, Engomi
P.O. Box 2006
Nicosia
Tel: 244-1730
Fax: 246-2051

CZECH REPUBLIC
National Information Center
prodejna, Konviktska 5
CS – 113 57 Prague 1
Tel: (2) 2422-9433
Fax: (2) 2422-1484
URL: http://www.nis.cz/

DENMARK
SamfundsLitteratur
Rosenoerns Allé 11
DK-1970 Frederiksberg C
Tel: (31)-351942
Fax: (31)-357822

ECUADOR
Facultad Latinoamericana de
Ciencias Sociales
FLASCO-SEDE Ecuador
Calle Ulpiano Paez 118
y Av. Patria
Quito, Ecuador
Tel: (2) 542 714; 542 716; 528 200
Fax: (2) 566 139

EGYPT, ARAB REPUBLIC OF
Al Ahram
Al Galaa Street
Cairo
Tel: (2) 578-6083
Fax: (2) 578-6833

The Middle East Observer
41, Sherif Street
Cairo
Tel: (2) 393-9732
Fax: (2) 393-9732

FINLAND
Akateeminen Kirjakauppa
P.O. Box 23
FIN-00371 Helsinki
Tel: (0) 12141
Fax: (0) 121-4441
URL: http://booknet.cultnet.fi/aka/

FRANCE
World Bank Publications
66, avenue d'Iéna
75116 Paris
Tel: (1) 40-69-30-55
Fax: (1) 40-69-30-68

GERMANY
UNO-Verlag
Poppelsdorfer Allee 55
53115 Bonn
Tel: (228) 212940
Fax: (228) 217492

GREECE
Papasotiriou S.A.
35, Stournara Str.
106 82 Athens
Tel: (1) 364-1826
Fax: (1) 364-8254

HONG KONG, MACAO
Asia 2000 Ltd.
Sales & Circulation Department
Seabird House, unit 1101-02
22-28 Wyndham Street, Central
Hong Kong
Tel: 852 2530-1409
Fax: 852 2526-1107
URL: http://www.sales@asia2000.com.hk

HUNGARY
Foundation for Market
Economy
Dombovari Ut 17-19
H-1117 Budapest
Tel: 36 1 204 2951 or
36 1 204 2948
Fax: 36 1 204 2953

INDIA
Allied Publishers Ltd.
751 Mount Road
Madras - 600 002
Tel: (44) 852-3938
Fax: (44) 852-0649

INDONESIA
Pt. Indira Limited
Jalan Borobudur 20
P.O. Box 181
Jakarta 10320
Tel: (21) 390-4290
Fax: (21) 421-4289

IRAN
Kowkab Publishers
P.O. Box 19575-511
Tehran
Tel: (21) 258-3723
Fax: 98 (21) 258-3723

Ketab Sara Co. Publishers
Khaled Eslamboli Ave.,
6th Street
Kusheh Delafrooz No. 8
Tehran
Tel: 8717819 or 8716104
Fax: 8862479

IRELAND
Government Supplies Agency
Oifig an tSoláthair
4-5 Harcourt Road
Dublin 2
Tel: (1) 461-3111
Fax: (1) 475-2670

ISRAEL
Yozmot Literature Ltd.
P.O. Box 56055
Tel Aviv 61560
Tel: (3) 5285-397
Fax: (3) 5285-397

R.O.Y. International
PO Box 13056
Tel Aviv 61130
Tel: (3) 5461423
Fax: (3) 5461442

Palestinian Authority/Middle East
Index Information Services
P.O.B. 19502 Jerusalem
Tel: (2) 271219

ITALY
Licosa Commissionaria Sansoni SPA
Via Duca Di Calabria, 1/1
Casella Postale 552
50125 Firenze
Tel: (55) 645-415
Fax: (55) 641-257

JAMAICA
Ian Randle Publishers Ltd.
206 Old Hope Road
Kingston 6
Tel: 809-927-2085
Fax: 809-977-0243

JAPAN
Eastern Book Service
Hongo 3-Chome,
Bunkyo-ku 113
Tokyo
Tel: (03) 3818-0861
Fax: (03) 3818-0864
URL: http://www.bekkoame.or.jp/~svt-ebs

KENYA
Africa Book Service (E.A.) Ltd.
Quaran House, Mfangano Street
P.O. Box 45245
Nairobi
Tel: (2) 23641
Fax: (2) 330272

KOREA, REPUBLIC OF
Daejon Trading Co. Ltd.
P.O. Box 34
Yeoeida
Seoul
Tel: (2) 785-1631/4
Fax: (2) 784-0315

MALAYSIA
University of Malaya Cooperative
Bookshop, Limited
P.O. Box 1127
Jalan Pantai Baru
59700 Kuala Lumpur
Tel: (3) 756-5000
Fax: (3) 755-4424

MEXICO
INFOTEC
Apartado Postal 22-860
14060 Tlalpan,
Mexico D.F.
Tel: (5) 606-0011
Fax: (5) 606-0386

NETHERLANDS
De Lindeboom/InOr-Publikaties
P.O. Box 202
7480 AE Haaksbergen

NEW ZEALAND
EBSCO NZ Ltd.
Private Mail Bag 99914
New Market
Auckland
Tel: (9) 524-8119
Fax: (9) 524-8067

NIGERIA
University Press Limited
Three Crowns Building Jericho
Private Mail Bag 5095
Ibadan
Tel: (22) 41-1356
Fax: (22) 41-2056

NORWAY
Narvesen Information Center
Book Department
P.O. Box 6125 Etterstad
N-0602 Oslo 6
Tel: (22) 57-3300
Fax: (22) 68-1901

PAKISTAN
Mirza Book Agency
65, Shahrah-e-Quaid-e-Azam
P.O. Box No. 729
Lahore 54000
Tel: (42) 7353601
Fax: (42) 7585283

PERU
Editorial Desarrollo SA
Apartado 3824
Lima 1
Tel: (14) 285380
Fax: (14) 286628

PHILIPPINES
International Booksource Center Inc.
Suite 720, Cityland 10
Condominium Tower 2
H.V dela Costa, corner
Valero St.
Makati, Metro Manila
Tel: (2) 817-9676
Fax: (2) 817-1741

POLAND
International Publishing Service
Ul. Piekna 31/37
00-577 Warzawa
Tel: (2) 628-6089
Fax: (2) 621-7255

PORTUGAL
Livraria Portugal
Rua Do Carmo 70-74
1200 Lisbon
Tel: (1) 347-4982
Fax: (1) 347-0264

ROMANIA
Compani De Librarii Bucuresti S.A.
Str. Lipscani no. 26, sector 3
Bucharest
Tel: (1) 613 9645
Fax: (1) 312 4000

RUSSIAN FEDERATION
Isdatelstvo <Ves Mir>
9a, Lolpachrui pereulok
Moscow 101831
Tel: (95) 917 87 49
Fax: (95) 917 92 59

SAUDI ARABIA, QATAR
Jarir Book Store
P.O. Box 3196
Riyadh 11471
Tel: (1) 477-3140
Fax: (1) 477-2940

SINGAPORE, TAIWAN, MYANMAR, BRUNEI
Asahgate Publishing Asia
Pacific Pte. Ltd.
41 Kallang Pudding Road #04-03
Golden Wheel Building
Singapore 349316
Tel: (65) 741-5166
Fax: (65) 742-9356

SLOVAK REPUBLIC
Slovart G.T.G. Ltd.
Krupinska 4
PO Box 152
852 99 Bratislava 5
Tel: (7) 839472
Fax: (7) 839485

SOUTH AFRICA, BOTSWANA
For single titles:
Oxford University Press
Southern Africa
P.O. Box 1141
Cape Town 8000
Tel: (21) 45-7266
Fax: (21) 45-7265

For subscription orders:
International Subscription Service
P.O. Box 41095
Craighall
Johannesburg 2024
Tel: (11) 880-1448
Fax: (11) 880-6248

SPAIN
Mundi-Prensa Libros, S.A.
Castello 37
28001 Madrid
Tel: (1) 431-3399
Fax: (1) 575-3998
http://www.tsai.es/mprensa

Libreria Internacional AEDOS
Consell de Cent, 391
08009 Barcelona
Tel: (3) 488-3009
Fax: (3) 487-7659

SRI LANKA, THE MALDIVES
Lake House Bookshop
P.O. Box 244
100, Sir Chittampalam A.
Gardiner Mawatha
Colombo 2
Tel: (1) 32105
Fax: (1) 432104

SWEDEN
Fritzes Customer Service
Regeringsgaton 12
S-106 47 Stockholm
Tel: (8) 690 90 90
Fax: (8) 21 47 77

Wennergren-Williams AB
P. O. Box 1305
S-171 25 Solna
Tel: (8) 705-97-50
Fax: (8) 27-00-71

SWITZERLAND
Librairie Payot
Service Institutionnel
Côtes-de-Montbenon 30
1002 Lausanne
Tel: (021)-320-2511
Fax: (021)-320-2514

Van Diermen Editions Technique
Ch. de Lacuez 41
CH1807 Blonay
Tel: (021) 943 2673
Fax: (021) 943 3605

TANZANIA
Oxford University Press
Maktaba Street
PO Box 5299
Dar es Salaam
Tel: (51) 29209
Fax: (51) 46822

THAILAND
Central Books Distribution
306 Silom Road
Bangkok
Tel: (2) 235-5400
Fax: (2) 237-8321

TRINIDAD & TOBAGO, JAMAICA
Systematics Studies Unit
#9 Watts Street
Curepe
Trinidad, West Indies
Tel: 809-662-5654
Fax: 809-662-5654

UGANDA
Gustro Ltd.
Madhvani Building
PO Box 9997
Plot 16/4 Jinja Rd.
Kampala
Tel/Fax: (41) 254763

UNITED KINGDOM
Microinfo Ltd.
P.O. Box 3
Alton, Hampshire GU34 2PG
England
Tel: (1420) 86848
Fax: (1420) 89889

ZAMBIA
University Bookshop
Great East Road Campus
P.O. Box 32379
Lusaka
Tel: (1) 213221 Ext. 482

ZIMBABWE
Longman Zimbabwe (Pte.)Ltd.
Tourle Road, Ardbennie
P.O. Box ST125
Southerton
Harare
Tel: (4) 662711
Fax: (4) 662716